Chagos islanders in Mauritius and the UK

Manchester University Press

New
Ethnographies

Series editor
Alexander Thomas T. Smith

Already published
Devolution and the Scottish Conservatives:
Banal activism, electioneering and the politics of irrelevance
Alexander Thomas T. Smith

Chagos islanders in Mauritius and the UK

Forced displacement and onward migration

Laura Jeffery

Manchester University Press
Manchester and New York

Distributed in the United States exclusively
by Palgrave Macmillan

Published by Manchester University Press
Oxford Road, Manchester M13 9NR, UK
and Room 400, 175 Fifth Avenue, New York, NY 10010, USA
www.manchesteruniversitypress.co.uk

Distributed in the United States exclusively by
Palgrave Macmillan, 175 Fifth Avenue, New York,
NY 10010, USA

Distributed in Canada exclusively by
UBC Press, University of British Columbia, 2029 West Mall,
Vancouver, BC, Canada V6T 1Z2

British Library Cataloguing-in-Publication Data
A catalogue record for this book is available from the British Library

Library of Congress Cataloging-in-Publication Data applied for

ISBN   978 0 7190 8430 0   *hardback*

First published 2011

Typeset in Minion with Futura display by
Special Edition Pre-press Services, www.special-edition.co.uk

Printed in Great Britain by
CPI Antony Rowe Ltd, Chippenham, Wiltshire

Contents

List of maps

Acknowledgements

This research was made possible by the support and collaboration of the leaders, members, and supporters of the various Chagossian organisations in Mauritius and the UK, many of whom have assisted my research in numerous ways. Among them, my special thanks go to the Chagos Refugees Group, especially Olivier Bancoult and Lisette Talate; the Chagossian Social Committee, especially Fernand Mandarin and Hervé Lassemillante; the Diego Garcia Island Council and Diego Garcian Society, especially Allen Vincatassin and Christian Ramdas; and the Chagos Island Community Association, especially Hengride Permal.

I am extremely grateful for the generous hospitality of the many people who welcomed me into their homes and families in Mauritius and Crawley. Among them, my warmest gratitude goes to Elena and Hervé Rabouine; Jenny and Joseph Bertrand; Marie-Josée Clément, Pamela Clément, and their family; Claudinette and Wessley Jules and their families; Mylene and Michel Leveque; Rita Elysée and Mimose and Cyril Furcy; Anne-Marie Alphonse, Rosemay Spéville, and Jean-Noel Louis; Charlesia Alexis; Maudea and Rosemond Saminaden, and Claudie Anselme; Louis-René France, Jean-Aurel France, and their families; Dick Kwan Tat and Sarochin Khunwongsa; Lindsey Collen, Ram Seegobin, and Ragini Kistnasawmy; and Dominique Pascal and family.

My family has supported me in numerous ways throughout this period of research and writing. My partner Andrew Clements accompanied me for the first year in Mauritius, and his presence and assistance greatly enriched my experience of fieldwork (as I discovered when I later conducted fieldwork alone). My parents Patricia and Roger Jeffery have engaged tirelessly with all stages of my work, from research proposal to final manuscript. I am further indebted to my parents and my parents-in-law Susan and Paul Clements for looking after their grandson Kenneth so that I could prepare the final transcript during my maternity leave.

The processes of thinking through and writing up my doctoral and post-doctoral research have also benefited from the support and input of numerous anthropologist friends and colleagues in Cambridge, Edinburgh, St Andrews, and beyond, especially my doctoral supervisor James Laidlaw; my PhD examiners Dan Rabinowitz and Harri Englund; inspiring teachers at Cambridge, particularly Yael Navaro-Yashin, Marilyn Strathern, Stephen Hugh-Jones, and Susan Bayly; my Cambridge housemates Joanna Cook, Gwyn Williams, and Matei Candea; my postdoctoral mentor Tony Good and other Edinburgh colleagues Toby Kelly and Richard Whitecross; my St Andrews mentor Nigel Rapport, and Hideko Mitsui; and fellow researchers who have worked with the Chagossian community, particularly David Vine and Iain Walker. I am also grateful to the New Ethnographies series editor Alex Smith for his unwavering confidence in this project, to Manchester University Press for its efficient peer review and publication process, and to three anonymous reviewers for their constructive criticism and insightful comments on my manuscript. None of the above bears responsibility for my neglect to incorporate some of their suggestions more fully.

My doctoral research amongst displaced Chagos islanders in Mauritius was supported by an ESRC Postgraduate Training Award (R42200134267) at the University of Cambridge (2001–5). My postdoctoral research amongst Chagos-sian migrants in the UK was supported by a Leverhulme Early Career Fellow-ship (ECF/2006/0122) at the University of Edinburgh (2006–8). Preparation of this manuscript was supported by a writing fellowship at the University of St Andrews (2008–9).

Parts I and II of this book are based on my doctoral research amongst dis-placed Chagos islanders in Mauritius (see Jeffery 2006a). Some aspects of the first two chapters are shared with book chapters I co-authored with David Vine (Vine & Jeffery 2009; Jeffery & Vine 2011), parts of Chapter 2 speak to my article in *History and Anthropology* (Jeffery 2006b), and Chapter 3 is based on my article in the *Journal of the Royal Anthropological Institute* (Jeffery 2007). The chapters in Part III are based on my postdoctoral research amongst migrant Chagossians in the UK, resonating with arguments explored in my article in the *Journal of Ethnic and Migration Studies* (Jeffery 2010). The first half of the Postscript is based on my comment published in *Anthropology Today* (Jeffery 2009).

Timeline

1500s	Portuguese stop at Mauritius *en route* between Cape of Good Hope and India
1598	Dutch East India Company starts to use Mauritius *en route* to East Asia
1710	Dutch East India Company abandons attempts to settle Mauritius
1715	France claims Mauritius and dependencies
1721	French colonists establish settlement on Mauritius with enslaved labourers from Africa and Madagascar
1740s	French establish settlements in Seychelles
1780s	French establish coconut plantations on Chagos Archipelago
1814	Treaty of Paris: Britain acquires Mauritius and its dependencies
1835	British emancipate enslaved labourers and introduce apprenticeship system
1962	Chagos-Agalega Ltd consolidates ownership of plantations on Chagos
1965	BIOT Order: UK excises Chagos Archipelago from Mauritius, and Aldabra Atoll, Farquhar Atoll, and Desroches Island (one of the Amirante Islands) from Seychelles, to form British Indian Ocean Territory (BIOT)
1966	UK and US Governments exchange notes on Diego Garcia for US military base
1967	UK Government purchases Chagos plantations from Chagos-Agalega Ltd
1968	Mauritius gains independence on 12 March
1971	BIOT Immigration Ordinance; *Nordvær* carries last islanders from Diego Garcia to Seychelles and Mauritius; US commences construction of military base on Diego Garcia
1972	*Nordvær* carries last islanders from Salomon Islands

1973	*Nordvær* carries last islanders from Peros Banhos Atoll
1976	Seychelles gains independence on 29 June; UK returns Aldabra Atoll, Farquhar Atoll and Desroches Island to Seychelles control
1978	UK Government awards compensation to Chagos islanders in Mauritius
1980	Mauritian Government reiterates claim to sovereignty of Chagos Archipelago
1982	UK Government awards compensation to Chagos islanders in Mauritius; Chagossian activists Charlesia Alexis, Lisette Talate and Olivier Bancoult form Chagos Refugees Group
1995	Chagossian Fernand Mandarin forms Chagossian Social Committee
1996	United Nations Working Group on Indigenous Populations recognises Chagossians as indigenous people
1997	Mauritian journalist publishes *Diego Files* in *Week-end* newspaper
2000	*Bancoult I* judicial review in High Court rules that depopulation of Chagos Archipelago was contrary to laws of BIOT; BIOT Immigration (Amendment) Ordinance permits return to Chagos Archipelago except Diego Garcia; Diego Garcian islander Allen Vincatassin forms Diego Garcia Island Council (subsequently renamed Diego Garcian Society)
2002	British Overseas Territories Act: UK Government awards UK citizenship to Chagos islanders and their children
2003–2004	*Chagos Islanders* litigation: High Court and Court of Appeal reject Chagossian compensation case
2004	UK Government uses Orders in Council to introduce new BIOT Immigration Order prohibiting return to Chagos Archipelago
2006	UK Government organises boat trip to Chagos Archipelago for 100 islanders; Hengride Permal forms Chagos Island Community Association
2006–2008	*Bancoult II* judicial review in High Court and Court of Appeal, overturned by House of Lords; case pending in European Court of Human Rights (2010)
2010	UK Government announces establishment of Marine Protected Area in BIOT, including a no-take marine reserve of 544,000 square kilometres with ban on commercial fishing

Abbreviations

AGOA	African Growth and Opportunity Act
BDT	British Dependent Territory
BIOT	British Indian Ocean Territory
BOT	British Overseas Territory
CBC	Crawley Borough Council
CEN	Chagos Environment Network
CICA	Chagos Island Community Association
CRG	Chagos Refugees Group (*Grup Refizyé Chagos*)*
CSC	Chagossian Social Committee (*Comité Social Chagossien*)
DGIC	Diego Garcia Island Council
DGS	Diego Garcian Society
ECHR	European Court of Human Rights
FAC	Foreign Affairs Committee
FCO	Foreign and Commonwealth Office
IST	Ilois Support Trust
ITFB	Ilois Trust Fund Board
IWF	Ilois Welfare Fund
LPT	Education For Workers (*Ledikasyon Pu Travayer*)
MBC	Mauritius Broadcasting Corporation
MLP	Mauritian Labour Party (*Parti Travailliste (PTr)*)
MMM	Mauritian Militant Movement (*Mouvement Militant Mauricien*)
MPA	Marine Protected Area
MSM	Militant Socialist Movement (*Mouvement Socialiste Militant*)
RRA	Rodrigues Regional Assembly
SAHRINGON	Southern Africa Human Rights NGO Network
UKCSA	UK Chagos Support Association
WGIP	Working Group on Indigenous Populations
WSCC	West Sussex County Council

French/Kreol name given in parentheses.

Map 1 – Indian Ocean

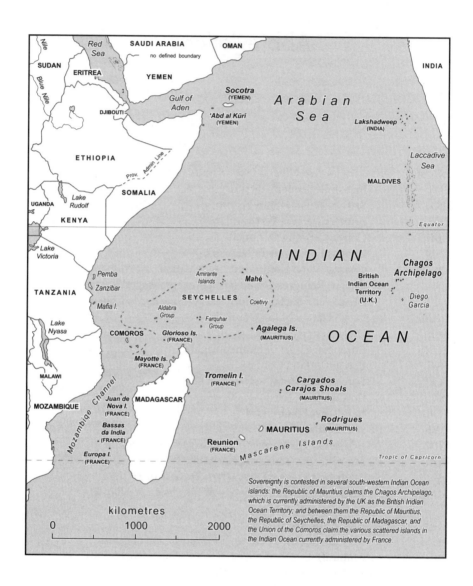

Sovereignty is contested in several south-western Indian Ocean islands: the Republic of Mauritius claims the Chagos Archipelago, which is currently administered by the UK as the British Indian Ocean Territory; and between them the Republic of Mauritius, the Republic of Seychelles, the Republic of Madagascar, and the Union of the Comoros claim the various scattered islands in the Indian Ocean currently administered by France.

Map 2 – Chagos Archipelago

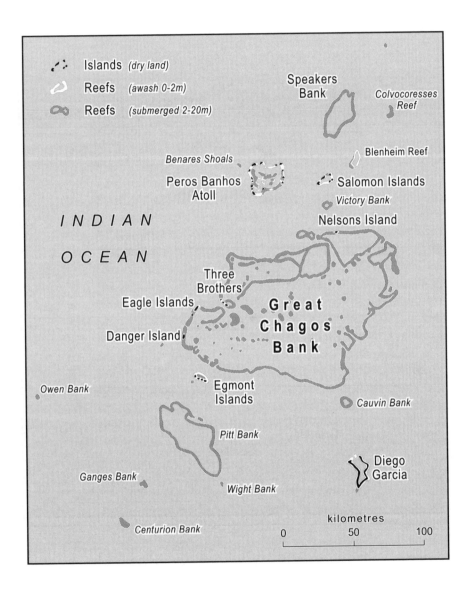

Islands *(dry land)*

Reefs *(awash 0-2m)*

Reefs *(submerged 2-20m)*

Speakers Bank

Colvocoresses Reef

Blenheim Reef

Benares Shoals

Peros Banhos Atoll

Salomon Islands

Victory Bank

INDIAN

Nelsons Island

OCEAN

Three Brothers

Eagle Islands

Great Chagos Bank

Danger Island

Owen Bank

Egmont Islands

Cauvin Bank

Pitt Bank

Diego Garcia

Ganges Bank

Wight Bank

kilometres

Centurion Bank

0   50   100

Map 3 – Mauritius

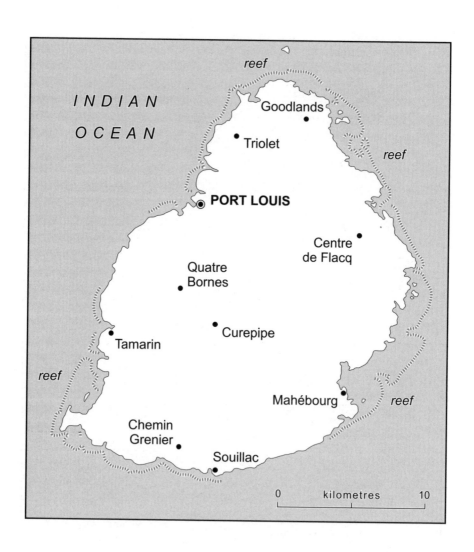

Map 4 – Port Louis

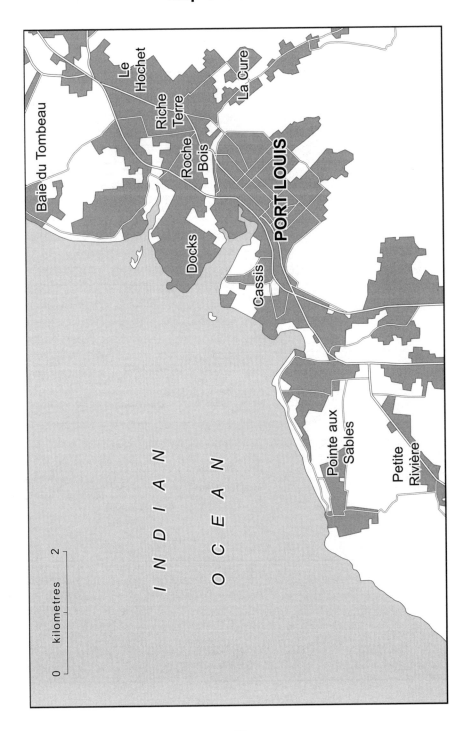

Map 5 – United Kingdom

Map 6 – West Sussex

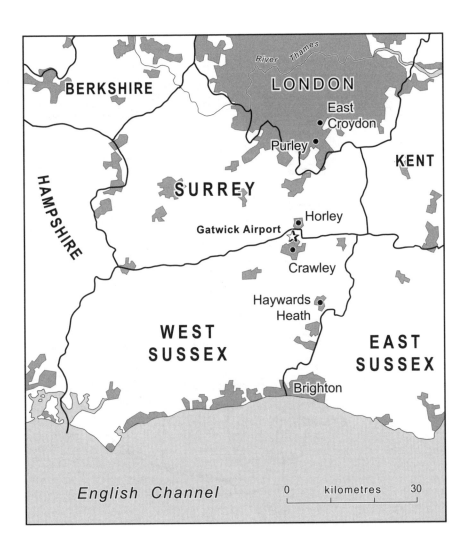

Map 7 – Crawley

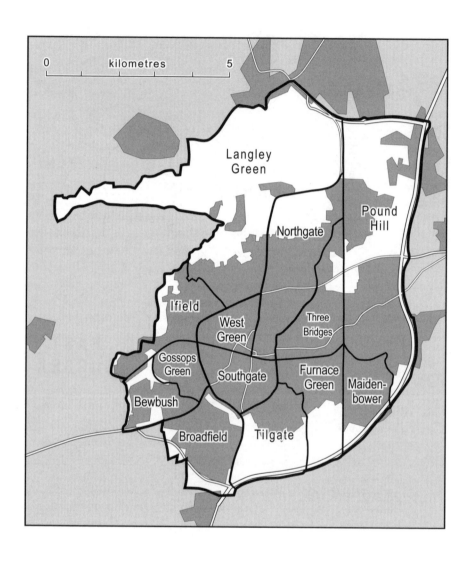

Series editor's foreword

At its best, ethnography has provided a valuable tool for apprehending a world in flux. A couple of years after the Second World War, Max Gluckman founded the Department of Social Anthropology at the University of Manchester. In the years that followed, he and his colleagues built a programme of ethnographic research that drew eclectically on the work of leading anthropologists, economists and sociologists to explore issues of conflict, reconciliation and social justice 'at home' and abroad. Often placing emphasis on detailed analysis of case studies drawn from small-scale societies and organisations, the famous 'Manchester School' in social anthropology built an enviable reputation for methodological innovation in its attempts to explore the pressing political questions of the second half of the twentieth century. Looking back, that era is often thought to constitute a 'gold standard' for how ethnographers might grapple with new challenges and issues in the contemporary world.

The *New Ethnographies* series aims to build on that ethnographic legacy at Manchester. It will publish the best new ethnographic monographs that promote interdisciplinary debate and methodological innovation in the qualitative social sciences. This includes the growing number of books that seek to apprehend the 'new' ethnographic objects of a seemingly brave new world, some recent examples of which have included auditing, democracy and elections, documents, financial markets, human rights, assisted reproductive technologies and political activism. Analysing such objects has often demanded new skills and techniques from the ethnographer. As a result, this series will give voice to those using ethnographic methods across disciplines to innovate, such as through the application of multi-sited fieldwork and the extended comparative case study method. Such innovations have often challenged more traditional ethnographic approaches. *New Ethnographies* therefore seeks to provide a platform for emerging scholars and their more established counterparts engaging with ethnographic methods in new and imaginative ways.

Alexander Thomas T. Smith

Note to readers

Until the late 1990s, when the community collectively adopted the term Chagossian, islanders born on Chagos had been known in Mauritius as *Ilois* [islander], a generic term which became increasingly derogatory. Throughout this book I refer to people born on the Chagos Archipelago as Chagos islanders rather than as *Ilois*, regardless of the time period under discussion. I use the term Chagossian to refer to members of the extended Chagossian community, which includes not only Chagos islanders but also their descendants born in exile.

I identify socio-politically active research participants by their real names, but I assign others first-name pseudonyms and describe them anonymously in terms of some of their characteristics, such as place of birth, age, sex, and profession. During interviews, I either took detailed notes or recorded the proceedings for later transcription into my field notes. All quotations from speech derive from interviews or conversations in Kreol, which I have translated into English.

Kreol in Mauritius is a French-based language also influenced by East African and South Asian languages. There is no official orthography, and there have long been tensions between the French-based orthography devised by the Catholic Church and the various phonetic orthographies favoured by radical political groups such as *Ledikasyon Pu Travayer* [Education for Workers], which produced a useful phonetic Kreol-to-English dictionary (Ledikasyon Pu Travayer 1993). When quoting other texts in Kreol I follow the original orthography, but otherwise I use LPT's phonetic orthography and translations. I also use LPT's phonetic principles to transcribe distinctively Chagossian Kreol words that are not found in Mauritian Kreol dictionaries. Most Kreol vocabulary comes from French, and French-speaking readers may find that reading Kreol quotes phonetically enables them to understand a high proportion of the words, although the grammar is different.

I also follow the (non-phonetic) practice, common amongst researchers working in Mauritius, of distinguishing between Creole (an ethnic category comprising those of partially, primarily or wholly African descent) and Kreol (the language) in order to avoid the tendency to assume a connection between the language (which is the first language of the vast majority in Mauritius) and one particular ethnic group (Baker 1972; see also Eriksen 1998: 21 note 27; Miles 1999: 221–223).

Introduction

Forced displacement and onward migration

> [Chagos] was like a paradise ... the sand is white and fine like flour, the coconut trees lie flat over the sea, and the fish and octopuses swim between the coconut branches so you can just step into the sea and catch them like this. (Janine, a Chagos islander displaced to Mauritius)

The Chagos Archipelago, a remote group of coralline islands in the middle of the Indian Ocean (see Map 1), is British territory. Chagos is routinely described as the archetypal idyllic island paradise, although since 1971, the largest island in the archipelago, Diego Garcia, has been occupied by a major US overseas military base. At the US Government's request, the UK Government removed all the inhabitants from all the islands in the archipelago, sending them to Mauritius and Seychelles. What happened to these people? How have they made sense of their disrupted lives? What has life been like for them in exile?

> There are lots of problems in Mauritius. Tourists live it up but those who actually live there have lots of problems. (Lucette, a Chagos islander displaced to Mauritius)

The Republic of Mauritius, in the south-western Indian Ocean, is best known in the UK as a popular honeymoon destination, and has had a reputation as Africa's postcolonial success story in terms of its democratic governance, peaceful multiethnic population, and capitalist economic development. At the same time, however, there is huge disparity of wealth and opportunity, with poverty concentrated in remote villages and around the capital, Port Louis, where people struggle to find jobs and support their families. Emigration is highly desirable. Migrating to the UK has become a real possibility for Chagos islanders and their children since 2002, when they became eligible for UK passports.

> We work harder here [in the UK] than we did in Mauritius, and we are more stressed about our expenses ... but we think of it as a sacrifice for our children, who reward us by doing well at school and getting good results. (Lydia, born in Mauritius to Chagossian parents, living in the UK)

On arrival in the UK, most Chagossians have settled in Crawley, a New Town in West Sussex near the south coast of Great Britain. It is three-quarters of an hour from London by train, and is a suburban commuter town which also supplies much of the labour to the nearby Gatwick Airport, the second busiest airport in the UK (see Map 5). Crawley also has extremely low rates of unemployment and is seen by many recent arrivals as a haven of opportunity, especially when compared with the places they have left behind.

The Chagos Archipelago provides the historic backdrop while Mauritius and Crawley are the ethnographic settings for this book, which seeks to convey the complexities of the lives of Chagos islanders and their descendants in exile. The book explores Chagossians' recollections of forced displacement, their re-formulations of the homeland, their challenging lives in exile, their experiences of onward migration, and their attempts to make home in successive locations.

From Chagos to Mauritius to Crawley

The Chagos Archipelago was unpopulated prior to European colonial expansion in the Indian Ocean from the late eighteenth century onwards, whereupon it was administered as a dependency of colonial Mauritius. French and British coloni-alists populated the archipelago with enslaved labourers and contract workers, mostly from East Africa and Madagascar via Mauritius. By the mid-twentieth century, the population numbered about two thousand. During the 1960s, the main island of Diego Garcia housed around half the total number of inhabitants, while under a third lived on Ile du Coin in the Peros Banhos Atoll and around a fifth on Boddam in the Salomon Islands (see Map 2). Diego Garcia is by far the largest island in the Chagos Archipelago: 27.20 square kilometres out of a total land mass of 63.17 square kilometres. In 1965, as part of the negotiations leading to Mauritian independence in 1968, the UK Government excised the Chagos Archipelago from colonial Mauritius and created the new British Indian Ocean Territory (BIOT). In 1966 the UK Government made Diego Garcia available to the US Government to build what quickly became a major overseas military base.

Between 1965 and 1973 the UK Government depopulated the Chagos Archi-pelago: first by preventing the return of islanders who had gone on trips to Mauritius and Seychelles, and later by restricting supplies, winding down work on the coconut plantations and finally coercing the remaining islanders onto crowded ships. About 1,500 islanders were relocated to Mauritius and about 500 were relocated to Seychelles. No resettlement programmes were put in place, and many Chagossian families have contended with chronic homelessness, underemployment and impoverishment in exile. The UK Government awarded limited compensation to Chagos islanders in Mauritius in 1978 and 1982, but those in Seychelles have yet to receive any compensation at all. In 2003, a coalition of Chagossian organisations led by the Chagos Refugees Group (CRG) in Mauritius lost a High Court case seeking further financial compensation. In 2004, the Court of Appeal rejected the Chagossian coalition's application for permission to appeal.

Yet, in 2000, a High Court judge had ruled that the depopulation of the Chagos Archipelago was contrary to the laws of the BIOT (laws that the UK Government itself had passed). The UK Government responded by enacting a new BIOT Immigration Ordinance which theoretically entitled Chagos islanders to return to all the islands in the Chagos Archipelago other than Diego Garcia. In 2004, however, the UK Government used the Orders in Council (a royal prerogative) to enact a new BIOT Immigration Order, which prohibited unauthorised people (including Chagossians) from entering any part of the Chagos Archipelago. Despite this, the UK authorities then permitted and orchestrated a long-awaited return visit for one hundred islanders in 2006. The Chagossians' legal team initially won judicial review of the Immigration Order in 2006, but the UK Government eventually won its appeal in the House of Lords in 2008. As I write, in 2010, the case is pending in the European Court of Human Rights.

Meanwhile, in 2002, the British Overseas Territories Act reclassified the British Dependent Territories (BDTs) as Overseas Territories and awarded full UK citizenship to citizens of such territories. Islanders born on Chagos when it was a British colony, who were eligible for BDT citizenship under the British Nationality Act 1981, thus became eligible for full UK citizenship through their place of birth. In response to a campaign by the CRG, the UK Government also introduced a supplementary section to provide for the transmission of UK citizenship to Chagos islanders' children born in exile (but not their grandchildren or subsequent generations born in exile). Chagossian groups estimate that more than one thousand people migrated from Mauritius and Seychelles to the UK in the first five years after becoming eligible for UK citizenship in 2002.

What does it mean to be forced to leave one's homeland, and how does this differ from choosing to leave the place where one was born and raised? What are the implications of different experiences of movement and mobility? How do such differences affect recollections of and relationships with places of birth, upbringing, and residence, and strategies for making home in new places of residence? This book compares Chagossians' recollections of their forced displacement from the Chagos Archipelago and their subsequent experiences in Mauritius with their reports of onward migration to the UK. It explores these questions through several key debates in the anthropology of displacement and migration studies.

Force and agency in displacement and migration

Numerous scholars have theorised human mobility as a continuum from relatively free to relatively forced, and have outlined this continuum through a range of oppositional terms such as voluntary versus involuntary (Richmond 1994), proactive versus reactive (Van Hear 1998), and migration versus displacement (Turton 2003). As David Turton has pointed out, 'forced' implies a lack of choice, whereas 'migration' carries associations of choice, agency, and purposive action, and the phrase 'forced migration' is thus an oxymoron (Turton 2003: 1, 9). 'Displacement', by contrast, implies being acted upon. 'Forced displacement' refers to movement induced by development projects, environmental change, conflict or militarisation – particularly within a country – resulting in internally displaced people who are often marginalised and living in a 'refugee-like situation' within their country of origin and nationality.

Cumulatively, the characteristics of forced displacement seem best to reflect the experiences of the Chagos islanders. Chagos islanders evoke their 'uprooting' [*derasinman*] and self-identify as 'an uprooted people' [*en lepep derasine*] living in 'exile' [*exil*] from their homeland or 'natal land' [*later natal*]. My use of a combination of these phrases – forced displacement, forcible uprooting, and exile – reflects that the Chagos islanders were given no choice concerning their removal from the Chagos Archipelago. This is emphatically not to conceptualise the Chagos islanders only as passive victims (cf. Turton 2003: 6–11); rather, it is to note that they were denied absolutely the option of remaining in Chagos. Their agency as 'purposive actors' (see Turton 2003: 9–10) comes into play in other aspects of their lives, such as in relation to their strategies for integration or mobilisation, which are a main focus of this book. Likewise, my description of the 'onward migration' of Chagossians from Mauritius and Seychelles to the UK both reflects that this movement is to a third location and implies an increased degree of choice in deciding whether or not to emigrate at all, and if so where to go.

The anthropologist Elizabeth Colson has asked why forced displacement is such a traumatic experience. Her response is multifaceted: alongside community dispersal and dislocation from one's familiar home environment, which can result in insecurity and disorientation, she also highlights the lack of agency, noting that those forcibly uprooted from their homeland often suffer as a result of their loss of control over their own destinies (Colson 1989: 13). She concluded that 'humans are in fact migratory animals in the sense that they treasure possibilities for mobility but at the same time see any attempt to force mobility upon them as an infringement of their personal space and upon their sense of integrity' (Colson 1989: 13). More recently, David Turton has concluded that 'the way people experience movement to a new place, and the extent to which this is a shocking and disruptive experience, is determined by the conditions under which they move', a crucial element of which is whether or not they experience their movement as desirable (Turton 2005: 275).

Research aggregating findings from hundreds of cases of forced displacement worldwide has shown that, in the absence of adequate preventative measures, forced displacement is likely to result in chronic impoverishment in exile (Cernea 2000: 12). Michael Cernea has demonstrated that 'the core content of unmitigated forced displacement is economic and social uprooting' (Cernea 1997: 1572). He identifies the most widespread risks of displacement as landlessness, joblessness, homelessness, marginalisation, food insecurity, increased morbidity, loss of access to common resources, and community disarticulation (Cernea 2000).

These insights are extremely helpful for understanding the experience of displaced Chagos islanders, who often described their lives in exile in terms of *sagrin*, *tristes*, and *mizer*: sorrow, sadness, and impoverishment. Social scientists, human rights researchers, government officials, and journalists have documented how the islanders were marginalised and impoverished by their forced displacement, suffering an array of economic, social, cultural, physical, and psychological harms (Anyangwe 2001; Botte 1980; Dræbel 1997; Madeley

1985; Prosser 1976; Sylva 1981; Vine 2006). Displaced islanders lost their land, houses, and other property; their jobs; their access to shared resources such as fish and seafood, coconut palms, and other edible plants and animals; and their access to common property such as the sea, beaches, and ancestral graveyards. Social networks, village ties, and cultural practices of sharing and socialising (such as the weekly music and dance parties) were ruptured through the dispersal of the community in Mauritius and Seychelles. Islanders' mental and physical health suffered from the stressful and traumatic experiences of displacement, relocation, and the ongoing dislocation from a society where they and their ancestors had lived and worked for generations. This resulted in significant numbers of deaths by suicide, miscarriage, and exposure to and susceptibility to diseases that were not common in Chagos, such as influenza and diphtheria. Chagos islanders' repeated use of the words *sagrin*, *tristes*, and *mizer* thus captures their material, social, and psychological suffering as a result of their forced displacement.

Marginalisation and mobilisation in exile

While emphasising the significance of the experience of forcible uprooting itself, it is also important to consider the significance of other factors such as treatment received and opportunities available at the destination (Kibreab 1999: 406). David Turton has pointed out that when relocation of a population is planned, the authorities ought to be able to take steps to minimise the disruptive impacts of the move on those displaced and to sustain their standard of living. Yet this is rare: those subjected to planned displacement – who are typically already 'amongst the poorest and politically most marginal members of society' – are also likely to become even more marginalised and impoverished as a result of displacement due to inadequately planned relocation and resettlement and increasing alienation from the authorities (Turton 2003: 3).

Chapter 1 provides a detailed historical background to the case study and outlines the history of decolonisation in Mauritius and its dependencies. It serves to highlight the challenging social, economic, and political conditions that confronted the displaced islanders upon their arrival in Mauritius, the main site of relocation. Focusing on three major problems – poor housing, underemployment, and ethnic discrimination – Chapter 1 shows how the demographic constraints, economic challenges, and ethnic tensions in Mauritius during the decades each side of independence in 1968 negatively impacted upon relocated Chagos islanders. First, Chagos islanders in Mauritius suffered from overcrowded living conditions in poor-quality houses in disadvantaged neighbourhoods with associated educational and social problems. Second, they were marginalised economically by the obsolescence of their skills in Mauritius, where they were exposed to unemployment, underemployment, and low wages. Third, they were marginalised socially through ethnic stereotypes and discrimination. Chapter 1 argues that marginalisation has inspired self-identification by Chagos islanders as a victimised community and has attracted external support, while intermarriage and integration into the Mauritian job-market were effective strategies for managing life in Mauritius. It concludes that strategies of integration and non-integration can be complementary rather than contradictory processes.

As the literature on 'long-distance nationalism' shows, however, traumatic experiences of displacement and marginalisation can also trigger the mobilisation of the disadvantaged community in exile (Anderson 1998; Fuglerud 1999). Key elements of such mobilisation include the development of collective identification as a victimised community and expressions of a shared political project such as the desire to return to the homeland (Al-Rasheed 1994: 201; Anwar 1979; Bascom 1998: 146–149; Jansen & Löfving 2009: 14; Watson 1977: 5; Zetter 1999: 6). Chapter 2 describes the mobilisation of Chagos islanders in Mauritius. Chagossian groups have historically been united concerning their desired ends, with a shared focus on compensation and the right to return to the Chagos Archipelago. Competing Chagossian groups have, however, disagreed on whether negotiation or litigation is the best means to achieve these aims. Chapter 2 outlines these tensions before focusing on the ideological and pragmatic disagreements within and beyond the community concerning two key issues. The first is debates about whether Chagos should be under British or Mauritian sovereignty. The second is debates about the legitimacy or otherwise of the US military base on Diego Garcia, which is seen by some as a necessary opportunity for employment and by others as conflicting with their visions for the resettlement of Chagos.

Narrating homeland, displacement, suffering, and loss

Elizabeth Colson has suggested that displacement provides a lens through which collective memory is reworked, and that 'the memory of shared experience of uprooting helps to create new forms of identity' in exile (Colson 2003: 9). Many displaced peoples 'display enduring and powerful images which evoke a familiar, idealized past and sustain the memory of collective loss' (Zetter 1999: 4). These 'semantics of exile', according to Pamela Ballinger, often take a similar form, following, like rites of passage, a tripartite structure: 'the original state of innocence, the liminal moment of rupture and transformation, and the phase of (partial) integration' (Ballinger 2003: 183). Liisa Malkki has shown how what she calls a 'mythico-history' can help to sustain self-identification amongst refugees as a victimised community standing together against perceived oppressors (Malkki 1995: 54–56).

Collective memories of the idealised homeland and of shared traumatic experiences of the displacement often provide displaced people with 'a wide frame of reference against which all subsequent experiences, even those of their descendants, could be interpreted' (Hirschon 1998: 17). Thus, from the perspective of displaced people, powerful moral narratives can enable subsequent generations – who did not experience the displacement at first hand – to 'identify with what others ("we") went through' (Ballinger 2003: 193). This can help to sustain collective identities and the desire to return over decades and generations in exile. Archetypal homeland discourses, then, evoke an idealised past interrupted by exposure to trauma, try to make sense of ongoing difficulties and sustain collective identification in exile, and project into the future by envisioning a triumphant return to the homeland.

Exactly such themes were routinely evoked in Chagossian homeland discourses. Chagossians recounted standardised collective narratives that romanticised and idealised the Chagos Archipelago as their homeland. They emphasised the collective and traumatic nature of their experiences of displacement from the Chagos Archipelago and of their chronic impoverishment, marginalisation, and suffering in exile. The proposed solution to their problems was the right of return to the Chagos Archipelago along with sufficient financial assistance to facilitate resettlement. These homeland discourses, however, existed not in a vacuum but in a context of dual strategies of mobilisation and integration in Mauritius, and were further complicated by challenges to the durability of the community over generations in exile and by the opportunity for Chagossians to migrate onwards to the UK instead of either remaining in Mauritius or resettling Chagos.

Chapter 3 engages with these Chagossian homeland discourses through an analysis of the changing lyrical content of songs composed on Chagos compared with Chagossian songs composed in exile. Whilst the lyrics of songs composed on the Chagos Archipelago concern the everyday sorrows and joys of life there, the lyrics of Chagossian songs composed in exile romanticise life on Chagos, highlight the suffering of the community in exile, and appeal for community solidarity and mobilisation in the struggles for compensation and the right to return to Chagos. Chapter 3 shows that such standardised homeland discourses have successfully elicited support from within and beyond the community, but that these collective representations of the experience of displacement have posed problems for Chagossian witnesses in court, where the laws of evidence require individual eyewitness accounts.

Chapter 4 concerns the politics of culture in exile, and in particular Chagossians' engagements with contrasting understandings of the characteristics of culture, from authenticity and continuity on the one hand to change, loss, and transformation on the other. In order to demonstrate that they remain an identifiable group in exile, Chagossians must emphasise the durable aspects of their culture that distinguish the Chagossian community from other communities. At the same time, however, in order to demonstrate their victimhood and establish that they deserve recompense and repatriation, Chagossians must show that they have suffered cultural loss in exile, where they have both struggled to sustain their own traditions and been influenced by interaction and intermarriage with non-Chagossians. Each of these aspects was incorporated into Chagossian music and cuisine, with cultural loss and cultural overlaps with others framed negatively and cultural distinctiveness and cultural revival framed positively. Such contrasting conceptualisations of culture do not imply contradictions but rather survival strategies in the face of severe structural disadvantage. Politicians, lawyers, judges and others in positions of power are therefore mistaken wilfully to misinterpret the diverse cultural practices of displaced and otherwise victimised groups as evidence for either local integration or inauthentic cultural production in exile.

Onward migration and making home in exile

Social scientists have recently challenged the assumption that 'home' is necessarily associated with a particular physical location (Blunt & Dowling 2006: 230; Mallett 2004: 79; Staeheli & Nagel 2006: 1600). Ethnographers have instead conceptualised 'home' in terms of lived processes and practices: how people seek to make themselves, as Michael Jackson has put it, 'at home in the world' (Jackson 2000; see also Jansen & Löfving 2009: 2–3; Olwig 1999: 83). Even amongst migrants, home may be as much about where one is going as about where one has come from (Mallett 2004: 77). As David Turton has put it, 'the experience of displacement is not only about the *loss* of a place, and the pain and bereavement this entails. It is also, and inevitably, about the struggle to *make* a place in the world' (Turton 2005: 278). This resonates with Staeheli and Nagel's suggestion (Staeheli & Nagel 2006: 1608) of a temporal and generational distinction for migrants between home as where one's parents belonged (in the past), home as where one participates (in the present), and home as where one's children belong (in the future).

For the extended Chagossian community, the struggle for the right of return to resettle Chagos has coexisted with a range of strategies for survival and integration in exile. A majority of those born to Chagos islanders in exile have one Chagossian and one non-Chagossian parent. An increasing proportion of 'the Chagossian community' is from generations born and brought up in exile, who have never been to Chagos. While many from the younger generations do identify as Chagossian, they are likely to see themselves as having multiple identifications and to define themselves as also Mauritian, Seychellois, British, or a combination of these. It would be implausible to seek to identify a single physical location as 'home' for the extended Chagossian community. It is more fruitful instead to engage with Chagossians' diverse strategies for making a place (or a home) for themselves in the world.

Such strategies have been complicated by Chagossians' eligibility for UK citizenship since 2002. Only Chagos islanders and their children born in exile are automatically eligible for compensation and for UK citizenship. Chagos islanders' grandchildren and subsequent generations are ineligible, despite pleas from the Chagossian leadership for their inclusion. Onward migration to the UK has been dominated by young working-age families (including the third and subsequent generations born in exile, who have to acquire visas). The vast majority have settled in or around Crawley, where most work nearby at Gatwick Airport.

Revisiting the themes in Part I, Chapter 5 reveals the similarities and differences between the Chagossians' forced displacement from the Chagos Archipelago and their onward migration to the UK. The 'echoes of marginalisation' include bureaucratic hurdles in acquiring citizenship status and the relevant identification documents, familial separation across continents, and the implications of relocation to an area of relative ethnic diversity, socio-economic deprivation, and educational challenges. The similarities go only so far, of course. In particular, unlike the high rates of unemployment in Mauritius in the 1960s, late 1970s to early 1980s, and again since the late 1990s, Crawley has had consistently extremely low rates of unemployment since its inception as a New Town in the 1960s. By and large, Chagossian migrants in Crawley have managed to find jobs and adequate housing, and have been able to access state welfare when required. Compared to their overwhelmingly negative assessments of their lives in Mauritius, they have reported a far wider range of experiences, both negative and positive, relating to education and employment, taxes and benefits, and racism and discrimination in the UK.

Echoing the concerns of Part II, Chapter 6 engages with Chagossians' changing relationships with their places of birth, upbringing, and residence. In Mauritius, the widespread desire to return to Chagos can be explained by the Chagossians' overwhelmingly negative experiences of forced displacement and the comparisons they highlighted between the good life in Chagos and their poor circumstances in Mauritius. Those who emigrated sought better education and employment prospects. By and large they continued to view Mauritius negatively, and they made much more varied (although generally less negative) assessments of life in the UK. Yet many nevertheless claimed that they wished to return to Mauritius one day. My conclusion is that this can only be explained by seeking to understand how experiences in the UK have challenged preconceptions about the UK, brought about subtle reformulations of conceptions of Mauritius (from 'host' to 'home'), and altered the focus of visions of the future. From the vantage point of Mauritius, life in Mauritius was depicted as uniformly inferior to life in Chagos. From the vantage point of Crawley, life in Mauritius was depicted as having certain benefits and drawbacks relative to life in the UK. In particular, the UK was generally seen as preferable to Mauritius in terms of standard of life and education and employment opportunities for young people, while Mauritius was generally seen as preferable in terms of quality of life, particularly for retired people. Among the younger generations at least, this reassessment of Mauritius has been accompanied by a concomitant reconfiguration of Chagos as ancestral homeland rather than viable future. The Chagossian case, then, reveals ethnographically how migrants' perspectives on the past and the future alike are relative to their positioning in the present.

Migration research and 'multi-sited ethnography'

Migration research often entails 'multi-sited ethnography' (Marcus 1995) in which an ethnographer conducts fieldwork in both the source and destination locations. In order to carry out this comparative study of Chagossian experiences in Mauritius and the UK, I lived and worked with the extended Chagossian community in several locations between 2002 and 2007. As detailed below, the bulk of my ethnographic data comes from extended periods of fieldwork in Mauritius and Crawley.

I lived in Mauritius for fifteen months between October 2002 and February 2004. For most of the first year I lived with my partner Andrew in a flat near the Chagossian housing estate *Cité Ilois* in Pointe aux Sables, to the south-west of the capital Port Louis (see Map 4).[1] For the final few months I lived with a family in Riche Terre, to the north-east of Port Louis, from where I had easy access to other areas inhabited by Chagossians. Chagossian and Mauritian families invited us to share family occasions such as birthday parties, baptisms, first communions, weddings, and funerals, and to join their celebrations of the New Year, Easter, Christmas, and other Catholic festivals. I conducted semi-structured interviews with Chagos islanders and their descendants. As detailed in Chapter 1, I also undertook a small-scale household survey on Chagossian living conditions.

After winning the judicial review in the London High Court in 2000 in the name of its leader, Olivier Bancoult, the CRG became the dominant Chagossian organisation, representing the vast majority of the extended Chagossian community. Throughout my fieldwork in Mauritius, the CRG's main financial support came from the Ilois Support Trust (IST), a UK charity that secured grant of £76,279 from Comic Relief (a UK charity committed to poverty reduction) for a two-year 'capacity building' project with Chagossians in Mauritius. The main institutional effect of the project was the establishment of a CRG office in Cassis, on the western outskirts of the Mauritian capital Port Louis (see Map 4).

On arrival in Mauritius, Andrew and I volunteered at the CRG office, which enabled us to get to know CRG members and to learn Kreol. After three months, I reduced my commitments at the CRG office in order to concentrate on fieldwork, but Andrew continued to work there for the rest of his year in Mauritius, producing a database of CRG members and preparing demographic statistics that were used in press releases and for organising the distribution of funding for social activities. At that time, the CRG database contained registration details for 843 native Chagos islanders and 3,139 of their second-generation descendants then still living in Mauritius.[2] I attended the meetings of the various CRG committees and participated in activities organised by the CRG and by other groups clustered under the CRG umbrella: its longstanding Chagossian Youth Group [*Grup Zanfan Zilwa*], the newly established Chagossian Women's Group [*Grup Fam Chagossienne*], and a newly established musical ensemble called the Chagos Tambour Group [*Grup Tambour Chagos*].

In my fieldwork, I was guided by my research subjects in terms of what cultural practices came to constitute my focus. What was most important to Chagossians became what was most important to me as an ethnographer. At the time of my fieldwork, members of two recently formed groups within the CRG – the Chagossian Women's Group and the Chagos Tambour Group – were preoccupied with remembering, enacting, and transmitting Chagossian culture. For them, Chagossian culture primarily took the form of cuisine and music. My ethnographic experience was thus dominated by activities such as cooking and eating together; recalling, learning, transcribing, and recording Chagossian song lyrics; practising and performing Chagossian instruments and Chagossian dance; and debating cultural authenticity in exile and cultural transmission to generations born in exile. Such issues consequently comprise a core focus of this book, to the inevitable exclusion of other manifestations of culture – such as religious beliefs, ritual practices, and kinship, for instance – which are no doubt equally interesting but were not (at the time) such major preoccupations for the people I encountered during my fieldwork.

I joined two CRG delegations to the Mauritian outer island of Rodrigues: first to assist the CRG on a networking visit to the devolved Rodrigues Regional Assembly in June 2003, and second to accompany the Chagos Tambour Group on tour to perform at the Creole Festival there in October 2003. Along with the IST, I helped organise and run a two-day residential young leaders' workshop with the Chagossian Youth Group. The IST subsequently employed Andrew and me to undertake the midpoint internal evaluation of its 'capacity building' project with the CRG, and later asked me to reconnoitre the Chagossian group in Seychelles to investigate the possibilities for a similar project there, which I did during a two-week visit to Seychelles in January 2004. I interacted socially with numerous CRG members as well as non-Chagossian supporters of the CRG, such as the group's Mauritian legal representatives and their families, and with Mauritian journalists.

I also formed good research relationships with the other main Chagossian organisations. I attended the Chagossian Social Committee's (CSC) monthly meetings and annual remembrance services, and conducted interviews with CSC members and the CSC's Mauritian barrister. I worked with the Diego Garcia Island Council (DGIC) by attending its meetings and press conferences and by interviewing its active members. I found that by declining to pass information between the groups, I was able to gain the trust of diverse Chagossians regardless of their political loyalties in the Chagossian struggle.

Beyond the Chagossian community, I attended political and cultural events organised by the marginal left-wing political party *Lalit* (from the French *la lutte*, meaning the struggle), its educational wing *Ledikasyon Pu Travayer* [Education for Workers], and its women's group *Muvman Liberasyon Fam* [Women's Liberation Movement]. My relationship with *Lalit* became invaluable in the latter half of my fieldwork when *Lalit* and the CRG collaborated briefly on a proposal to organise a boat trip to Diego Garcia (which never came to fruition). I also built on my links with social scientists at the University of Mauritius by participating in their development of the Mauritius wing of the Organisation for Social Science Research in Eastern and Southern Africa (OSSREA) and presenting a paper on the Chagossian case study at their conference on Poverty in Mauritius when I returned to Mauritius in 2007. Through the University of Mauritius and *Lalit* I met Mauritian and foreign journalists, lawyers, academics, and other anthropologists with whom to discuss research issues. Finally, I accessed primary historical sources at the Mauritius Archives in Coromandel, secondary historical sources and Mauritian newspaper archives at the University of Mauritius Library in Moka, and national statistical data courtesy of the Central Statistics Office in Port Louis.

During the first year of fieldwork in Mauritius, Andrew and I ran a series of conversational English courses (held in the *Centres Ilois* in Pointe aux Sables and Baie du Tombeau, and in the CRG office in Cassis) for those Chagos islanders and their descendants who intended to migrate to the UK. When I began my fieldwork with Chagossian migrants in the UK, these participants and their families became my first Chagossian contacts in the UK. In 2006–7 I conducted a total of five months of fieldwork with Chagossian migrants in Crawley, where I rotated between three families from Mauritius. In Crawley (as in Mauritius), I attended family celebrations and religious festivals, conducted semi-structured interviews, and observed Chagossian migrants' relationships with other Chagossians from Mauritius and Seychelles and with other migrants, locals, colleagues, employers and representatives of local authorities. I participated in campaigns and Chagossian community-building projects organised by the Diego Garcian Society (DGS, formerly DGIC), the new Chagos Island Community Association (CICA), and local civil society organisations. I also attended the hearings and judgments of several court cases in London.

For several reasons, my fieldwork experiences in Mauritius and Crawley were quite different from one another. In Mauritius a much larger proportion of the Chagossian community was retired, unemployed, or mobilised in the Chagossian struggle. Many social activities took place at community centres (such as the CRG office and the two *Centres Ilois*), and people spent a lot of time outdoors in gardens or on the street. It was extremely easy to make contacts and be introduced to new people, especially in my own neighbourhood of Pointe aux Sables, where there was a high concentration of Chagossian households, and where life in the *Cité Ilois* was characterised by frequent interaction between households. In Crawley, by contrast, the extended Chagossian community was predominantly of working age. A higher proportion of women were employed, including women who had been housewives in Mauritius. Additionally, the colder climate, longer shifts and longer school hours, and the dispersal of Chagossian households across the town meant that many people in Crawley returned directly to their houses after work and did not reconvene in the evenings. This meant that I often set up meetings and interviews in advance, in comparison to the frequent spontaneous interactions I was used to from my fieldwork in Mauritius.

In a sense, this book is based on so-called 'multi-sited ethnography': my fieldwork consisted of what George Marcus would call 'follow[ing] the people' as they migrated from Mauritius to the UK (Marcus 1995: 106). My methodological approach, however, differs significantly from 'jet lag' (Hage 2005: 465) or 'jet-set ethnography' (Olwig 2007: 22), which is characterised by a consecutive series of transitory stays in multiple geographical locations. By contrast, I conducted fifteen months of fieldwork amongst the extended Chagossian community in Mauritius (i.e. the main site of relocation following their displacement from Chagos) and then, several years later, five months of fieldwork amongst some of the same people, plus others, in Crawley (i.e. their main site of relocation following emigration from Mauritius and Seychelles). Two key features of my approach – the sustained character of my two periods of fieldwork, and the fact that I engaged with many of the same people in both fieldsites – enable me to overcome the concern that 'foreshortened', multi-sited ethnography is likely to produce 'shallower' data than the 'thick description' produced through long-term, intensive fieldwork in a single geographical location (Falzon 2009: 7–10;

Marcus 1995: 100, 106). A by-product of my method is that my data are not only spatially divided (between Mauritius and the UK) but also temporally divided between two distinct periods of time (2002–4 and 2006–7 respectively) (see also Gallo 2009; Leonard 2009).

Notes

1 At the time when the *Cité Ilois* housing estates were established in the mid-1980s, Chagos islanders were still known as *Ilois* [islanders]. For a detailed discussion of the collective name change from *Ilois* to Chagossian in the late 1990s, see Chapter 4.

2 The CRG database also contained registration details for 22 native Chagos islanders and 168 of their second-generation descendants then living in the rest of the world (except Seychelles, where about 154 native Chagos islanders and 300 of their second-generation descendants were registered by the separate Chagossian organisation based in Seychelles). The number of native Chagos islanders is in steady decline, whereas the number of subsequent generations of descendants born in exile is increasing. A decreasing proportion of the Chagossian community lives in Mauritius and Seychelles as large numbers emigrate to the UK and beyond.

I

Marginalisation and mobilisation

1

Marginalisation in Mauritius

My father didn't like Mauritius. He told us that life in Mauritius was not the same [as life in Chagos]. We didn't understand because we were children, and we always said that we wanted to go to Mauritius. Our father told us that life in Mauritius was hard; even the Mauritian people were very poor. I was little when we came here for the first time. I was seven years old. At that time all the children liked Mauritius and we said that we wanted to stay, but my father didn't like it so after a month we returned to Chagos. Then we came to Mauritius in 1968 and at the office my mother was told that the islands had been sold. We had lots of problems here. One day my father asked me if I understood why he didn't like Mauritius; why he said that life in Mauritius is hard. I've never forgotten that. I always remember my father said that. (Mimose, born on Peros Banhos to Chagossian parents)

This chapter outlines the history of colonisation, settlement, and decolonisation in Mauritius and the Chagos Archipelago. It shows that the inhabitants of the Chagos Archipelago were already marginal within colonial Mauritius, and that their marginality was compounded by their relocation to Mauritius during the decade around independence, which was a period of social, economic, and political unrest.

Colonising Mauritius[1]

Malay and Arab or Swahili traders explored the south-west Indian Ocean (see Map 1) over a thousand years ago. However, many of the smaller islands of the Indian Ocean – including Mauritius and Rodrigues, the Chagos Archipelago, Réunion, and the Seychelles islands – were unpopulated prior to European colonial expansion in the region from the end of the fifteenth century onwards. In the decades following Vasco da Gama's trip around the Cape of Good Hope in 1498, Portuguese navigators rediscovered the islands now known as Mauritius, Réunion, and Rodrigues, which they collectively named the Mascarene Islands after a Portuguese navigator. The Portuguese used Mauritius as a stopping place between the Cape and India, but did not establish a permanent settlement on any of the Mascarenes. Portuguese navigators also explored – but did not settle on – several distant archipelagos further north in the Indian Ocean, including Chagos, Agalega and Cargados Carajos Shoals (St Brandon), and the Seychelles. The Dutch East India Company used Mauritius as a stopping place between Europe and East Asia from 1598 onwards, and claimed the island in 1638, naming it after the ruling prince Maurice van Nassau. But the Dutch found it difficult to maintain the small and remote settlement, and by 1710 the island had been abandoned. The French, who had occupied Réunion since 1642, then claimed Mauritius in 1715 and Seychelles in 1742. In 1810, during the Napoleonic wars, the British captured the Mascarenes. Realising the military significance of the natural harbours on Mauritius, the British retained Mauritius and its dependencies – including Rodrigues, the Chagos Archipelago, and the Seychelles – but returned Réunion to French control.

These successive European colonists attempted to turn Mauritius into an economically viable colony (see Allen 1999; Allen 2004; Barnwell & Toussaint 1949; Benedict 1965; Carter 1995; Teelock 2001). The Dutch introduced sugarcane to Mauritius in the mid-seventeenth century, finding the crop resilient and well suited to the rainy and windy climate. Following French experimentation with coffee, cotton, indigo, and spices, the British again favoured sugarcane. Britain raised its quota for imports of Mauritian sugar to match the West Indies quota in 1825, and sugar accounted for 85 per cent of the value of Mauritian exports by the 1830s.

The fact that the Mauritian economy quickly became dependent on sugar in particular had implications for the type of plantation society that developed there. Comparative historians of European plantations in the Caribbean and the Pacific and Indian Oceans have argued that variations in mortality rates depended less on the era and nature of employment contract, the nationality of the colonial power, or the character of the estate manager, than on the technical relations of production. The production of sugar is extremely labour-intensive, and conditions on sugar estates were arguably worse than those on plantations growing crops such as tea, coffee, cocoa, coconuts, spices, cotton, and rubber (Higman 1984; Tinker 1974). The sugar estates on Mauritius were characterised by particularly hard physical labour, poor remuneration, and the widespread use of punishments – violence and the withholding of rations or wages – to extract labour (Allen 1999: 13–14; Tinker 1974: 17–18). High rates of desertion and high mortality rates that outstripped birth rates posed challenges for estate owners, who continually imported overseas workers to supplement their labour forces (Allen 1999: 13–15, 175–176; Teelock 2001: 119).

The settlement of Mauritius began under the French, who brought enslaved labourers mainly from Africa and Madagascar. The British abolished the slave trade in 1807 and emancipated enslaved labourers in Mauritius in 1835. They compensated the slave owners financially and replaced slavery with an apprenticeship scheme entitling the former slave owners to continued labour for a maximum of six years. The apprenticeship scheme proved unpopular and was eventually terminated prematurely in 1839, after which many labourers in Mauritius rejected the employment terms offered by their former owners. They left the sugar estates for nearby vacant land, towns, and marginal coastal areas, where they supported themselves through small-scale commercial agricultural cultivation, non-agricultural manual labour or domestic servitude, and fishing (Allen 1999: 112,129; Carter 1995: 19; Vaughan 2005: 267).

From the late eighteenth century onwards, French and later British colonists also brought enslaved and convict labourers from British India. After the 1835 emancipation of enslaved labourers, estate owners supported indentured labour as a way to keep labour costs low, arguing that indentured labourers would work for longer hours at lower wages than formerly enslaved labourers (see Allen 1999: 148–149; Carter 1995: 16–17). The rate of immigration from India increased dramatically, such that Indian immigrants comprised one-third of the population of Mauritius by the mid-1840s and stabilised at two-thirds during the 1860s (Allen 1999: 17; Benedict 1961: 17; Benedict 1965: 17; Carter 1995: 271). A slump in sugar prices led many Franco-Mauritian estate owners to sell plots of their land from about 1875 onwards. By this time, Indian labourers had largely replaced African labourers on the sugar estates, and many were able to purchase smallholdings, which became rural villages and small plantations dominated by Indo-Mauritians (Benedict 1961: 27–31; Teelock 2001: 294). European contractors also recruited labourers from China from 1860 onwards. Once emigration had been legalised, many Chinese sought to escape the economic depression in China during the second half of the nineteenth century (Ly-Tio-Fane Pineo 1985: 22–24). Immigration from China peaked following the Maoist revolution in 1949, and people of Chinese origin constituted over 3 per cent of the Mauritian population by 1952 (Central Statistics Office 2003a: 15–16).

The particular history of settlement via African slavery and Asian indenture in colonial Mauritius resulted in a relatively durable ethnic division of labour, which has to a large extent persisted in postcolonial Mauritius. Indo-Mauritians continue to be over-represented in agriculture and Afro-Mauritians in non-agricultural manual labour, while Sino-Mauritians are over-represented in business and Franco-Mauritians still own the large sugar estates (Benedict 1965: 25–28; Eriksen 1998: 64, 110, 118; Mauritius Research Council 1999: 30; Salverda 2004; Simmons 1982: 10–11; Srebrnik 2002: 277–278). As we shall see below, this ethnic division of labour had particular implications for the Chagos islanders when they arrived in Mauritius in the 1960s and 1970s.

Two centuries of settlement on the Chagos Archipelago

Economic activity, settlement and administration on the Chagos Archipelago were conducted by commercial companies through concessions granted by the government of Mauritius (Scott 1961: 96–101). From about the 1770s onwards, French planters began to populate Chagos with enslaved labourers brought mostly from mainland East Africa and Madagascar via Mauritius (Ly-Tio-Fane & Rajabalee 1986; Scott 1961: 120–121; Toussaint 1966: 64, 272; Walker 1986). They established coconut plantations on the larger islands – including Diego Garcia, the Salomon Islands and Peros Banhos Atoll – producing copra (dried coconut flesh), from which was extracted coconut oil used in the generation of electricity and manufacture of soap in Mauritius and beyond. This gave rise to an alternative name for the archipelago: the Oil Islands (Toussaint 1977: 11).

The copra companies controlled the land use, owned the buildings and other infrastructure, and were responsible for administration, which they often devolved to an onsite manager or administrator (Scott 1961: 136, 153). From 1835 onwards, the government of Mauritius periodically sent magistrates to visit the dependencies, check the conditions for the labourers, arbitrate disputes and administer justice, and report to the governor of Mauritius (Scott 1961: 139, 159–160). Reports by a series of nineteenth-century magistrates – Charles Anderson (1839), Charles Farquharson (1864), E. Pakenham Brooks (1875), J. H. Ackroyd (1878), and Ivanoff Dupont (1884) – along with reports of visits during the mid-twentieth century by a Roman Catholic priest, Roger Dussercle (1934), and a governor of Mauritius, Robert Scott (1961), comprise a fascinating (if limited) resource on working life on the colonial Chagos Archipelago.

Labour on the coconut plantations was gendered and varied by island and estate (Scott 1961: 163–164). Generally, men and women alike speared and gathered coconuts; men stripped off the husks using a wooden stake topped with a metal blade; women used a curved blade to break open the shells, scraped the flesh from the shells, and laid the flesh out to dry in the sun or in furnaces to form copra; men worked the machines pressing copra to extract coconut oil; men loaded the produce (dried copra and pressed coconut oil alike) onto ships destined for Mauritius and beyond; men and women alike gathered palm leaves for various purposes; and a few labourers rose to the rank of commanders or overseers (Ackroyd 1878; Brooks 1875; Dussercle 1934: 9–10). Outwith copra production, women worked as domestic servants in the plantation managers' houses; men and women cut and gathered palm leaves and grass to make baskets; and men were employed as fishermen, stablemen, gardeners, cooks, boat manufacturers, brewers, carpenters, coopers, blacksmiths, stonemasons, rat-catchers, watchmen, and hospital attendants (Ackroyd 1878; Brooks 1875). Throughout the settled history of the archipelago, commercial activity was dominated by copra production, although by the twentieth century other exports from Chagos islands to Mauritius included guano, salt fish, timber, surplus grain, brushes and brooms, rope, wooden toys, and turtles (Scott 1961: 253–255, 274–275, 287–288).

Copra production is much less labour intensive than sugar production, and during the period of apprenticeship the magistrate Charles Anderson reported that workloads in the dependencies were much more manageable than those in mainland Mauritius (Anderson 1839: 78). Additionally, workers were permitted to plant crops and raise animals, which, Anderson remarked, gave them 'self interest' in the land (Anderson 1839: 77). As Anderson predicted, a far larger proportion of former enslaved labourers accepted work contracts to remain on the plantations in the dependencies after the termination of the apprenticeship scheme than was the case in mainland Mauritius. As a result, people of African origin were always in the majority in Chagos, although there were continuous flows of people around Mauritius and its dependencies throughout the colonial period (Anderson 1839: 63–64; Benedict & Benedict 1982: 122; Dussercle 1934: 9–10; Todd 1969: 19–20, 29, 33; Toussaint 1977: 22–23). Since the islands were run by copra companies that issued work contracts for the islanders, unemployment was not a problem on Chagos, although employers could – and sometimes did – dismiss and deport those workers who were considered to be workshy or troublemakers.

Workers received rations and bonuses that varied by island and estate but included rice, maize, lentils, coconuts, coconut oil, salt, rum, coconut toddy, and tobacco (Brooks 1875; Farquharson 1864). Wages were low, although overtime was often available, and pay could be spent in the company shops on additional foodstuffs and other supplies, or else banked to fund trips to Mauritius to visit relatives or purchase items unavailable in Chagos (Ackroyd 1878: 22; Brooks 1875: 64–75; Farquharson 1864). Proprietors were required to provide workers with basic housing or building materials. Islanders often had access to plots of land on which they could plant food crops and raise animals such as poultry and pigs, and they supplemented their diets with fish, seafood, turtles, and seabirds (Ackroyd 1878: 23–30; Brooks 1875; Dussercle 1934; Farquharson 1864). Proprietors were also required to provide basic healthcare and primary education.

The magistrates' reports depict conditions on Chagos that vary somewhat by date, island and estate, the character of the manager, and the temperament of the magistrate himself. Farquharson (1864) and Dupont (1884) reported that the Chagos islanders were generally content and did not have substantial complaints, and concluded that they benefited from a light workload, regular payment of rations and wages, proportionate punishment for misdeeds, well-stocked stores, and adequate hospitals. Dupont also detailed numerous cases of imprisonment for disturbances such as murder, violence and the threat of violence, attempted rape, theft, drunkenness, desertion, insolence and insubordination. Brooks (1875) and Ackroyd (1878) reported that islanders had substantial grievances against their managers: excessive workloads; irregular provision of rations and wages; excessive punishment (including fines, deduction of wages, detention, imprisonment and violence) for offences such as theft, absence from work, lateness and non-completion of tasks; the absence of written work contracts detailing ration entitlements; the detention of islanders who wished to go to Mauritius; inadequate housing and a lack of hospitals; restrictions on fishing, hunting seabirds, and raising pigs to force islanders to purchase foodstuffs from company stores instead; and excessive price hikes on imported items sold in those stores. Successive commentators were concerned about the gender imbalance, low rates of marriage, competition between men for the limited women, circulation of women between men, and resulting violence and abuse (Scott 1961: 149, 161).

In sum, these reports reveal that the colonial Chagos Archipelago can be characterised by paternalistic management, underlying violence and disruption, and basic living conditions throughout its settled history. Importantly, however, both the magistrate Charles Anderson and the priest Roger Dussercle – whose visits took place almost a century apart – remarked that conditions in Chagos were better than those in many other plantations, including those on mainland Mauritius. In comparison with Mauritius, Chagos was characterised by a less arduous workload in return for adequate rations and the freedom to volunteer for paid overtime or instead to use the abundant leisure time to fish, hunt, grow crops, and raise animals for consumption.

These features are reflected in Chagos islanders' recollections of life on Chagos as akin to a form of slavery [*esklavaz*], but one in which the workload was manageable and islanders could choose how to spend their plentiful time off work. As Rosemond, a Chagossian man in his sixties, put it, on Chagos 'we lived like slaves [*esklav*] – we weren't free – but we could do whatever we wanted to do'. When I asked him if they had to work hard, Rosemond replied 'not really' since working hours were concentrated in the morning and early afternoon, leaving the rest of the day free. Others complained that their tasks were physically demanding and could be dangerous (because of sharp tools), their pay was low, and their employers could be domineering [*domineer*], but added that they had benefited from guaranteed employment on the islands and did not have to contend with unemployment. Yvonne, a Chagossian woman in her sixties, recalled that 'life was hard over there – we had to work to get everything we needed – but we all had work'. Most Chagossians I spoke with felt that their low wages were more than offset by the provision of free houses and food rations, which meant that they did not have to worry about money. Raphael, another Chagossian man in his sixties, expressed it as follows: in terms of 'money we were poor, but food we weren't poor' [*larzan nu ti mizer, me manze nu pa ti mizer*].

Excision and depopulation of the Chagos Archipelago

This way of life was brought to an end between 1964 and 1973. During the Cold War, the US sought to establish a military presence in the Indian Ocean, favouring the Chagos island of Diego Garcia on account of its administration by British allies, its small and politically insignificant population, its central but isolated location, its natural harbours, and its potential to build a runway (Jawatkar 1983: 44; Vine 2009: 61). In 1965 – as part of negotiations leading to Mauritian independence in 1968 – the UK Government excised the Chagos Archipelago from colonial Mauritius and created the new British Indian Ocean Territory (BIOT). In exchange for what was in effect a US$14 million discount on the Polaris missile system, the UK Government agreed to depopulate the Chagos Archipelago and lease Diego Garcia to the US Government (Bandjunis 2001: 26–27; Jawatkar 1983: 17; Vine 2009: 87–88).

The residents of the Chagos Archipelago had been accustomed to making periodic trips to Mauritius to renew work contracts, purchase supplies, receive medical treatment, take holidays or visit family. From 1967 onwards, however, Chagos islanders in Mauritius were refused return passages and were told that the Chagos Archipelago had been 'sold' and the islands 'closed'. They were thus stranded in Mauritius, sometimes separated from family members who had remained in Chagos. In Chagos, proprietors gradually reduced the importation of supplies, wound up copra production, and did not renew employment contracts once they had expired.

Diego Garcia was the first to be depopulated, in 1971. The BIOT administrator, John Todd, called a meeting to announce to the islanders that they would have to leave Diego Garcia (Vine 2009: 108–109). They were told they could either move to one of the settlements on the other Chagos atolls of Salomon and Peros Banhos, or leave the Chagos Archipelago and be taken to Mauritius or Seychelles. Many islanders recall being told they would receive assistance – land; housing, animals, and financial compensation – upon arrival in Mauritius. The authorities deployed several tactics to intimidate islanders into obeying orders to leave (Vine 2009: 112–114). Firstly, the plantations had been wound down, food and medical supplies were already low, and ships no longer replenished supplies. Secondly, the US military moved in and commenced the construction of its military base. Thirdly, the BIOT Commissioner, Bruce Greatbatch, ordered that the islanders' dogs be destroyed: the dogs were rounded up and burned in the building used to dry copra. Islanders feared for their own survival.

Some of those who made the journey from Diego Garcia to Mauritius via Seychelles were housed in a prison during their stopover in Seychelles. Those who had chosen to remain on other Chagos islands soon learned that this was only a short-term solution. The remaining plantations on Salomon and Peros Banhos were wound down and supplies continued to dwindle. Salomon was depopulated in 1972, and Peros Banhos in 1973. The *Nordvær*, the ship that made the final voyages from Chagos, could not comfortably accommodate the numbers of people who were to be moved. People were allowed to take some small items but had to leave most of their larger belongings behind. Passengers suffered seriously overcrowded and insanitary conditions, lacking in adequate food and water supplies. On some journeys, passengers died, miscarried, or committed suicide, and dead bodies were thrown overboard (Vine 2009: 118–120). Thus, two centuries after Chagos was populated via slavery, the archipelago was similarly depopulated via forced removals and traumatic upheavals.

Ethnic politics and decolonisation in Mauritius

The excision and depopulation of the Chagos Archipelago aside, Mauritian decolonisation is usually analysed in terms of ethnic politics. As outlined above, European colonial administrators and estate owners in Mauritius and its dependencies created populations with diverse ancestral origins and societies in which ancestral, ethnic, religious, and class affiliations have been central to social, political, and economic life. Slave owners had routinely classified their workers by geographical area of origin until the emancipation of enslaved labourers in 1835, after which census enumerators were responsible for recording a respondent's 'population group' (Central Statistics Office 2003a: 15). During the remainder of the British colonial period, the population classifications used were changed to reflect that the main sources were no longer East Africa and Madagascar but rather India and China. At the same time, an increasing proportion of the population was now born in Mauritius rather than elsewhere. The term 'Creole', which originally referred to all those who had been born in the colony, gradually came to refer to those of primarily African or mixed ancestry (Benedict 1965: 14; Eriksen 1998: 176–177; Eriksen 2002: 79–80; Miles 1999: 212 note 7; Teelock 1999: 3; Vaughan 2005: 2–3, 272). A subcategory of 'Afro-Creole' reflects the collective cultural identity of those who emphasise their shared African (i.e. enslaved) ancestry in contradistinction to people of European and/ or Asian ancestry (Eriksen 2002: 75–76; Vaughan 2005: 264).

In 1962 and 1972, census enumerators in Mauritius were instructed to ask respondents to assign themselves to a particular 'community'. The categories offered were 'Hindu' and 'Muslim' (both of South Asian origin), 'Sino-Mauritian' (of Chinese origin), and the residual 'General Population' (all others: 'Creoles' and 'Franco-Mauritians'). These censuses reported that the Mauritian population comprised approximately 50 per cent Hindus, 16 per cent Muslims, 31 per cent General Population and 3 per cent Sino-Mauritians (Central Statistics Office 2003a: 16). In the 1983 census, the practice of classifying respondents according to ethnic or religious affiliation was discontinued in the hope of reducing ethnic tension (see Dinan 2002: 81). The census continued to record citizens' names, religious background and ancestral language. In 2000 the Central Statistical Office extrapolated from these data to estimate that the balance had remained fairly constant. The Mauritian population of nearly 1.2 million comprised 66 per cent Indo-Mauritians (Hindus and Muslims forming approximately 52 per cent and 14 per cent of the total population respectively), 31 per cent General Population (Creoles and Franco-Mauritians forming approximately 29 per cent and 2 per cent of the total population respectively), and 3 per cent Sino-Mauritians (Central Statistics Office 2000: 2; see also Eriksen 1998: 183).

Accounts of the late colonial period in Mauritius have noted that decolonisation was highly controversial and that ethnic and religious affiliations played a large part in political affiliations (Benedict 1965: 60–67; Simmons 1982; Teelock 2001: 373–399). The Mauritian Labour Party (MLP) was established in 1936 with the intention of uniting estate labourers and small planters – regardless of ethnic or religious community – by focusing on their shared working-class interests. By the mid-twentieth century, however, the MLP had turned from class-based to communal politics, and was dominated by high-caste Hindus who focused on the campaign for independence from Britain. Many non-Hindus feared that independence would result in domination by majority Hindu interests. In 1955 a group of Franco-Mauritian planters and urban Creoles and Sino-Mauritians, who opposed the MLP, formed the rival Mauritian Party to campaign against independence (see Carroll 1994: 312; Eriksen 1998: 10; Mauritius Research Council 1999: 7; Selvon 2001: 382–385).

In 1965, the debate about independence sparked riots between Creoles and Hindus. In 1966, the MLP created an Independence Party by forming an alliance with two Hindu parties and a Muslim party. General elections were held in Mauritius in 1967 and won by the Independence Party. This paved the way for independence in 1968, although 44 per cent of the electorate had voted for the Mauritian Party's anti-independence coalition (Eriksen 1998: 10, 151–152; Miles 1999: 215; Srebrnik 2002: 279). In January 1968 (just prior to independence in March), major inter-ethnic rioting broke out in the north of Port Louis between Creoles and Muslims over control of the constituency. The riots resulted in over twenty-five deaths, hundreds injured, thousands fleeing their homes and the declaration of a state of emergency (Eriksen 1998: 151–152; Simmons 1982: 186–188; Teelock 2001: 396). After independence on 12 March 1968, there was no major inter-ethnic violence for the next thirty years.

In February 1999, however, there were four days of inter-ethnic violence across Mauritius. This violence was sparked by the death in police custody of Reginald Topize (also known as Kaya), a popular Afro-Creole *seggae* [Kreol-language reggae] singer. He had been arrested for use of marijuana following his participation in an event campaigning for the legalisation of marijuana (Miles 1999: 211). Perceiving that Kaya's death had been ethnically motivated, and blaming it on the Hindu-dominated police force, Creoles attacked police stations. Hindus retaliated by burning houses owned by Creoles. The riots resulted in the deaths of at least four civilians and one police officer. Over one hundred people were injured, fifty homes were lost, and a state of emergency was imposed (Carroll & Carroll 2000: 139; Chateau 2000; Srebrnik 2002: 282).

Some social scientists (e.g. Carroll 1994; Salverda 2004) have portrayed Mauritius as a multiethnic success story. Others (e.g. Eriksen 1998; Hills 2002) have argued that an overarching Mauritian national identity increasingly offers 'common denominators' that take precedence over particularistic ethnic or religious identities. The recent recurrence of violence, however, recalls the warnings of earlier social scientists (cf. Benedict 1965; Simmons 1982) that ethnic and religious communalism lay not far beneath the peaceful surface of Mauritian society and remain underlying currents in Mauritian social, political, and economic life. Anthropological accounts of ethnicity in Mauritius in the twenty-first century (e.g. Boswell 2006; Eisenlohr 2006) have demonstrated that the prospect of an overarching Mauritian national identity is threatened by the official valorisation of (Indian) ancestral heritage over local (Creole) hybrid traditions. The social, political, and economic dominance of Indo-Mauritians and the durability of ethnic categorisation reinforce the marginalisation of Creoles in Mauritius. Discrimination, in the form of institutional racism, ethnic stereotyping, and ethnic nepotism, has restricted opportunities for many Creoles and particularly Afro-Creoles. The resultant 'Creole malaise' is characterised by low educational achievement, high unemployment, poverty, low standards of living, high rates of substance abuse and crime, and a lack of solidarity within Afro-Creole communities (Boswell 2006: 77–78; Eriksen 2002).

This history of colonisation, decolonisation, and ethnic tensions provides the backdrop for the arrival of the Chagos islanders in Mauritius during the 1960s and early 1970s. The remainder of this chapter deals with the implications for the Chagos islanders relocated to Mauritius. It addresses the ways in which Chagos and the Chagos islanders were already marginal within colonial Mauritius; how this pre-existing marginality was compounded by the ethnic, social, economic, and political challenges that confronted Chagos islanders upon their arrival in Mauritius during the years on each side of independence; how they dealt with these challenges; and how their situation has changed over time.

Housing shortages

The Mauritian census shows a slow rate of population growth throughout the first half of the twentieth century, rising from 371,000 in 1901 to 419,000 in 1944 at a rate of less than 0.5 cent per year. After the Second World War, however, the population grew much faster, rising from 501,000 in 1952 to 681,000 in 1962 at a rate of between 2 and just over 3 per cent per year, resulting in a population density of 367 people per square kilometre by 1962 (Bowman 1991: 50–51). At independence in 1968, Mauritius was widely considered to be a Malthusian time bomb because of high population growth and limited land and resources (Bowman 1991: 112–113; Toussaint 1977: 82–83, 91).[2]

By the time the Chagos islanders started to arrive at the docks in the capital Port Louis, Mauritius in general and Port Louis in particular were suffering from a severe shortage of housing stock. This was the result of high population growth and density plus the devastating effects, especially on poor-quality housing, of recent cyclones, particularly cyclone Carol in 1960.[3] Upon arrival in Mauritius, most Chagos islanders were homeless, had to seek new accommodation, and had to pay for accommodation (unlike in Chagos). Chagossian families who had left Chagos to visit Mauritius in the early-to-mid 1960s – and who did not know until later that they would be unable to return to Chagos – often stayed with their extended families and other acquaintances in Mauritius. Their hosts tended to live in the already crowded neighbourhoods of Port Louis and its environs: Cassis to the west of the city centre, Roche Bois to the north-east, and Petite Rivière to the south-west of the city (see Map 4). Others had nobody to accommodate them in Mauritius and sought cheap or temporary accommodation in disadvantaged neighbourhoods.

In May 1973, the penultimate boatload of 125 Chagos islanders deported from Peros Banhos on the cargo ship the *Nordvær* refused to disembark on the quayside in Port Louis. They demanded that they be returned to the Chagos Archipelago or be offered compensation and housing. Eventually, after almost a week on board, the Mauritian Government offered them accommodation in the dockers' flats in Baie du Tombeau or in government housing in Cité la Cure, two disadvantaged neighbourhoods to the north and east of Port Louis (*L'express* 1973; *Le Mauricien* 1973). Chagossian families recall the unsanitary and dilapidated state of the accommodation, much of which lacked running water and glass in the windows.

No resettlement programmes were put in place. Chagos islanders received no immediate compensation or assistance finding employment. All sources agree that they faced severe socio-economic difficulties throughout the subsequent decades. For example, in a report for the UK Government, Russell Prosser noted in 1976 that housing was the main problem for relocated Chagos islanders, who were 'living in deplorable conditions' (Prosser 1976: 6). A Mauritian social worker, Françoise Botte, wrote in 1980 that unemployment and underemployment, lack of understanding of money, low educational achievement, and housing problems had led to alcoholism, gambling, prostitution, and stealing (Botte 1980: 43–49). A 1981 report by Hervé Sylva likewise concluded that the main problems for Chagos islanders were poor housing and unemployment, and that poverty had given rise to problems such as alcoholism, gambling, and crime (Sylva 1981). In a 1985 report for the Minority Rights Group, the investigative journalist John Madeley described the Chagos islanders as living in 'abject poverty' and noted that housing and unemployment remained major problems (Madeley 1985: 3, 10–11). Iain Walker devoted one chapter of his 1986 anthropological report on the Chagos islanders in Mauritius to a discussion of unemployment, under-employment and poor housing (Walker 1986: 20–27).

In 1972, the UK Government paid the Mauritian Government £650,000 to meet the costs of resettling the Chagos islanders in Mauritius (de l'Estrac 1983: 73). Most of this was not distributed until 1978, and the Mauritian Government retained the interest it had accrued in the interim (de l'Estrac 1983: 78). In 1978, each Chagossian adult was entitled to receive Rs.7,590 (about £650 at the time, according to Madeley 1985: 7) and Chagossian children under eighteen were entitled to between Rs.1,000 and Rs.1,500 depending on their age at the time (de l'Estrac 1983: 77). Many families (including all Chagos islanders in Seychelles) received no money. Even for those who received the payments, the money proved 'hopelessly inadequate' (Madeley 1985: 7). It paid off some debts incurred since their arrival but generally was insufficient to purchase land or a house.

Further negotiations between Chagossian groups in Mauritius, the Mauritian Government, and the UK Government produced another compensation package in 1982. This time, the UK Government contributed £4 million, and the Mauritian Government contributed land in Baie du Tombeau and Pointe aux Sables worth £1 million. The Mauritian Government also set up the Ilois Trust Fund Board (ITFB) to administer the distribution of this compensation.[4] Each Chagos islander was immediately entitled to receive Rs.10,000 (about £600 at the time, according to Madeley 1985: 10). Adults then received a further Rs.36,000, while children under 18 received a further Rs.23,000, much of which was used to pay off debts or pooled by families and put towards the purchase of land or a house.[5] Final instalments of Rs.8,000 were released in 1983. Between 1982 and 1985, over one hundred Chagossian-headed households moved to Pointe aux Sables or Baie du Tombeau to live in houses in the purpose-built Chagossian housing estates called *Cités Ilois* or to build on the land allocated to Chagos islanders in *Morcellements Ilois*.

The size of the plots of land and concrete houses in the *Cités Ilois* varied according to the number of claimants: one Chagossian claimant was entitled to a smaller plot and fewer rooms than a household made up of two or more eligible Chagossian claimants. The original houses were two, three, or four main rooms for living and sleeping (the number of main rooms depending on the number of eligible Chagossian claimants in the household), plus a kitchen and a toilet. Most houses in the *Cités Ilois* have subsequently been extended horizontally or vertically (or both), and many plots are now cluttered with additional houses built by subsequent generations. The fate of the *Morcellements Ilois* has been much more varied: many plots were sold by their original Chagossian owners or were seized by loans companies; other plots remain vacant; and only a minority are inhabited by Chagossian families. Their houses range from basic wooden frames covered with corrugated iron, to small but sturdy concrete houses akin to those in the *Cités Ilois*, to substantial multi-storey concrete brick houses complete with garages.

In 2003–4, I conducted a socio-economic household survey of seventy-six Chagossian households in Mauritius. I defined a Chagossian household minimally as one in which at least one of the senior male or female residents was born in Chagos. Many such households comprised a Chagossian couple and sometimes even a subsequent generation born in Chagos. I surveyed the forty Chagossian households in the *Cité Ilois* in Pointe aux Sables to the south of Port Louis, where the original Chagossian inhabitants or their descendants still own forty-two of the forty-four houses (95.4 per cent).[6] I also surveyed a total of thirty-six Chagossian households in other areas around Port Louis with significant Chagossian populations, including elsewhere in Pointe aux Sables, Cassis, Baie du Tombeau's *Cité Ilois* and *Morcellement Ilois*, Roche Bois, Cité La Cure, and Le Hochet (see Map 4). Not surprisingly, the rate of house ownership outwith the designated *Ilois* neighbourhoods was slightly lower: 84.8 per cent, corresponding more closely to the national rate of 86.5 per cent (Central Statistics Office 2003b: 19). Given the relative poverty within the Chagossian community, this level of house ownership can be explained if many Chagos islanders who did not take a house or land in compensation eventually used their compensation money and/or savings to buy houses elsewhere.

My respondents estimated that those who took and kept the compensation land or houses tended to be in a better financial situation now than those who had used their compensation money in other ways such as paying off pre-existing debts. I found that living standards in both of the *Cités Ilois* varied within a much narrower middle range by comparison with the wider variation in housing standards in other areas. A survey led by David Vine in 2001–2 estimated that about two-thirds of Chagossian houses were made of concrete, while about a third were made of a combination of building materials, including concrete bricks, corrugated metal, and wood (Vine *et al.* 2005: 155). The concrete buildings (which include the compensation *Cité Ilois* houses) are generally secure and structurally sound, whereas the mixed-fabric houses are at particular risk from destructive weather such as cyclones (Vine *et al.* 2005: 162–164). Thus the standard of Chagossian housing began to improve during the 1980s when they received compensation and could access sturdier housing, but securing structurally sound accommodation remained and remains a problem for many Chagossian families.

High unemployment

From the eighteenth century onwards, as we have seen, the economy of mainland Mauritius was dominated by sugarcane production. Colonial government reports from the 1960s indicated that the main economic problems were its extreme dependence on the sugar industry and resulting vulnerability to the fluctuations of the sugar market, and its rapid population growth resulting in high unemployment and increased pressure on resources (Bowman 1991: 112–113). This precarious economic situation had particular implications for Chagos islanders' attempts to enter the Mauritian labour market. British government officials predicted that Chagos islanders would have difficulties integrating into the Mauritian economy because of the already high levels of unemployment and because of the Chagossians' lack of experience in the sugar industry. In 1969 the then High Commissioner to Mauritius, Arthur Wooller, sent a telegram to inform the Foreign and Commonwealth Office (FCO) that the Mauritian Government was reluctant to accept the Chagos islanders. After all, he noted, Mauritius faced 20 per cent unemployment and the influx of 250 Chagossian families would increase pressure on social services. He suggested that the Chagos islanders would be faced with the 'near impossibility of finding suitable employment' because they were trained only in the copra industry, which was absent in Mauritius.[7] A letter to the FCO from the BIOT Commissioner, Hugh Norman-Walker, reinforced this viewpoint:

> It is important when dealing with the problem of the *Ilois* [islanders] from Chagos to appreciate what type of people they are. They are extremely unsophisticated, illiterate, untrainable and unsuitable for any work other than the simplest labour tasks on a copra plantation. This is not altogether surprising as they have spent all their lives on remote islands.[8]

This letter illustrates that the authorities anticipated that the Chagossians' efforts to find jobs would be hampered both by existing high levels of unemployment and by the islanders' lack of training for the jobs that were available. Particularly when times were tight, Chagos islanders observed that Mauritian employers – like employers elsewhere – had a general preference for hiring experienced local workers rather than inexperienced outsiders with whom they had no connection. Chagos islanders frequently criticised the authorities for having sent them to Mauritius at a time of acute job shortages. This, they argued, compounded their existing problems such as their lack of formal education, their lack of experience in the sugar industry, and the obsolescence of many of the skills they had brought with them from Chagos. During his fieldwork amongst the Chagossian community in Mauritius in the mid-1980s, Iain Walker noted that many of those Chagos islanders who did manage to get jobs on arrival in Mauritius were later disadvantaged by 'last in, first out' policies implemented by Mauritian employers during economic downturns (Walker 1986: 33).

The Mauritian economy was helped by global demand for sugar and rises in sugar prices, and the unemployment rate fell to around 7 per cent in 1976, but the end of the sugar boom in the mid-1970s and highly destructive cyclones in

1975 and 1979–80 once again precipitated high unemployment in Mauritius, rising back up to 15 per cent in 1982 (Bowman 1991: 112–122). Throughout the 1970s and 1980s, Mauritius underwent a major transformation as successive governments diversified the economy. The textiles industry quickly became the single largest employer and exporter, followed by tea and tobacco for export, large-scale fishing, tourism, and offshore finance (Benedict 1965: 5–7; Bowman 1991: 122–137; Central Statistics Office 2003b; Eriksen 1998: 19). Unemployment fell sharply to around 3 per cent by the late 1980s, and by the 1990s Mauritius was being hailed as *the* African postcolonial multiethnic political and economic success story (Bowman 1991: 137–140; Eriksen 1998: 13).

Contrary to this conventional narrative, however, and despite the significant increases in levels of employment as a result of the growth in the textiles and tourist industries in particular, unemployment and underemployment have remained problems. For many of the poorest in Mauritius, and especially Afro-Creoles, securing stable jobs has proved difficult. Even at the height of Mauritian employment growth, in 1986, more than 30 per cent of the labour force was working in the informal sector (Lamusse 2001: 41). The expansion of the Mauritian economy had relied on cheap labour throughout the 1980s and early 1990s. As Mauritian workers became more expensive in the mid-1990s, large employers – especially in the textiles industry – increasingly moved their factories abroad or imported cheap labour such as Chinese workers (Mauritius Research Council 1999: 3). This resulted in a reduction in the number of jobs in industry for Mauritians, particularly among the unskilled urban working classes. In the late 1990s, the Mauritian economy slowed and unemployment rose every year from just over 5 per cent in 1995 to over 10 per cent in the early 2000s, falling gradually to hover around 7 per cent by the end of the decade (Central Statistics Office 2003a; Central Statistics Office 2010).

'At the bottom of the socio-economic scale,' noted the Mauritius Research Council in 1999, are 'Hindu plantations workers, Muslims working in petty jobs within the informal sector, and Black Creole factory workers, dockers, and fishermen' (Mauritius Research Council 1999: 30). This latter category includes the Chagossian community. A series of surveys indicates that the Chagossian community has suffered disproportionately from chronic underemployment and unemployment. In particular, a significant proportion of Chagossian men has remained underemployed and a significant proportion of Chagossian women has remained unemployed (Botte 1980; Jeffery 2006a: 50–53; Sylva 1981; Vine *et al.* 2005: 116–119). While the Mauritian economy was expanding and diversifying, then, the Chagossian community was structurally disadvantaged in ways that inhibited Chagossians from accessing the wider macroeconomic prosperity.

Ethnic division of labour

In addition to their lack of education, relevant skills, and local networks, Chagossians also encountered problems as a result of the dominance of Indo-Mauritians and the durability of ethnic categorisation and stereotyping in Mauritius.

After independence, Hindu Mauritians controlled many sectors of Mauritian society, including government and public-sector employment. Like other Afro-Creoles in Mauritius, Chagossians routinely described the archetypal employer in Mauritius as a Hindu who would discriminate in favour of other Hindus. Many Afro-Creoles have reported that if a Hindu and a non-Hindu applied for the same job, a Hindu employer would be likely to give the job to the Hindu applicant even if the non-Hindu applicant was better qualified (see Eriksen 1998: 62–67; Mauritius Research Council 1999: 10, 60). Chagossian interviewees told me that they believed that it was 'normal' or 'natural' for employers to discriminate in favour of employing members of their own ethnic or religious community. Indeed, Chagossian employers in the fishing and construction trades hired workers on a similar basis, tending to favour fellow Chagossians and particularly family members or those with similar political affiliations.

Employers were also perceived to be likely to discriminate against members of other communities about which they held negative stereotypes stemming from a history of slavery, racial classifications, and ethnic discrimination. Some Mauritians of Indian, Chinese or European descent hold negative stereotypes of, and discriminate against, people of primarily African origin (i.e. Afro-Creoles). Thomas Eriksen found that many non-Creoles held stereotypes of Creoles as 'lazy, merry, careless' (Eriksen 1998: 54). Rosabelle Boswell similarly reported that non-Creoles perceived darker-skinned Creoles to be 'lazy, atavistic and present-oriented' (Boswell 2002: 2). According to William Miles, 'Creoles are stereotypically regarded, by themselves as well as by other Mauritians, as those Mauritians who have adopted an epicurean philosophy, enjoy partying, eschew savings, and put little stock into education' (Miles 1999: 219). Many of my Chagossian and Mauritian Creole acquaintances asserted to me that 'Creoles are lazy'. As evidence, they would cite the fact that Roman Catholics would take extra days off work following public holidays and Christian festivals, whereas members of other religious groups would return to work straight after their own religious festivals. According to the anti-communalist Mauritian politician and playwright Dev Virahsawmy, Mauritius is characterised by institutional racism up to government level, and many Indo-Mauritians see Afro-Creoles as inherently less employable than other ethnic groups. Concurring with this analysis, many Afro-Creoles reported to me that discrimination made it difficult for them to find jobs, forced them to take jobs below their training or ability, and meant that they were less likely later to be promoted up the hierarchy and pay scale.

Most Chagossians are of primarily African descent (or mixed African, South Asian, and/or European descent). As such, they are physiognomically indistinguishable from other Afro-Creoles in Mauritius. On arrival in Mauritius, Chagos islanders were generally slotted into a subset of Afro-Creoles known as *ti-kreol* [literally, 'small Creole'], who tend to be marginalised and in low-status and low-paid jobs (Eriksen 1998). The problem for Chagos islanders was that, as one Chagossian woman put it to me, 'we are too dark, our hair is short-short': that is, they share phenotypes such as dark skin and Afro hair with already marginalised peoples of African descent.

Chagos islanders were identifiable by their accents, dress, and place of birth listed on identification cards. Stereotyping of Afro-Creoles in general was compounded by stereotyping of Chagos islanders – then known simply as *Ilois* [islanders] – for being uneducated and uncivilised. As Josephine, a retired Chagossian woman, explained to me:

> It was difficult when we came here to look for work. Why? [Mauritians said:] 'The *Ilois* [islanders] don't know how to read. Don't pay attention to them. They're savages.' That's not easy. When we came to Mauritius we came to a foreign country. How to adapt? We're humans too, so instead of treating us in that way, they could have welcomed us, but instead they were mostly bad … They said 'the *Ilois* have left their islands and come to take all the work here'. For getting work it was the same: when they knew that you are *Ilois* it was difficult, and they wouldn't give you work except as a housemaid. So many people were mistreated. Dogs are treated better in Mauritius than we are.

Several researchers have confirmed these claims, showing how Chagossians suffered discrimination in their searches for employment and in the low salaries they received (Botte 1980: 38–39; Dræbel 1997: 36; Walker 1986: 21–22).

Madeleine, a Chagossian woman in her early forties, recalled that when a group of Chagos islanders was moved to a housing estate outside Port Louis, a local Mauritian resident exclaimed: 'the Zulus are coming to Mauritius to eat us!' Madeleine went on to say: 'we were treated very inhumanely, we weren't treated like humans. [Mauritians] mistreated Chagossians'. Characterisation of the Chagos islanders as (foreign) Zulus highlights that discrimination stemmed both from their stigmatised African origins and from their outsider status. Thus from a Chagossian perspective, their maltreatment at the hands of Mauritian employers was a result of a combination of factors. Firstly, Mauritian employers preferred to hire members of their own family, ethnicity, or religious group. Secondly, Afro-Creoles in general and the Chagossians in particular suffered discrimination on the basis of criteria such as laziness, lack of education or training, and ideas about a racial hierarchy.

Given their residential concentration around Port Louis, their lack of contacts and skills relevant to the Mauritian job market, and their stigmatised status as Afro-Creoles and Chagossians, it is not surprising that the extended Chagossian community have gradually been incorporated into a predominantly Afro-Creole urban workforce made up of low-paid workers who can be easily hired and fired. The 190 workers – comprising Chagos islanders and their descendants – sampled in my survey of Chagossian households in and around Port Louis were over-represented at the bottom end of the employment spectrum. The vast majority worked in low-wage, low-status, often insecure jobs, and a very small percentage – compared to national averages – worked in the service industries and the professions (Jeffery 2006a: 52–53). In this sample, men worked in the largest numbers as construction workers, followed by lorry helpers, fishermen, dock workers, carpenters, and factory workers. Meanwhile, women worked in the largest numbers as factory workers followed by housemaids, shop helpers, and cleaners. Thus by the early twenty-first century most in the extended Chagossian community were employed in archetypal urban Afro-Creole working-class jobs. As such their disadvantages in terms of education and skills were compounded by their ethnic and geographic alignment with an already marginalised sector of Mauritian society, and the double discrimination they faced as Afro-Creoles and as Chagossians.

Ambivalence towards Mauritius

Chagossians also have reason to be circumspect about the Mauritian nation-building project since Mauritian independence was achieved via the excision and consequent depopulation of the Chagos Archipelago. Seewoosagur Ramgoolam, the Mauritian politician at the centre of the independence negotiations in 1965, later reported that the UK Government had coerced him into agreeing to the detachment of the Chagos Archipelago to ease and speed up the process of decolonisation (de l'Estrac 1983: 9–11). He told the Select Committee on the Excision of the Chagos Archipelago:

> A request was made to me. I had to see which was better – to cede out a portion of our territory of which few people knew, and independence. I thought that independence was much more primordial and more important than the excision of the island which is very far from here, and which we had never visited, which we could never visit … If I had to choose between independence and the ceding of Diego Garcia, I would have done again the same thing. (de l'Estrac 1983: 22)

Ramgoolam's account reveals the marginality of the Chagos Archipelago within colonial Mauritius. Most people in Mauritius knew little about the territory and its inhabitants, and the political elite 'considered that the excision of a distant archipelago, and the expulsion of some poor illiterate Creoles, was a small price to pay for state power, with British support, in decolonisation' (Houbert 1992: 471).

In Mauritius, Ramgoolam is often affectionately referred to as 'father of the nation' [*père de la nation*] (Eriksen 1998: 146; cf. Teelock 2001: 415), but, not surprisingly, many Chagossians dissent from this accolade. Several told me that they did not celebrate Mauritian independence because it came at their expense. Josephine expressed the problem as follows:

> Mauritian independence is something that has brought great sadness … we have suffered too much. This whole community suffered, people died of sadness and poverty, all because of Mauritian independence. Mauritius got its freedom but we are still suffering, we have nothing, we're still slaving away … Mauritius got its independence and became a republic on our backs. The country was developed with a university and all that, all on our backs. [Look at] the courage of my elders, they suffered and died because of poverty and missing the islands. Look at our dark poverty [*mizer nwar*], our sacrifice for independence.

Chagossians thus tend to feel ambivalent at best about the Mauritian post-colonial nation-building project.

Another arena in which Chagossians tend to dissent from the standard national narrative is in relation to the relative significance of displacement and immigration for the various populations that make up Mauritius. As previously explained, Mauritius was unpopulated prior to European colonial settlement in the Indian Ocean, and all of the early settlers were uprooted – voluntarily or forcibly – from their native lands in Asia, Africa, and Europe. Thus all Mauritians are descended from ancestors who experienced dislocation and relocation. In public speeches at Chagossian events, Mauritian politicians routinely emphasised this, and attempted to conflate the historical displacement of Mauritians' ancestors with the Chagos islanders' first-hand experiences of displacement. For instance, in November 2003, the then Minister of Arts and Culture, Motee Ramdas, declared at the unveiling of a monument to commemorate the displacement of the Chagos islanders: 'displacement is the history of our country: slavery, indentured labour, and this more recent displacement [of the Chagossians]'.

Many Chagossians, however, emphasised the distinction between the displacements that led to the populating of Mauritius on the one hand and the displacement of the Chagos islanders on the other. Madeleine, who was born in the late 1960s and was a young girl when her family was forcibly removed from Peros Banhos in 1973, remarked that there was a significant difference: 'It wasn't just my ancestors who were uprooted; I myself was uprooted, so I feel it more'. Pauline, also born in Peros Banhos in the late 1960s, pointed out that, in contrast to the historical displacements of slavery and indenture – during which only certain proportions of the local populations were relocated – in this case 'the entire Chagossian people were uprooted'. Thus both women rejected the notion that their displacement was just another example of the population movements that created Mauritius, because the Chagossian case has two differentiating features. Firstly, it occurred during living memory and formed part of lived experience. Secondly, the entire population was removed from Chagos.

Thus it is not surprising that many Chagossians find it difficult to engage with the Mauritian nation-building project. Their engagement, however, has been complicated by their relationships with non-Chagossians and the subsequent birth and upbringing of their children in Mauritius. In my household survey, over half of the Chagos islanders who had formed cohabiting or marital relationships since coming to Mauritius had partners born in Mauritius. Of the seventy-six Chagossian households surveyed, forty-eight were headed by couples.[9] Of these, fifteen households were headed by couples in which both partners were born on Chagos. Meanwhile, thirty-three households were headed by couples in which one partner was a Chagos islander and the other was a non-Chagossian born elsewhere in the Republic of Mauritius.[10] Most of the Chagossian–Chagossian couples were older people who had already been partners on Chagos. Most of the younger Chagos islanders who formed marital or cohabiting relationships since their arrival in Mauritius did so with partners born in Mauritius rather than Chagos. The Mauritius-born descendants of Chagos islanders likewise overwhelmingly tended to take non-Chagossian partners. Thus there seems to have been no particular valorising of Chagossian–Chagossian partnerships, but Chagos islanders and their descendants have generally taken partners who fall within categories that can be considered taxonomically close. Most (but by no means all) of their Mauritius-born partners were also urban working class Afro-Creole Roman Catholics, and indeed many were from the same neighbourhood, secondary school, or church (cf. Nave 2000: 330).

Given these marriage patterns, most of those born to Chagos islanders in Mauritius have one Chagossian and one Mauritian parent, and most of those with Chagossian grandparents have fewer Chagossian than Mauritian grandparents. At a Chagossian youth leadership workshop, participants were asked to choose between being a 'young Chagossian' or a 'young Mauritian', which several refused to do on the grounds that they had both Chagossian and Mauritian parentage and grand-parentage and had been born and raised in Mauritius. They agreed that they wanted to learn Chagossian history and culture, but asserted that they were also Mauritian. Integration through geographical proximity, interaction, and marriage with Mauritians has resulted in an increasing proportion of the younger generations of the Chagossian community considering themselves to be (also) Mauritian. Thus Chagossians remain marginalised in Mauritian society, but have generally integrated socio-economically into the (also marginalised) Afro-Creole urban working classes through such practices as work and civic participation, leisure and religious activities, and marriage and child-rearing.

Marginalisation in Mauritius

Throughout the colonial period, the Chagos Archipelago was a marginal dependency of Mauritius, and its inhabitants were thus already marginalised prior to the displacement. Their marginality was compounded by their displacement, which uprooted Chagos islanders from their homes, jobs, and livelihoods, and which relocated them during a time of social upheaval, political competition, economic insecurity, and housing shortages in Mauritius. Chagos islanders lacked contacts, education, training, and experience relevant to the job market in Mauritius. They were further disadvantaged by overlapping ethnic discrimination against Afro-Creoles in general and Chagossians in particular. In combination, these factors had detrimental effects on their ability to find adequate housing and jobs in Mauritius. Chagossian families have consequently suffered disproportionately from the concomitants of poor housing in disadvantaged neighbourhoods and of unemployment and underemployment. These have included low levels of educational achievement and high rates of teenage and unplanned pregnancy, alcoholism and drug abuse, and prostitution (Anyangwe 2001; Dræbel 1997; Vine *et al.* 2005).

On the one hand, Chagossians frame their experience in Mauritius in terms of their initial experiences of discrimination and their ongoing lack of identification with the Mauritian nation-building project. This is not least because independence came at the cost of the excision and depopulation of the Chagos Archipelago. On the other hand, however, Chagossians have gradually integrated into the urban Creole working classes. Over time, Chagossians seem to have achieved a relative 'insider' status, at least when compared to more recent newcomers. The Chagossian community's early experiences of resettlement in Mauritius, for instance, have been echoed by the experiences of recent migrants from the

Mauritian island of Rodrigues, who have likewise suffered stigmatisation as Afro-Creoles and have likewise struggled to secure decent houses and jobs in Mauritius (see Boswell 2006: 151).

When asked when and why they thought the situation for Chagossians in Mauritius had started to change, the vast majority of my respondents referred to a series of Chagossian successes over the past decade or so. They cited the popularisation by the Chagossian Social Committee of the collective noun Chagossian (instead of the generic and derogatory term *Ilois*) during the late 1990s, Olivier Bancoult's successful High Court case against the UK Foreign and Commonwealth Office in 2000, the UK Government's granting of UK citizenship to Chagossians in 2002, and, more generally, recognition of the 'value' of the community derived from the Chagos Refugee Group's campaigns for compensation and the right to return. These developments are the focus of Chapter 2.

Notes

1 This section draws extensively on work by historians of colonial Mauritius, particularly Richard Allen, Marina Carter, Auguste Toussaint, Vijaya Teelock, and Megan Vaughan.

2 Population growth rates slowed from the 1970s onwards, and had fallen to an annual growth rate of less than 1 per cent by the 2000 census, which recorded a population of over one million people, but Mauritius remains one of the most densely populated countries in the world (Dinan 2002: 107–109).

3 According to the Mauritius Meteorological Services (http://metservice.intnet.mu), Carol is still 'the most devastating cyclone on record'. It uprooted crops, killed forty-two people, destroyed 40,000 houses, and left thousands homeless. As a result of this destruction, the Central Housing Association set up the Cyclone Housing Scheme, which built 14,000 subsidised houses (of which 6,000 were on urban housing estates) between 1961 and 1970 (www.unhchr.ch/tbs/doc.nsf/(Symbol)/7d47498c72a3ab758025655a004 e46e7). Cyclone Gervaise destroyed 13,000 houses in 1975, and the Government commissioned another 10,000 subsidised homes to be built between 1975 and 1980.

4 At the time when the Ilois Trust Fund Board was established in the early 1980s, Chagos islanders were still known as *Ilois* [islanders]. For a detailed discussion of the collective name change from *Ilois* to Chagossian in the late 1990s, see Chapter 4.

5 *Chagos Islanders v Attorney General and HM BIOT Commissioner* [2003] EWHC QB 2222: paragraphs 77–80.

6 There are technically forty-four houses in the *Cité Ilois* in Pointe aux Sables, but during my fieldwork three were uninhabited by their Chagossian owners (in at least one case the family was in Agalega) and one had been sold to a non-Chagossian Mauritian family. These four houses were not included in the detailed household survey. Of the forty *Cité Ilois* houses I surveyed, two were no longer owned by their Chagossian inhabitants. One had been seized by a loans company while the former owner (who still lived there) paid off her debts. The other was owned by the descendants of the original Chagossian owner, who rented the house to another Chagossian family.

7 Quoted in *Chagos Islanders v Attorney General and HM BIOT Commissioner* [2003] EWHC QB 2222: appendix paragraph 221.

8 *Ibid.*: appendix paragraph 312.

9 The remainder were headed by Chagossians who were divorced or separated, widowed, or single.

10 Of these, twenty-six were born in Mauritius, five in Agalega, and two in Rodrigues.

2

Mobilisation in exile

In the previous chapter, I described how the Chagos islands and the Chagos islanders were already marginal within colonial Mauritius, and showed that the socio-economic, political, and ethnic tensions in mainland Mauritius in the 1960s and 1970s negatively affected the Chagos islanders' experiences of relocation. In this chapter I show how Chagossians have responded to their chronic marginalisation and impoverishment in exile through mobilisation in the form of struggles led first by Chagossian women in Mauritius and later by Chagossian organisations in Mauritius, as well as (to a lesser extent) Seychelles and (more recently) the UK. Historically, most Chagossian organisations have agreed that their primary aims are adequate compensation and the right to return to the Chagos Archipelago. Chagossian groups have, however, disagreed about the best means to achieve these ends, whether through political negotiation or through legal cases. Additionally, Chagossian organisations in exile have not functioned in isolation from local political processes. On the contrary, successive Chagossian organisations have been constituted by their changing relationships with political parties and advocacy groups in Mauritius and elsewhere. These changing alliances have had important implications for the ideological and pragmatic stances taken by Chagossian groups on two key issues. These are, firstly, whether the Chagos Archipelago should be under British or rather Mauritian sovereignty, and secondly, the legitimacy or otherwise of the US military base on Diego Garcia.

Mobilisation of the Chagossian community

From the beginning, Chagos islanders rejected the fact and the terms of their removal from Chagos. In 1971, when the administrator of BIOT announced that Diego Garcia would be closed and all of its inhabitants uprooted, islanders protested against being made to leave. In 1973, as described in Chapter 1, the penultimate boatload of Chagos islanders to arrive in Mauritius refused to disembark until the Mauritian Government offered accommodation (*L'express* 1973; *Le Mauricien* 1973). In 1975, Chagos islanders in Mauritius petitioned the UK Government, citing the broken promise made by British officials in

Chagos that the islanders would receive resettlement assistance and financial compensation on arrival in Mauritius. The petition urged the UK Government to ask the Mauritian Government to provide land, housing, and jobs, or else to return the islanders to the Chagos Archipelago. This petition went unheeded, along with numerous subsequent pleas to the Governments of the UK, the USA, Mauritius, and Seychelles. Nevertheless, these small-scale early protests reveal a history of periodic resistance in the form of demonstrations, hunger strikes, negotiation, and litigation.

In 1972, as detailed in Chapter 1, the UK Government paid the Mauritian Government £650,000 to compensate the displaced Chagos islanders. However, the Mauritian Government did not distribute the money until 1978, after a group of Chagossian women had led a protest lasting several months. Later that year, a cyclone destroyed much poor-quality accommodation, and the Mauritian Government subsequently evicted some Chagossian families from their emergency accommodation. After living with their families under tarpaulin sheets for two months, a group of eight Chagossian women started a three-week hunger strike and protestors distributed flyers reading: 'Give us a house; if not, return us to our country, Diego' (*Le Mauricien* 1978). Four Chagos islanders were later jailed for resisting the police when Mauritian authorities tore down their accommodation (Madeley 1985: 7). These protests yielded few concrete results but they did add to mounting awareness of the Chagos islanders' plight and mobilised political support from a new left-wing political party, the Mauritian Militant Movement (MMM), which had been formed in 1969.

In 1979 the MMM assisted a group of Chagos islanders to engage a British lawyer, Bernard Sheridan, to negotiate with the UK Government for additional compensation. Sheridan was already suing the UK Government on behalf of a Chagossian man, Michel Vincatassin, who charged that he had been forcibly removed from his ancestral homeland. British officials reportedly offered to pay an additional £1.25 million if Vincatassin would drop his case and Chagossian recipients would sign deeds 'in full and final settlement', waiving all their 'claims and rights (if any) of whatsoever nature to return to the British Indian Ocean Territory' (Madeley 1985: 6, 8, 15). Sheridan visited Mauritius to offer this deal of money in exchange for these renunciation forms, which were written in English. Initially some Chagos islanders – many of whom were not literate and did not know English – did sign or thumbprint these forms. When other Chagossian leaders and MMM activists heard the terms of the deal, however, they halted the process and sent Sheridan back to the UK. A support group of Chagossians and Mauritians (many MMM members) wrote to Sheridan that the Chagos islanders who had signed or thumbprinted the forms had done so without 'alternative legal advice' and 'as a mere formality' to obtain the compensation, rather than out of agreement with the conditions, and no money was disbursed (Madeley 1985: 8).

Chagos islanders continued to demonstrate in Port Louis in 1980 and 1981. Led again by women who repeatedly faced police intimidation, violence, and arrest, hundreds of Chagossians marched to the British High Commission, protested in front of government offices, and slept on pavements in the Mauritian capital. They demanded the right to return to Chagos, immediate compensation, decent housing, and jobs. A broad coalition of Mauritian political groups – including *Lalit*, a marginal leftist wing of the MMM that eventually separated from the MMM in 1982 – supported the Chagos islanders under the rallying cry *Rann Nu Diego* [Give Us Back Diego]. This phrase united the Chagossian struggle with the desire of some Mauritians to return Chagos to Mauritian sovereignty and to close the military base on Diego Garcia (Lalit 2002: 113–117; Vine & Jeffery 2009).

After an eighteen-day hunger strike and violent clashes resulting in the arrest of eight women – six Chagos islanders and two members of *Lalit* – the then Mauritian Prime Minister, Seewoosagur Ramgoolam, left for London to meet the then British Prime Minister, Margaret Thatcher. Representatives of the two Governments held talks with Chagossian representatives including Charlesia Alexis, Lilette Naïck, and Christian Ramdas (*L'express* 1982; *Le Mauricien* 1982a, b, c). After two rounds of negotiations, the UK Government agreed to provide £4 million in compensation and the Mauritian Government agreed to contribute land valued at £1 million. The final instalments of cash were released in 1983 only on condition that the recipients would sign or thumbprint English-language renunciation forms to indemnify the UK Government from further claims for compensation or the right to return (Madeley 1985: Appendix 2). Since the majority of Chagos islanders were not literate and did not know English, the fact that the renunciation forms were produced in English and were not adequately translated or explained indicates that they were extracted without appropriate informed consent.

Accounts by journalists, advocates, and social workers report that Chagossian women were well represented in the hunger strikes, demonstrations, clashes with police, and negotiations with the UK and Mauritian Governments in the early 1980s (Botte 1980; Collen & Kistnasamy 2002; Madeley 1985: 8). Even at this stage, however, it seems that rather than having been overwhelmingly dominated by women, Chagossian activism could be characterised by its relative balance in the socio-political status of men and women.[1] Indeed, the Chagossian activist Charlesia Alexis told me that men and women alike participated enthusiastically in demonstrations and negotiations. According to her, the reason why only women were arrested in 1982 was that the demonstrators understood that the police would react more violently towards men than towards women, and so the women took the frontlines. Men and women have been well represented on the committees of Chagossian organisations, and, among the general memberships, men and women have participated in Chagossian socio-political activities to an approximately equal degree. This analysis of the Chagossian socio-political movements as incorporating men and women alike rather than being dominated by either sex reflects how the objectives of Chagossian campaigns have appealed to both sexes.[2]

Negotiation versus litigation

In the wake of the controversial 1982 compensation agreement, many Chagos islanders felt that their interests had not been well represented by some of their Mauritian spokespeople. Two prominent Chagossian leaders and former hunger strikers, Charlesia Alexis and Lisette Talate, along with Olivier Bancoult (the then eighteen-year-old son of Rita Elysée, another Chagossian leader), together created the first solely Chagossian support organisation, called the Chagos Refugees Group (CRG). Throughout the 1980s and 1990s the CRG fought for additional compensation and the right to return to Chagos, but the group made little progress, gradually losing support within the community due to lack of results.

In 1995, a Chagossian man called Fernand Mandarin, together with a Mauritian barrister called Hervé Lassemillante, set up a new group called the Chagossian Social Committee (CSC). Lassemillante investigated the possibility of taking a case for compensation to court in the UK, but concluded that this would acknowledge that British courts had the jurisdiction to rule on the Chagos Archipelago, thus acquiescing to UK sovereignty and damaging the Mauritian Government's claim over the territory. He therefore initiated out-of-court negotiations between the CSC and the Governments of the UK, Mauritius, and the USA (Lassemillante 2001a). The CSC also popularised the collective noun Chagossian (to indicate their link to the particular territory of the Chagos Archipelago) rather than their previous name *Ilois* (a generic and increasingly derogatory term meaning 'islander'), and gained recognition for the Chagossians as an indigenous people before the UN in 1996.[3] However, the CSC's negotiations made little tangible progress towards compensation and the right of return, and by the late 1990s support within the community was declining.

Meanwhile, after the release of official UK Government documents from the 1960s under the Public Records Act, a Mauritian journalist called Henri Marimootoo uncovered exchanges of hitherto secret notes between UK officials concerning the depopulation of the Chagos Archipelago. Marimootoo's discoveries were published between May and August 1997 in the weekly Mauritian newspaper *Week-end* as a series entitled the *Diego Files*. Amongst quotes from senior civil servants describing the Chagos islanders as 'Tarzans' and 'Man Fridays', the documents also revealed that UK officials had knowingly attempted to maintain 'the fiction' that the inhabitants of the Chagos Archipelago were merely transient 'contract workers' in order to prevent the UN from seeking to protect their rights as 'belongers' (Marimootoo 1997). The exchange of notes thus provided the evidence required to show that the UK Government knew at the time that the islanders were a settled population and that uprooting them was contrary to international law.

Prompted by a British solicitor called Richard Gifford, who had looked into Bernard Sheridan's activities in the 1980s, the Sheridans law firm decided to take on the case. Given Lassemillante's opposition to working within the British court system, Gifford turned to the CRG, by now led by Olivier Bancoult. In 2000, the London High Court ruled in favour of the Chagos islanders. The judge, Lord Justice Laws, ruled that section 4 of the BIOT Immigration Ordinance 1971, which had legitimised the exile of the Chagos islanders, contradicted section 11(1) of the pre-existing BIOT Order 1965, which guaranteed the 'peace, order and good government' of BIOT:

Section 4 of the Ordinance effectively exiles the *Ilois* from the territory where they are belongers and forbids their return. But the 'peace, order and good government' of any territory means nothing, surely, save by reference to the territory's population. They are to be governed not removed.[4]

Lord Justice Laws declared section 4 of the BIOT Immigration Ordinance to be invalid under section 11(1) of the BIOT Order and thus quashed the BIOT Immigration Ordinance.

The UK Government immediately implemented a new BIOT Immigration Ordinance which entitled Chagossians to return to the Chagos Archipelago except Diego Garcia. In response, islanders from Diego Garcia, including the former CRG activist Charlesia Alexis and members of the Ramdas and Vincatassin families, established a new Chagossian organisation called the Diego Garcia Island Council (DGIC) to campaign for the right to return to be extended to include Diego Garcia (Vincatassin 2001). From their perspective, the right to return only to what they termed 'outer islands' – such as the Peros Banhos Atoll and Salomon Islands (see Map 2) – was insufficient, and the ruling was a hollow victory because it did not result in people from Diego Garcia winning the right to return to their particular native island (Marimootoo 2002). The DGIC campaigned for the inclusion of Diego Garcia in all negotiations and litigation concerned with the right to return.

At the same time, the High Court ruling had made possible further court action seeking compensation and the right to return on the grounds that the depopulation of the Chagos Archipelago had been contrary to the laws of the BIOT. The CRG took the leading role, registering the vast majority of Chagos islanders plus their children born in exile – totalling over four thousand people – to be included in the court proceedings. The CRG then formed a coalition with two smaller Chagossian organisations: the DGIC (then representing about sixty islanders born on Diego Garcia) and the Chagossian committee in Seychelles (representing most of the Chagossian community in Seychelles, totalling about 450 people). In 2002, Sheridans launched a preliminary hearing in the London High Court on behalf of the Chagossian coalition to investigate whether some Chagos islanders and their descendants might be eligible to claim further compensation from the UK Government. In 2003, however, the judge, Mr Justice Ouseley, ruled against the Chagossian coalition, and in 2004 three Court of Appeal judges rejected the Chagossian coalition's application for leave to appeal (see Jeffery 2006c).[5]

Meanwhile, also in 2004, the UK Government used the Orders in Council (a royal prerogative) to implement a new BIOT Immigration Order prohibiting all unauthorised persons (including Chagossians) from entering BIOT on the grounds of national security. This removed by political means the legal right to return established by the judicial review. In 2006, the BIOT Immigration Order 2004 was repealed following another successful judicial review, and in 2007 the UK Government's appeal was rejected, but in 2008 the House of Lords ruled in favour (by three votes to two) of the UK Government (see Jeffery 2009).[6] The Chagossians have appealed to the European Court of Human Rights.

Changing immigration legislation aside, Chagossian groups have successfully campaigned for brief return visits to the Chagos Archipelago including Diego Garcia. In late 2000, the CRG leader Olivier Bancoult made a brief visit along with two other senior CRG members, Rosemond Saminaden and Raphael Louis. More significantly – in light of the more restrictive BIOT immigration legislation since 2004 – the UK authorities organised a long-awaited large-scale return visit to the main Chagos islands (including Diego Garcia) for one hundred Chagos islanders in 2006. As the largest group, the CRG sent seventy-five people, while the CSC sent ten and the Seychelles group sent fifteen. Small-scale visits by eight and eighteen CRG members took place in 2008 and 2009 respectively, and the UK-based DGS, which was not included in the 2006 visit, was granted visits for six members in 2008 and 2010.[7]

When I returned to Mauritius in 2007 I interviewed several of those who went on the trip to Chagos in 2006. The group spent a day each on Boddam in the Salomon Islands, Ile du Coin in the Peros Banhos Atoll, and finally Diego Garcia, all of which had changed dramatically in their absence. They found Diego Garcia transformed by the military base, although residents have tended the chapel and cemetery there, whereas the unpopulated islands of Boddam and Ile du Coin were overgrown, so the group spent most of their days there clearing the chapels and cemeteries. Some people managed to find their former homes, and a few even collected personal items that had been abandoned when they left Chagos, but others were unable to reach their homes through the overgrowth. Returnees uniformly commented on the abundance of coconut palms, crabs, fish, and octopus, all of which they enjoyed eating during their visit. The official Royal Navy film of the trip shows islanders weeping, prostrating themselves on the ground, collecting earth samples, reciting prayers, singing songs, and erecting stone monuments to commemorate their visit. The trip evoked conflicting emotions in all of those I interviewed. They were overwhelmed by the return to their homes after such a long absence, the overgrown islands and derelict buildings, the brevity of the visit, and the fact that they could not remain there. As one elderly woman put it, 'I'm happy that I managed to see the place where I was born and visit the cemetery where my grandmother and grandfather are buried, but I'm sad that I can't stay there'.

Political patrons

Chagossian organisations campaigning for compensation and the right to return to Chagos have not acted in isolation from mainstream political processes in Mauritius and beyond. On the contrary, Chagossian groups have been profoundly constituted by their changing relationships to political parties and advocacy groups in Mauritius and elsewhere. As I will show in the final sections of this chapter, these pragmatic alliances have had important implications for the changing standpoints taken by Chagossian organisations with regard to ideological issues such as sovereignty over the Chagos Archipelago and the legitimacy or otherwise of the US military base on Diego Garcia. First, though, this section introduces more fully some of the key political actors who have been sometime collaborators of Chagossian groups.

Recent politics in Mauritius can be characterised as a multi-party demo-cracy comprising largely centrist political parties that routinely need to forge coalitions to form government, although these coalitions are subject to frequent realignments at and between elections. The Mauritian Labour Party (MLP), which had been instrumental in achieving independence, was in government – either alone or as leader of a coalition – from independence in 1968 until 1982, when it was defeated by the MMM led by Anerood Jugnauth. The MMM had been established in 1969 by Paul Bérenger and Dev Virahsawmy as a left-wing party opposed to the ethnic, religious, and caste-based politics of the exist-ing political parties. In 1982, as Deputy Prime Minister and Finance Minister, Paul Bérenger represented the Mauritian Government in the negotiations that resulted in the compensation deal for Chagos islanders. To facilitate the distribu-tion of the compensation package, the Mauritian Government set up the ITFB, which initially comprised a chairperson selected by the Prime Minister, five civil servants representing Mauritian government departments, and five Chagossian representatives selected by the Prime Minister.

Following the MLP's 1982 electoral defeat, Anerood Jugnauth was Prime Minister from 1982 until 1995, first as leader of the MMM, and after 1983 as leader of a splinter party, the Militant Socialist Movement (MSM). In 1995, an MLP–MMM coalition defeated the MSM, and Seewoosagur Ramgoolam's son Navin Ramgoolam (who had become leader of the MLP in 1991) was Prime Minister until 2000. During the late 1990s, when the CSC dominated Chagos-sian politics, Ramgoolam worked with the CSC's barrister Hervé Lassemillante to launch negotiations for compensation and the right to return, but, as noted above, the negotiations were inconclusive. More tangible progress was on a much smaller scale: in 1999, under pressure from the CSC, the Mauritian Govern-ment rebranded the ITFB as the Ilois Welfare Fund (IWF), expanded member-ship to seven representatives of Mauritian Government departments and seven Chagossian representatives elected by Chagos islanders, and agreed to provide Rs.500,000 (about £13,250 in 1999) per year for community projects. The first bi-ennial elections to the IWF took place in March 2001, after the 2000 High Court ruling in Bancoult's name, and Bancoult's CRG won a landslide victory against Mandarin's CSC, taking all seven of the seats with about 70 per cent of the vote overall (*L'express* 2001). When the CSC boycotted the second IWF election in 2003, the CRG again won all seven seats, which it has retained in subsequent elections.

Meanwhile, in the general election in 2000, the new coalition MMM–MSM Government struck a leadership deal in which the MSM leader Anerood Jug-nauth was Prime Minister for the first half of the five-year term before being re-placed by the MMM leader Paul Bérenger. As Deputy Prime Minister from 2000 to 2003, Bérenger assisted the CRG-led IWF by increasing the government funds to Rs.2 million per year, renovating the community centres in the two *Cités Ilois*, and introducing a funeral grant of Rs.2,000 for the families of deceased Chagos islanders. In the general election in July 2005, however, the MMM–MSM coalition lost to a coalition led by the MLP, and Navin Ramgoolam once again became Prime Minister. Ramgoolam remained Prime Minister after the MLP won the 2010 general election in coalition with the MSM and another party called the Mauritian Social Democrat Party.

Thus historically there have been ties between the CSC and Navin Ramgoolam, leader of the MLP since 1985, and between the CRG and Paul Bérenger, sometime leader of the MMM. In particular, several commentators have remarked upon the mutually beneficial relationship between Bérenger and Bancoult. The MMM was originally established to champion class-based politics, but has become an increasingly mainstream centre-left party. The MMM co-founder, Dev Virahsawmy, told me that his former colleague Paul Bérenger used the Chagossian cause to demonstrate that he had not abandoned the Creole working classes in favour of majority Indo-Mauritian, middle-class, or capitalist interests. The Chagossian struggle has a high profile in Mauritius, and the IWF can be run relatively cheaply. From Bérenger's perspective, supporting the Chagossian cause was likely to increase his own and his party's support base amongst Chagossians and perhaps even across a wider urban Creole working-class voting bloc. For his part, Bancoult's critics in Mauritius had claimed that recognising the jurisdiction of the London courts amounted to acquiescing to UK sovereignty, and thus they accused him of acting against the interests of the Republic of Mauritius. Bancoult was able to demonstrate his loyalty to Mauritius through his close relationship to Bérenger and by proudly displaying the national Order of the Star and Key honours awarded to him by the Mauritian Government following the High Court victory in 2000. The close relationship between Bancoult and Bérenger was not uncontroversial among Chagossians, however, many of whom remarked to me that several Mauritian politicians had manipulated Chagossians in the past, and claimed that Bérenger himself had encouraged Chagos islanders to sign the controversial renunciation forms in return for compensation in 1982.

There has also been significant cooperation between several Chagossian groups and *Lalit*, a marginal left-wing party which had functioned as a subgroup within the MMM until 1982, when it separated in protest when the MMM formed an alliance with a sectarian rural Hindu party. In the 1982 compensation negotiations, *Lalit* members advised Chagossian representatives against agreeing to the compensation deal precisely because it entailed the controversial renunciation forms. *Lalit* portrays the Chagossian case as emblematic of campaigns for decolonisation, demilitarisation, and human rights.[8] One of *Lalit*'s long-running campaigns has been to promote the return of the Chagos Archipelago to Mauritian democratic control, which *Lalit* activists have defined not as a case of claiming sovereignty but as the last step in decolonisation and the reunification of the Republic of Mauritius (Lallah 2002: 222). *Lalit* has campaigned consistently for the demilitarisation of the Indian Ocean, and in 2003 the group organised demonstrations against the war in Iraq, at which participants simultaneously called for the closure of the US military base on Diego Garcia, which was used to launch bombing raids in Iraq. *Lalit* has also supported the claim for the Chagossians' right to return to the whole of the Chagos Archipelago, including Diego Garcia (Kistnasamy & Collen 2002). Thus *Lalit* members have related to the Chagossians as victims of contemporary global geopolitics dominated by the USA and the UK. Furthermore, they consider that the Chagossian struggle has the potential to unite global social justice movements against their perceived common enemy: US and UK imperialism and warmongering (Vine & Jeffery 2009).

Sovereignty

Tensions between Chagossian groups and the main Mauritian political parties revolve primarily around the issue of sovereignty over the Chagos Archipelago. In 1983, a Select Committee on the Excision of the Chagos Archipelago reported that the excision had been contrary to two UN declarations (de l'Estrac 1983: 4–5). Firstly, the 1960 UN Declaration on the Granting of Independence to Colonial Countries and Peoples had declared: 'any attempt aimed at the partial or total disruption of the national unity and the territorial integrity of a country is incompatible with the purposes and principles of the Charter of the United Nations' (Article 6). Secondly, following the creation of BIOT, a 1965 UN declaration on the Question of Mauritius reminded the UK Government of its responsibility not to 'dismember the Territory of Mauritius and violate its territorial integrity' (Article 4). Since 1980, successive Mauritian governments have repeatedly reiterated the sovereignty claim, and in 1982 the revised Mauritian Constitution included the Chagos Archipelago as Mauritian territory (Dinan 2002: 96). The UK Government, however, does not recognise the Mauritian Government's sovereignty claim, although it has theoretically agreed to return the Chagos Archipelago to Mauritian control once the territory is no longer required for US defence purposes (Foreign and Commonwealth Office 1999: 51).

Many high-profile socio-political groups in Mauritius have campaigned for the restitution of the Chagos Archipelago to Mauritian sovereignty. Participants in the Southern Africa Human Rights NGO Network (SAHRINGON) workshop in Mauritius in 2002 – including Olivier Bancoult (CRG), Fernand Mandarin (CSC), and several *Lalit* representatives – called for 'the complete decolonisation of Africa through the disbanding of BIOT and the reunification of the Republic of Mauritius' (reproduced in Lalit 2002: 222). Further, the SAHRINGON resolution recommended that 'the Mauritian government proclaims the Chagos Archipelago as the 22nd electoral constituency in the Republic of Mauritius', thus suggesting that the territory ought to be repopulated and brought under Mauritian democratic control (Lalit 2002: 223). In this formulation, the reincorporation of the Chagos Archipelago into the Republic of Mauritius would enable the resettlement of the islands by Chagossians and other Mauritian citizens.

Several Mauritian critics have argued that taking cases to British courts has demonstrated implicit recognition of UK sovereignty over the Chagos Archipelago, and they have accused the CRG of acting against Mauritian interests (Boolell 2001; Chateau 2002; Lassemillante 2000; Marimootoo 2000;

Minerve 2000; Poché 2000). According to the CRG's Mauritian barrister Siva Mardemootoo, however, the CRG's court cases in the UK neither help nor hinder the Mauritian sovereignty claim since the court cases relate to private law while the question of sovereignty is a matter for international public law (Anyangwe 2001: 26; Chinniah & Dhunputh 2002: 84). From this perspective, application to the London High Court for compensation was a pragmatic approach to achieving the desired ends through one channel that was open to the Chagossian community.

Official UK Government publications provide contradictory visions of the future of the Chagos Archipelago, making incompatible statements regarding the retention of the BIOT, the prospect of ceding the islands to Mauritian sovereignty, and the possibility of establishing the BIOT as a self-governing territory (Foreign and Commonwealth Office 1999: 4, 12, 51). In 2003, Olivier Bancoult organised a CRG visit to the newly established Rodrigues Regional Assembly to learn directly about possible forms that governance might take in the event of resettlement of the Chagos Archipelago. Throughout my fieldwork in Mauritius in 2002–4, Bancoult remained undecided as to whether his preferred solution would be to achieve autonomy for Chagos through a Regional Assembly within the Republic of Mauritius or through the establishment of the BIOT as a self-governing UK Overseas Territory. Since then, however, Bancoult has increasingly aligned himself with Mauritius. The leaders of Chagossian groups based in the UK, by contrast, say they would prefer Chagos to remain British territory.

Under the British Overseas Territories Act 2002, the UK Government granted full UK citizenship to Chagos islanders and their children born in exile. Many Mauritian commentators have been concerned that if the UK Government were to resettle the Chagos Archipelago as a British Overseas Territory, it would only allow entry by UK passport holders, thus entrenching UK sovereignty and restricting non-Chagossian Mauritians' access to the territory (Boolell 2001; Lassemillante 2002; Marimootoo 2002; Minerve 2000; Prosper 2000). Thus the determination of sovereignty over the Chagos Archipelago could have significantly different consequences for Chagos islanders on the one hand and for non-Chagossian Mauritians on the other.

By contrast, whilst there was widespread support in Mauritius for Mauritian sovereignty over the Chagos Archipelago, many Chagos islanders who were relocated to Seychelles opposed Mauritian sovereignty. From their perspective, Mauritian politics and business are controlled by Indo-Mauritians for their own interests to the exclusion of Creoles and other ethnic groups in Mauritius. In this formulation, resettlement of the Chagos Archipelago under Mauritian sovereignty would be controlled by Mauritian business interests, and Chagossians might not be given the opportunity to return to the Chagos Archipelago, or they might be enabled to return only as cheap unskilled manual labour. Furthermore, Chagos islanders in Seychelles suggested to me that if the Chagos Archipelago were Mauritian territory, controlled by Mauritian immigration laws, Seychellois Chagossians might find themselves unable to resettle there since they do not hold Mauritian passports. The solution to both of these problems suggested by

Seychellois Chagossians was that the Chagos Archipelago should continue to be administered as a UK Overseas Territory, in which all UK passport-holding Chagossians would be entitled to residency.

Diego Garcia

The question of sovereignty over the Chagos Archipelago is intimately linked to debates about the use of Diego Garcia as a US military base, which have been another source of tension between Chagossian groups and their allies in mainstream Mauritian politics. Jean-Claude de l'Estrac, who served in coalition governments as MMM Foreign Minister in 1982–83 and 1990–91, told me that the MMM's position on the US military base on Diego Garcia changed dramatically during the 1980s. Mauritian politicians received widespread support for their sovereignty claim at both the 1980 Organisation of African Unity meeting and the 1983 Non-Aligned Summit. This was because participants opposed military expansion during the Cold War and supported a vision of the Indian Ocean as a Zone of Peace (de l'Estrac 1983: Appendices E, X). By the time B-52 bombers destined for Iraq were launched from Diego Garcia during the first Gulf War in 1991, however, MMM leaders no longer officially opposed the US military base on Diego Garcia (Anyangwe 2001: 48). Many commentators, including de l'Estrac and members of *Lalit*, have explained the Mauritian Government's silence regarding sovereignty and the US military base as a result of economic incentives offered in return for not vocalising complaints. *Lalit* has campaigned against the African Growth and Opportunity Act (AGOA), the trade agreements between African states and the USA initiated by Bill Clinton in 2000 and subsequently extended by George W. Bush.[9] AGOA awards lucrative deals and large quotas for clothes exports to the USA to textile companies in African countries (including Mauritius) provided that their governments meet certain conditions. These conditions include African states having to guarantee not to undermine American national security policies, thus preventing the Mauritian Government from challenging the US military base on Diego Garcia (Lallah 2002: 62, 65).

Several senior members of the coalition MMM–MSM Government seemed to oppose the US-led war in Iraq which began during my fieldwork in 2003 (Marimootoo 2003; *Week-end* 2003a). Nevertheless, the then Deputy Prime Minister, Paul Bérenger, and the then Foreign Minister, Anil Gayan, also announced that the Mauritian Government was not opposed to the US military base on Diego Garcia or its use in the Iraq war. At the same time, both insisted that the Mauritian Government had made progress in its sovereignty claim (Tally 2003; *Week-end* 2003a). Commentators (e.g. Anyangwe 2001) hinted that the official MMM–MSM stance on the US military base derived from the Mauritian Government's intention to claim rent from the USA if Mauritian sovereignty over the Chagos Archipelago were recognised internationally. Many Mauritians agree that sovereignty over the Chagos Archipelago is therefore potentially highly significant for the Mauritian economy. At the time, several high-profile political actors such as Navin Ramgoolam, then leader of the opposition, and

Cassam Uteem, the former President of the Republic of Mauritius, criticised the MMM–MSM Government for acquiescing to the use of Diego Garcia by the US military (Antoine 2003; see also Anyangwe 2001; e.g. *Week-end* 2003b).

Similarly, in addition to calling for the return of the Chagos Archipelago to Mauritian control, participants in the SAHRINGON workshop called for the closure of the military base on Diego Garcia (see *Le Mauricien* 2002). In 2003, *Lalit* organised a coalition of left-wing movements and trades unions into an anti-war platform, and produced a pamphlet asserting that since Diego Garcia was Mauritian territory and Mauritius was not involved in the war, Mauritians should campaign for the closure of the US military base. Furthermore, as *Lalit* members have pointed out, Mauritius signed the Pelindaba Treaty for nuclear non-proliferation in Africa, and the Indian Ocean was declared a Zone of Peace (Subron 2002; *Week-end* 1997a). Thus there are sharp tensions in Mauritian politics about the use of Diego Garcia as a US military base.

Divergent opinions on Diego Garcia led to tensions between *Lalit* and the CRG. *Lalit* has consistently campaigned for the demilitarisation of the Indian Ocean and the establishment of the Indian Ocean as a UN Zone of Peace through the closure of the military base on Diego Garcia (Lalit 1986: 4, 15; Lalit 1987: 8, 19; Lalit 2002: 9; Lallah 2002: 64–65; Subron 2002). The CRG's participation in campaigns for the demilitarisation of Diego Garcia has been more sporadic. In 1998, *Lalit* and the CRG jointly initiated the Return Diego committee, which called 'for the dismantlement of the military and nuclear base on Diego Garcia' (Lalit 2002: 211; *Week-end* 1998). In 2002 both groups participated in the SAHRINGON workshop, which called 'for the immediate closure of the US military base on Diego Garcia' (Lalit 2002: 222; *Le Mauricien* 2002). *Lalit* and CRG together popularised the Mauritian Kreol slogan *Rann Nu Diego* [Give Us Back Diego], but *Lalit* members and Chagossians have subtly different interpretations of this phrase. Bancoult explained to me that from the perspective of the Chagossians, 'Diego is our native land', but from the perspective of *Lalit* members, 'Diego belongs to Mauritius'. Thus *Lalit* members interpreted *Rann Nu Diego* to mean 'return Diego to Mauritian sovereignty', whereas for many Chagossians the phrase has always meant 'repatriate us to Diego' (see also Collen & Kistnasamy 2002; Vine & Jeffery 2009).

Lalit mobilised opposition to the war in Iraq and led an anti-war demonstration in March 2003. The CRG declined to participate, however, having decided that they had, as Bancoult put it to me, 'no problem with the military base on Diego Garcia'. This disagreement soured relations between the CRG and *Lalit*, but the relationship was temporarily renewed later in 2003, when a former Greenpeace and Rainbow Warrior activist, Martini Gotje, contacted both groups to set up a coalition to organise a boat trip to Diego Garcia to raise awareness of and support for the Chagossian struggle (*Le Mauricien* 2004). *Lalit* and CRG members met Gotje at the 2004 World Social Forum, a gathering held by alternative globalisation movements in response to the annual World Economic Forum. Divisions between *Lalit* and the CRG re-emerged when Bancoult declined to endorse the No US Bases campaign to close US military bases overseas including Diego Garcia (see Vine & Jeffery 2009).

The CRG and *Lalit* subsequently distanced themselves from one another as the CRG became increasingly clear in its position that, in the event of resettlement of the Chagos Archipelago, the military base should provide jobs for resettled Chagossians. Leaders of the CRG and DGIC alike noted that military bases all around the world co-exist with and employ local populations, and criticised the discriminatory employment practices on Diego Garcia. The military base employed Filipinos, Singaporeans, and even non-Chagossian Mauritians (Bowman & Lefebvre 1985), but not, until recently, Chagossians. Many second- and third-generation Chagossians likewise suggested that the US military base should remain on Diego Garcia to provide employment for resettled Chagossians in the future. Another suggestion was that since the US military base occupies only a small proportion of the land area of Diego Garcia, it could be allowed to continue to operate as normal, whilst Chagossians could use the portion of the island that is not currently in use, as well as resettling the other islands in the archipelago.

In support of the military base and the war in Iraq, one senior CRG member told me: 'I feel proud because my country is doing good work'. Likewise, a young DGIC member claimed: 'I firmly believe that the construction of this Military Base was a must for the world's protection against terrorism and any other mischievous enemy' (Ramdas 2003). Another DGIC member insisted that it would be wrong to oppose the US military base on Diego Garcia since it was built for the benefit of humankind. Chagos islanders and their descendants who supported the war in Iraq told me that the Chagossian community ought to receive financial recompense on the grounds that their island was being used to protect the world from international terrorism, and thus, as one put it, their country was 'helping the whole world'.

Many Chagos islanders, however, oppose the use of Diego Garcia as a US military base on the grounds that, as one elderly islander from Diego put it: 'They took the humans who lived there and removed them from their land in order to make a base to destroy human life, taking innocent lives'. Similarly, an islander from Peros Banhos remarked: 'I am sad because I live in poverty in Mauritius and cannot go to my island because the Americans use it for war'. And another elderly islander from Salomon commented eloquently: 'I am living in poverty in Mauritius while America uses my homeland for war. My homeland is a pearl for America, but they should have considered us to be pearls too'. Other Chagossians oppose the military base for reasons of their own security: if the Chagossians return to the Chagos Archipelago, the presence of the US military base on Diego Garcia could endanger their lives and should therefore be closed down. Chagossians worry that, as one young man put it, 'if America can bomb Iraq from Diego Garcia, then Iraq could bomb Diego Garcia too'. However, such viewpoints have become marginalised as the CRG leadership increasingly takes the line that the military base would provide much-needed employment in case of resettlement.

Diego Garcia has also affected relations between Chagossian groups. Whilst the CRG has tended towards pragmatic acceptance of the US military base, the UK-based Chagos Island Community Association (CICA), established in Crawley in 2006, has received considerable support from the Workers Revolutionary Party and politically engaged trades unions including Unite and GMB,[10] and has taken an ideological stance against the US military base. Tensions between CRG and CICA emerged in 2007 when CICA members arrived in London to support the CRG's protests on the Strand and outside Downing Street against the UK Government's Court of Appeal hearing against judicial review of the 2004 Immigration Order. CRG banners reiterated generally: 'We've the right to live in our homes', while CICA banners proclaimed boldly: 'We will return to Diego Garcia – it's our right!' CICA's preoccupation with Diego Garcia was the reason given by the CRG leadership for refusing to support the CICA demonstration in Crawley the following weekend. A meeting organised by the Mauritian Society at the London School of Economics in 2007 became the forum for a debate between the CICA leader Hengride Permal and Olivier Bancoult's solicitor Richard Gifford. Whilst Gifford remarked that 80 per cent of the extended Chagossian community was represented by the CRG, which viewed cohabitation with the US military base as the basis for a resettled economy, Permal claimed to speak for Chagos islanders of her parents' generation:

> Who wants a military base on their land especially given Iraq? We would like to live in peace. The new generation speaks for the dying natives who are illiterate … My parents were born on Diego Garcia and don't want to live with a military base on their island so Americans can pay them … Richard Gifford said 80 per cent in Mauritius want to live with the military base but that's not true, we don't want that … We don't want to be victims of war again.

It is evident that many of the older Chagos islanders do not relish the notion of resettled cohabitation with the US military base. On the other hand, many have indeed been swayed by the CRG's logic that the closure of such a significant military outpost is so unrealistic that directing energy towards such a demand hampers the islanders' campaign for the right to return to the archipelago at all.

Human rights, indigenous rights, and refugee status

Chagossian representatives have often deployed human rights language and concepts in everyday speech and in public presentations. Fernand Mandarin and Olivier Bancoult have both made frequent and explicit references to the right to remain in one's birthplace, citing the UN Declaration on Human Rights as prohibiting the expulsion of a person from his or her native land. Lawyers, academics, social workers, politicians, and journalists have likewise identified the Chagossian case in terms of human rights violations. In November 2003, the then Prime Minister, Paul Bérenger, unveiled a monument in the Port Louis docks to commemorate the suffering of the Chagossian community. The then Deputy Prime Minister, Pravind Jugnauth (son of the former Prime Minister and incumbent President of Mauritius, Anerood Jugnauth) spoke publicly of the displacement as a violation of the Chagos islanders' human rights by the UK Government. On Human Rights Day on 10 December 2003, the CRG organised a day-long demonstration outside the British High Commission in Port Louis, seeking to bring the UN's attention to the fact that the Chagos islanders were victims of human rights abuses by the UK and the USA. The implications of the European Convention on Human Rights for the Chagossians will be a key feature of the forthcoming case in the European Court of Human Rights (ECHR).

Whilst Mauritian politicians have endorsed the Chagossian story as a case of human rights abuses, they have been less supportive of Chagossian appeals to indigenous rights. When the United Nations began to consider the plight of indigenous peoples in the 1980s, indigenous populations were conceived as those 'having a historical continuity with pre-invasion and pre-colonial societies that developed on their territories' (Martinez Cobo 1986: paragraph 379). This definition excluded many parts of the world, including the south-western Indian Ocean, where there were no precolonial populations and where colonists popu-lated the islands initially with enslaved labourers from Africa and later with indentured labourers from Asia. Attempting to sustain peaceful ethnic relations amongst their inhabitants and to prevent pleas for preferential treatment, suc-cessive Mauritian governments have insisted that Mauritius had no indigenous population.

In the 1990s, however, the UN adopted a more inclusive concept of indigeneity to include those who have the earliest claim to a territory, whether or not this pre-dated colonial settlement. The concept was also extended to incorporate elements such as cultural distinctiveness, self-identification, and identification by others as a group, and experience of discrimination (Daes 1996: 22). This more inclusive definition has had limited implications so far for the Chagossian community. Fernand Mandarin attended the 1996 meeting of the UN Working Group on Indigenous Populations (WGIP) and successfully appealed to have the Chagos-sians recognised as indigenous people. For Lassemillante, 'the fundamental right of the Chagossian native to return and reside on his homeland' was non-negotiable regardless of the 'full and final' 1982 agreement (Lassemillante 2002: 90). As Mandarin has put it, indigenous Chagossians have the right to return because they have never 'sold' their rights to their native land (*Week-end* 1997b). A CSC leaflet, showing Mandarin participating in the fourteenth session of the WGIP, proclaims 'To live on our land of origin: a sacred right, wherever our origin!' (Chagossian Social Committee 1997).

On the other hand, Mauritian politicians, including Paul Bérenger, have pub-licly used the more restrictive definition of indigeneity strategically to deny that the Chagos islanders were indigenous to the Chagos Archipelago since Mauritius and its dependencies had no precolonial indigenous populations and were popu-lated only through European colonial policies of slavery and indentured labour. At the unveiling of the aforementioned commemorative monument in Novem-ber 2003, for instance, the then Minister for Arts and Culture, Motee Ramdass, reiterated the Mauritian Government's stance that the Republic of Mauritius was built through immigration. Therefore, he asserted, Mauritians and Chagossians were 'not authochthonous, not an indigenous population'. Since the UN encourages indigenous populations to seek self-determination, classifying the Chagos islanders as indigenous to the Chagos Archipelago could potentially have negative implications for Mauritian sovereign control over the territory if it were resettled by Chagossians in the future. Thus Mauritian politicians have rejected the claim that Chagossians are an indigenous population deserving special treatment. In any case, since the 2007 UN Declaration on the Rights of Indigenous Peoples is non-binding, recognition as an indigenous people would not necessarily bring any tangible benefits to the Chagossian community.

Refugee status similarly seems not to offer much hope. The 1951 UN Convention Relating to the Status of Refugees defined a refugee as someone who is 'outside the country of his nationality'.[11] This definition entails a notion of clear-cut state boundaries and uncontested sovereignty and citizenship that is problematic in relation to the Chagos Archipelago. Despite a 1960 United Nations declaration in favour of the preservation of 'territorial integrity' during decolonisation processes, the UK Government excised the Chagos Archipelago from colonial Mauritius in 1965 during negotiations for Mauritian independence in 1968. Chagos islanders were thus forced to leave the British Chagos Archipelago and sent to Mauritius during the final years of British rule and the early years of Mauritian independence. Chagos islanders in Mauritius were then granted Mauritian citizenship under the Mauritian Constitution in 1968, and thus do not meet the UN Refugee Agency (UNHCR) definition of refugees as people outside their country of nationality. In 1982, however, the choice of group name by the founding members of the Chagos Refugees Group reflected their self-definition as refugees by dint of being a people forcibly dislocated from their homeland and marginalised in exile. From the perspective of the Mauritian Government, though, classifying the Chagossians as refugees would entail conceding that they had come from outwith Mauritius, thus acquiescing to UK sovereignty over the territory. In 2003, the CRG's legal team at Sheridans approached UNHCR to inquire about having the Chagossians recognised as refugees, but Bérenger refused Bancoult's request for state support since the Mauritian Government's official stance was that Chagossians were Mauritian citizens internally displaced within Mauritian territory.

Additionally, the question of refugee status raises somewhat different issues for Chagos islanders in Seychelles. The Republic of Seychelles has no territorial claim over the Chagos Archipelago, and therefore could not use national sovereignty as a reason not to support the Seychelles Chagossians' request to be recognised as refugees. Politicians in Seychelles, however, routinely insisted upon non-discrimination in an attempt to guarantee the equal treatment of all Seychellois citizens. They consequently rejected Chagossian requests for positive discrimination such as compensation or appeals to refugee status. Thus for several reasons refugee status has been elusive for displaced Chagos islanders.

Chagossian mobilisation in exile

This chapter has explored the history of the struggles led by successive Chagossian groups in Mauritius. It has revealed the three main ideological and pragmatic conflicts amongst competing Chagossian organisations. The first is the disagreement about the relative values of political versus legal approaches to compensation and the right to return. The second is the debate about British versus Mauritian sovereignty over the Chagos Archipelago. And the third is the question of the legitimacy or otherwise of the US military base on Diego Garcia. Crucially, these conflicts have taken form and played out not in a vacuum but rather in the context of local political concerns and changing alliances between Chagossian groups and their non-Chagossian supporters.

Notes

1 This distinguishes Chagossian groups from their Mauritian counterparts, most of which have always been both led by and numerically dominated by men.
2 For a discussion of the role of women in the Chagossian community in terms of gendered cultural responsibility and the Chagossian Women's Group, see Chapter 4.
3 For a detailed discussion of this process, see Chapter 4.
4 *R (Bancoult) v Secretary of State for Foreign and Commonwealth Affairs* [2000] QB 1067: paragraph 57.
5 *Chagos Islanders v Attorney General and HM BIOT Commissioner* [2003] EWHC QB 2222; *Chagos Islanders v Attorney General and HM BIOT Commissioner* [2004] EWCA Civ. 997.
6 *R (Bancoult) v Secretary of State for Foreign and Commonwealth Affairs* [2006] EWHC 1038; *Secretary of State for Foreign and Commonwealth Affairs v R (Bancoult)* [2007] EWCA 498; *R (Bancoult) v Secretary of State for Foreign and Commonwealth Affairs* [2008] UKHL 61.
7 DGS website: http://diegogarciansociety.org/visithomeland.aspx.
8 See www.lalitmauritius.org.
9 See www.agoa.gov and www.agoa.info.
10 Unite is the UK's largest trade union, with around two million members (www.unitetheunion.com); GMB is Britain's General Union, with 610,000 members (www.gmb.org.uk).
11 See www2.ohchr.org/English/law/refugees.htm.

II

Narrating homeland, displacement, suffering, and loss

3

Singing the homeland

Poverty here is poverty, poverty there was pleasure. [*Mizer isi mizer, mizer laba plezir.*] (Marguerite, a Mauritian woman who lived and worked on Chagos)

Displaced Chagos islanders are not only embroiled in political mobilisation and protest: they also participate in cultural expression in exile. This chapter illustrates how representations of a homeland in song lyrics and oral narratives have been transformed through experiences of displacement and relocation, and asks to what extent such transformed representations help or hinder political and legal struggles in exile. Focusing on the relationship between displacement and musical production, this chapter reveals the changing structure and thematic content of Chagossian song lyrics by comparing the lyrics of songs composed by Chagos islanders while living on the colonial Chagos Archipelago with those composed by displaced Chagos islanders living in exile. The latter songs form part of an emergent collective historical imagination motivated by the political and legal struggles (detailed in Chapter 2) for compensation and the right to return to Chagos. How Chagos is remembered by public representatives – lyricists, community leaders, and other activists – has particular implications for these struggles, and a romanticised collective historical narrative has successfully mobilised the Chagossian community and elicited support for the Chagossian cause from diverse sources. In legal contexts, however, such a standardised narrative has hindered rather than helped their cause.

Re-imagining the homeland

Many anthropological studies of displacement have illustrated how displaced people's representations of their homelands may be transformed by their subsequent experiences of uprootedness, loss, and life in exile. Palestinians in refugee camps in Lebanon reconfigured Palestine as paradise in comparison to the refugee camps, and their previous analyses of poverty and class oppression in historical Palestine were replaced in exile by affirmations of historical solidarity and strong ties to the land (Sayigh 1979: 10–12). The former residents of a village evacuated to create a reservoir on the Yellow River in China likewise did not dwell on historical hardships, but rather transmitted to their descendants a nostalgic image of a past characterised by community solidarity and abundant supplies in comparison to a present characterised by dislocation, poverty and famine (Jing 1996: 69–86). For exiled Palestinians and uprooted Chinese villagers alike, harsh experiences of displacement and resettlement generated romanticised and standardised representations of the homeland.

Anthropologists have also highlighted how physical or political alienation from the homeland is often expressed in terms of suffering and harm to cultural heritage. Islanders displaced from Rongelap in the Marshall Islands testified that dislocation from their lands resulted in a 'loss' of their cultural knowledge (Kirsch 2001). Similarly, Palestinians' dislocation from their ancestral lands generated a 'common memory of loss' and a sense of Palestinian solidarity within Israel (Rabinowitz 1994: 28). For Burundians in exile, a common sense of loss was the 'glue' that held individuals together into a diasporic community with shared objectives of return, rights, and political inclusion (Turner 2008: 746). Amongst Chagossians, as we shall see, a romanticised portrayal of the Chagos Archipelago as an idyllic island paradise and expressions of loss and suffering in exile promote a particular way of remembering the homeland and contribute to attempts to create a united community of people suffering in exile.

Harsh experiences of displacement and relocation, however, do not necessarily result in standardised or romanticised visions of the homeland. Liisa Malkki's research among Burundian Hutus in Mishamo, an isolated refugee camp in Tanzania, complicates the relationship between dislocation and romanticisation. Interviewing Hutu refugees in Mishamo about their past in Burundi, Malkki identified a standardised collective narrative that she called 'mythico-history'. To start with, the 'exhaustively detailed narratives generally corresponded to records of events, processes and relationships published in colonial and post-colonial historical texts on Burundi' (Malkki 1995: 54). Moreover, the narratives were centrally concerned with 'the ordering and reordering of social and political categories, with the defining of self in distinction to the other, with good and evil' (Malkki 1995: 55). Hutu refugees in Mishamo slotted accounts of their own personal experiences of fleeing Burundi into standardised narratives of the collective experience based on a few main themes, thus conflating the individual with the community (Malkki 1995: 109). They attempted to make sense of crucial episodes in the history of Burundi and their experiences in the refugee camp in Tanzania by creating moral analogies, firstly between their historical oppression in Burundi and their contemporary problems in the refugee camp, and secondly between the Tutsi rulers in Burundi and the Tanzanian camp authorities (Malkki 1995: 52–152). While the refugees romanticised the Hutus' ancient and aboriginal origins in historical Burundi, they also recalled their recent exploitation by Tutsis and were therefore not nostalgic about contemporary Burundi; instead, they glorified their future envisaged in terms of the eventual defeat of the Tutsis and the Hutus' heroic return to the aboriginal homeland (Malkki 1995: 230). Thus, Malkki writes, 'the mythico-historical narratives ingested events, processes, and relationships from the past and from the lived conditions of the present and transformed them within a fundamentally moral scheme of good and evil' (Malkki 1995: 244).

Chagossian collective imagination shares many of the characteristics of Malkki's concept of mythico-history, understood as narratives that deploy elements from personal experience and the historical record but are formalised into moralistic and standardised collective narratives for rhetorical and political purposes. Firstly, Chagossian cultural expressions of their experiences of displacement and relocation broadly complement historical records from the time, taking the form of didactic moral tales in which the Chagos islanders were wronged by diverse outsiders ranging from the British colonial administrators on Chagos to successive Mauritian governments and local Mauritians in Mauritius. Secondly, Chagossian historical narratives similarly order and try to make sense of the past and the present within a moral scheme, in this case by starkly comparing the idealised abundance, sharing, and simplicity of life enjoyed on Chagos with the unemployment, poverty, and social exclusion faced by Chagossians in Mauritius. Thirdly, Chagossian narratives have become highly standardised, using particular sets of phrases and examples to evoke the Chagossians' shared experiences of displacement, dislocation, and suffering. Fourthly, the Chagossian collective re-imagining of the homeland similarly developed in the context of a political and legal struggle by Chagossian organisations for compensation and the right to return to the Chagos. This has encouraged particular romanticised and standardised portrayals of life on Chagos, experiences of the displacement, and life in exile. I illustrate these points through a comparison of songs composed by Chagos islanders on Chagos and songs composed by Chagos islanders in exile.

Processes such as historical re-imagination, romanticisation of the homeland, evocations of suffering, and community mobilisation are often clearly identifiable in musical production amongst displaced peoples. In their introduction to a special issue on music and migration, Baily and Collyer note that:

> Music may be used to recreate the culture of the past, to remind you of the place from which you come, but migration can lead to cultural innovation and enrichment, with the creation of new forms which are indicative or symptomatic of the issues facing the immigrant, and which help one in dealing with a new life in a place of settlement and in the articulation of new identities. (Baily & Collyer 2006: 174)

Thus musical performance in exile can evoke the homeland and the past whilst also reflecting the current concerns of those now living in exile (see also Kaiser 2006: 186).

Similarly, through her work with Tibetan refugee musicians in India, Keila Diehl has shown that 'exilic performances comprise a continual ritual re-enactment of the memories of displacement, violence and loss that are central to the shared experience of exile' (Diehl 2002: 14–15). Diehl's research principally concerned refugees' differential engagements with diverse musical styles, but she also devoted one chapter of her book to the changing lyrical content of Tibetan songs. Folk songs from pre-1950 Tibet, she argued, 'addressed a wide variety of topics and served many purposes (setting the rhythm for manual labour, negotiating marriage arrangements, expressing political satire, and so on)' (Diehl 2002: 221). By contrast, Tibetan songs composed in exile have been 'limited to their use as a musical medium for expressing the specific experience of displacement out of which the genre was born' (Diehl 2002: 221). Exilic lyrics vocalise the community's pain, sadness, pride, and right of political self-determination. The 'ritual re-enactment' of exile 'preserves and reanimates (and certainly alters and sometimes even creates) the shared memories of displacement, violence, loss, and vulnerability that are central to feelings of solidarity in the Tibetan diaspora' (Diehl 2002: 221). Accordingly, this chapter focuses ethnographically on the changing lyrical content of Chagossian songs, comparing the lyrics of songs composed on Chagos with those of songs composed by Chagos islanders in exile.

Chagossian *sega* music

The history of *sega* music in the Indian Ocean stretches back to Saturday nights on the colonial plantations, when enslaved labourers played music, danced, and sang lamentation and protest songs to resist their everyday hardship and domination (Boswell 2006: 61–62; Lee 1990: 22–33). *Sega* lyrics protest against unfavourable social, political, and economic conditions; lament personal suffering; depict joyful occasions; or jest via suggestive sexual *double entendres* (Boswell 2006: 61–65; Lee 1990: 27, 31, 74–76). Traditional *sega* instruments (still in use today) include goatskin drums called *ravanne*, rainmakers (made with wooden frames filled with seeds) called *maravanne*, and metal triangles [*triang*] (Ballgobin & Antoine 2003: 77–80; Lee 1990: 35–40).

Historically associated with Creoles due to its origins in slavery, *sega* was long officially denigrated by the Roman Catholic Church as primitive, low class, and associated with wild and alcohol-fuelled sexual and morally questionable behaviour (Boswell 2006: 62; Dussercle 1934; Lee 1990: 45–49; Miles 1999: 220). By the 1980s, however, *sega* gained prominence and respectability due to the adoption by *sega* musicians of electronic instruments and the popularity of *sega* as a key element of the booming Indian Ocean tourist trade (Boswell 2006: 63–64; Lee 1990: 69–78; Miles 1999: 220). Nowadays *sega* is officially recognised in Mauritius, Seychelles and Réunion alike as a national music form and is frequently performed not only in homes but also by professional *sega* troupes at hotels, parties, weddings, national celebrations, and Creole festivals (see Chapter 4).

As on other islands in colonial Mauritius, *sega* was popular on the Chagos Archipelago, where it was similarly a matter of concern to European commentators: the Roman Catholic priest Roger Dussercle, who visited Chagos in 1933–34, associated *sega* parties with African roots, wild drunkenness, and frenzied sexual activity (Dussercle 1934; Edis 2004 [1993]: 60–61, 66–67). In Chagossian *sega*, a principal narrative voice starts to sing solo before the *ravanne* players join in with their accompaniment, usually in 6/8 time and consisting of three quavers of drumbeats repeated continuously throughout the rest of the song. The solo singer repeats the same lines several times before being joined by other singers singing in unison. Verses are interspersed with la-la-la choruses and with occasional cheers and calls from the singers. The musicians are accompanied by women and men dancing with one another, the women holding out their skirts and twirling while the men, often holding out their straw hats, circle around them. At the end of the song, the singers and dancers stop before the *ravanne*s gradually peter out.

Sega has remained popular amongst Chagossians in exile. As part of its two-year 'capacity building' project with the CRG, the IST helped to set up a Chagossian Women's Group [*Grup Fam Chagossienne*] encompassing a mixed-sex music ensemble called the Chagos Tambour Group [*Grup Tambour Chagos*]. The Chagos Tambour Group performed Chagossian *sega* music and dance at events such as Creole cultural festivals, Chagossian community fund-raising days, and *soirées* hosted by the CRG for its supporters and potential supporters. There were particular gendered roles in the Chagos Tambour Group. Women led most of the songs, and most in the chorus were women, although men led a couple of songs. Only men played *ravanne*, while men and women alike sometimes added percussion by playing triangles or using cutlery to tap glass bottles or pieces of metal. The male *ravanne* players sat in a curved row, and the women took turns as solo singer, chorus singers, percussion players, and dancers. There was no overall group leader or coordinator, and group members decided on the playlist collectively through negotiation, although there were occasional disputes among the singers about who was entitled to sing which songs composed by particular deceased forebears. These roles in the Chagos Tambour Group seem to match Chagos islanders' descriptions of historical musical practices on Chagos, but there is little documentation available for comparison.

In late 2003, whilst recording their songs for an album that was released in Mauritius in 2004, several Chagos Tambour Group members asked me to transcribe the lyrics of their elders' and their own *sega* songs so that they could register the lyrics with the Mauritius Society of Authors to establish their copyright.[1] While listening to, discussing, and attempting to transcribe and translate Chagossian songs, I noticed several differences between the lyrics of songs composed on Chagos and of songs composed since the displacement. First, songs from Chagos were polyphonic, often containing several interwoven stories, making these songs difficult to translate and interpret. By contrast, songs composed by Chagos islanders since the displacement had a clearer narrative structure and were more didactic, making them easier to follow, understand, and explain. Second, as I shall illustrate below, the representations of Chagos in lyrics composed on Chagos were significantly different from the representations of Chagos in lyrics composed since the displacement and in oral historical narratives.[2]

Chagossian musical production was not, of course, restricted to the *sega* of the Chagos Tambour Group. In this chapter I also refer to *sega* songs composed or sung by other Chagos islanders, including the professional *segatye* [*sega* musicians] Claude Lafoudre and Serge Elysée, and the veteran Chagossian activists Charlesia Alexis (Mauritius) and Jessy Marcelin (Seychelles). Moreover, other

Chagossians were also involved in alternative local music styles. Following the emergence during the 1970s of Rastafarianism and reggae in the Caribbean, the USA, and the UK, the 1980s also saw the development in the Indian Ocean of *seggae*, a combination of *sega* and reggae (Assone 2003; Boswell 2006: 65–68; Eriksen 1998: 88–89, 102 note 9). Whereas *sega* harks back to slavery (and thus appeals to tourists seeking 'authentic' slave dances), *seggae* integrates young Afro-Creoles in the Indian Ocean into a politicised, postcolonial, black African diaspora. Thus *sega* and *seggae* (as well as other more recent local music forms such as Kreol-language ragga and rap) each connect the Indian Ocean to variants of an imagined Africa. Crudely, *sega* was more popular with older generations, and *seggae* with younger generations. The most commercially successful Chagossian musician in Mauritius was the professional *seggae* singer Olivier Sakir (also known as Ton Vié), whose lyrics I also discuss below.

Representing Chagos in songs composed on Chagos

Historians of the Indian Ocean have highlighted how social unrest was widespread within and between the various immigrant communities in colonial Mauritius and its dependencies (Allen 1999; Vaughan 2001; Vaughan 2005: 178–201). Administrative records indicate that the smaller dependent islands were less turbulent than mainland Mauritius, but that they were nonetheless somewhat unsettled (Scott 1961). Leper convicts were sent from Mauritius to be imprisoned on Diego Garcia during the mid-nineteenth century (see Anderson 2000: 42). British magistrates' reports from the second half of the nineteenth century document the imprisonment of workers on the Chagos islands for disturbances such as murder, violence or the threat of violence, attempted rape, theft, drunkenness, desertion, insolence, and insubordination (Ackroyd 1878: 14; Dupont 1884; Farquharson 1864: 2).

During interviews, several Chagos islanders recounted to me their memories of social unrest and economic exploitation on the Chagos Archipelago in the early to mid-twentieth century. For a start, elderly Chagos islanders told me about a form of retributive justice in which groups of islanders organised their own punishments (sometimes violent) for those seen to have deviated from the local moral code. Additionally, those islanders who had left Chagos voluntarily in the 1950s and 1960s (before the forced evacuation of the islands) told me that they had done so because of the domineering [*dominer*] treatment meted out by European employers to African employees, or because of the comparatively low wages in relation to mainland Mauritius. Thus colonial records and elderly Chagos islanders' personal recollections represent the colonial Chagos Archipelago as a plantation settlement with the associated problems of social unrest, retributive justice, racial hierarchies, and economic exploitation.

Such concerns were dominant themes in songs composed on Chagos. Members of the Chagos Tambour Group revived a dozen or so *sega* songs composed on Chagos by their older relatives, all of which recounted aspects of everyday life on a colonial plantation settlement. A couple of these songs described joyous events

– *Bigorno* [Shellfish] describes the weekly dancing parties, and *Sone sone laklos* [Ring ring the bell] depicts the return of fishing boats from the smaller islands – but the majority expressed personal difficulties.

In *Serin rose* [Pink canary], composed by the late Elégie Jaffar and recorded by her granddaughter Léonide Jaffar, the singer laments:

The Second-in-Command Mr Talbot	*Segonn Talbot*
sends out his roll-call,	* fann so lapel,*
My pink canary goes into exile,	*Mo serin roz al eksile,*
In two or three months he'll return.	*Dan de-twa mwa li ava turne.*

Léonide told me that the 'pink canary' was the narrator's partner, and 'exile' referred to his being stationed as a fisherman on a distant Chagos island for a period of two to three months. This reference to exile and separation within the Chagos Archipelago is a reminder that dislocation from the 'homeland' and separation from family members have always been a central part of life for Chagos islanders and their ancestors. After all, the Chagos Archipelago was first populated with slaves forcibly displaced from mainland Africa and Madagascar, who were often separated from their families in the process.

Similarly, in *Ferlevenn* [Make mischief], composed by Rita Elysée and recorded by her daughter Mimose Furcy, the singer observes:

When the Commander cries:	*Kumander letan kriye:*
'Passengers, embark!'	*'Lapay passaze! Ambark passaze!'*
That woman's husband goes,	*Madam-la so mari ale,*
She stays behind.	*Li reste.*
Stop crying, woman,	*Ase plore madam,*
Your tears will flood the passenger list	*To larm lizye pu kuver lalis*
of the *Mauritius*	Mauritius,
Captain Lionnet won't come back	*Kapiten Yone li pa pu vire*
to collect you.	* ramass twa.*

Elsewhere in this song, the narrator also accuses a sexual competitor of trying to harm her through voodoo. In other songs, female narrators accuse their employers of trying to take advantage of them in various ways. In *Mama Sandrine*, composed by the late Alexandrine Petrisseur and recorded by her granddaughter Mimose Furcy, the narrator complains about her boss demanding overtime:

Mr Caboche tells me to stay,	*Misye Caboche dir mwa reste,*
I won't stay:	*Mo pa pu reste:*
I have two children at home	*Mo lakaz mo ena de zanfan.*

In *Baboo diaman* [Respected diamond], composed by Rita Elysée and recorded by Lisette Talate, the narrator recalls that her husband was correct to be wary of a ship's Second-in-Command because of his sexual interference with young women and girls. In *Felonn jabulo* [Diabolical outlaw], composed by Rita Elysée and recorded by her daughter Mimose Furcy, the narrator pleads with another woman about unsolicited sexual attention from the latter's son:

Madam, speak to your child:	Madam koz ek u piti,
What he's doing isn't good.	Seki li pe fer na pa bon.
Every evening he knocks on my door,	Tuleswar li tap mo laport,
Now my husband has heard him.	La mo mari inn tande.
He tells me to lift up my skirt,	Li dir mwa lev mo zip an ler,
To let him look at my calves.	Less li get mo mole.
My calves shouldn't concern him:	Mo mole na pa konsern li:
My calves belong to my husband.	Mo mole konsern mo mari.

In *Leoncine*, composed by the late Alexandrine Petrisseur and recorded by Marina Tiatous, the narrator accuses another woman of stealing her husband:

My good friend Leoncine,	Leoncine mo bon kamarad,
Liked to come to my house ...	Kontan vin dan mo lakaz ...

When she arrived she took
    my husband,
	Arrive li pren
	    mo mari,

Up above the granary furnace.	La-o grenye kalorifer.
That husband isn't yours alone,	Mari-la pa pu to tusel,

That husband belongs to
    the Company.
	Mari-la pu
	    la kompani.

We'll split the money in two,	Larzan nu partaz en de,
You keep his underpants for yourself.	Lamores to gard pu to tusel.

Most of these songs point to recurrent complaints about the harsh requirements of plantation society. These include separation from loved ones, the power dimensions of the social and racial hierarchy between the African labourers and the European plantation owners, the sexual exploitation of Chagossian women by their bosses and by male islanders, and social problems amongst islanders such as accusations of sexual infidelity and voodoo. The lyrics of *sega* songs composed on Chagos, then, paint a nuanced picture of the complexities and turbulence of colonial plantation life.

Romanticising Chagos in songs composed in exile

Songs composed in exile by Chagossian singer-songwriters, by contrast, tend to idealise the Chagos Archipelago as an idyllic island paradise. They highlight the positive characteristics of life there and imply stark contrasts with their negative experiences of life in Mauritius. In her song *Dan Diego* [On Diego], composed in Mauritius, Léonide Jaffar – who was born on Salomon in 1945 and left Chagos aged 22 in 1967 – describes Diego Garcia's natural heritage as follows:

Over on Diego there are pretty colours,	Dan Diego laba, zoli zoli koloriye,
I want to return there with all my heart ...	Mo leker demann turne ...
When you see its sea,	Kan u get so lamer,
When you see its beach,	Kan u get so laplaz,
When you see its shells,	Kan u get so kokiyaz,
Your heart wants to return.	U leker demann turne.

Other Chagossian songs composed by displaced islanders depicted the natural and free lifestyle on Chagos through wildlife metaphors. In *Payanke dan lizur* [Tropicbird in the light], Jessy Marcelin – who was born on Diego Garcia in 1934 and left Chagos aged 36 in 1970 – describes life on Diego as follows:[3]

When I lived in Diego,	*Letan mo ti viv dan Diego,*
I was like a tropicbird in the light:	*Mo kuma payanke dan lizur:*
We lived freely,	*La nu ti viv partu,*
We were like birds without branches.	*Nu pare en zwazo pena brans.*

Other Chagossian singers likewise evoke in their lyrics their appreciation of the natural attributes of the Chagos Archipelago. In 2002, Olivier Sakir (Ton Vié), who was born on Peros Banhos in 1957 and left Chagos aged ten in 1967, released a commercially highly successful album named *Peros vert* [Green Peros] after the Chagos atoll of his birth. In the title song, he describes how 'Green Peros is surrounded by white [sand]' [*Peros vert, tutotur li blan*] and recalls: 'I spent all day by the sea' [*Tut lazurne, mo lavi fini bor lamer*]. In his song *Zilois* [Islander], Ton Vié characterised life on Chagos as follows:

We gathered water in cans,	*Nu ti tir dilo dan pit,*
We had our straw houses.	*Nu ti ena nu lakaz lapay.*
We slept on coconut husk mattresses,	*Nu ti dormi lor kassiya,*
We lived the African way.	*Nu ti viv nu lavi afriken.*
There were no problems on	*La pena problem dan*
the islands,	*lezil,*
For us, the Chagossian inhabitants.	*Pu nu ban abitant chagossien.*
On our islands, we had plenty of food.	*Laba dan nu zil, manze labondans.*
On our islands, we shared what	*Laba dan nu zil, seki nu ena nu partaze.*
we had.	

With these clear and descriptive lyrics he evoked a vision of a simple, idealised 'African' lifestyle characterised by abundant supplies and a sharing mentality. In the final two lines he implicitly contrasted this lifestyle with that in Mauritius.

The lyrics of songs about Chagos composed by Chagos islanders since the displacement, then, do not depict the negative aspects of life on Chagos. References to racial hierarchies, employment hardships, community tensions, and sexual exploitation – which were common themes in lyrics composed and performed on Chagos – were omitted in more recent compositions, which instead portrayed life on Chagos as simple, free, natural, abundant, and harmonious. The stark contrast between Chagos and Mauritius, which remains implicit in the song lyrics quoted above, was made explicit in everyday conversations. Chagos islanders routinely juxtaposed images of Chagos as a place where people lived in harmony with nature and with one another against images of Mauritius as a place where people suffered material hardship and social isolation.

The idealisation of Chagos in terms of natural abundance is best exemplified by islanders' recollections of the plots of land on which they grew crops and raised animals for consumption, and of the fact that they could freely harvest coconuts, fish, seafood, turtles, and seabirds. Chagos islanders often told me that the sandy Chagos soil nourished crops without the need for any fertilisers, whereas Mauritian soil produced poor-quality vegetables, and anyway Chagossians tended not to have their own plots, nor could they afford to eat properly in Mauritius. Chagos islanders and healthcare professionals alike have attributed the disproportionately high levels of high blood pressure and diabetes amongst Chagossians in Mauritius to the contrast between their fresh and varied diets on Chagos and their impoverished diets in Mauritius, which rely on processed and starchy foods.

Chagos islanders correlated the abundance of freely available food in Chagos with a community spirit of sharing, which had become increasingly difficult to sustain in Mauritius, where poverty had meant that Chagossian families put their own material interests first. Nadia, a Chagossian woman in her fifties, recalled:

> Over there we lived as one family. If you were still at work but I'd gone fishing, I would save fish for you, cook for you. Here everyone looks after themselves, because here you have to put your hand in your pocket. Over there everything was abundant. You put your hand in the water, you get a fish.

Evoking a community living together in harmony, Josephine told me that on Chagos,

> We all lived peacefully as one big family, just like they say here 'one people, one nation' [enn sel lepep, enn sel nasyon]. There, it was like that: one people, one nation … Everyone knew everyone else [tu dimunn kon so kamarad] … We didn't have enemies so we didn't fear anyone, not like here in Mauritius … Everything was good there.

Similarly drawing a contrast between harmony in Chagos and disharmony in Mauritius, Elsie informed me that 'on the islands there was no fighting, no disturbances, no problems, no nothing [pena lager, pena tapaz, pena traka, pena narniya], not like here in Mauritius'.

Chagos islanders frequently illustrated the contrast between solidarity in Chagos and isolation in Mauritius by describing different approaches to death on Chagos and Mauritius. They reported that on the occasion of a death on one of the Chagos islands, the whole community came together: neighbours and other islanders would collectively raise funds to purchase provisions for the wake in order to relieve the bereaved family of this responsibility, and any celebrations that had been scheduled during the mourning period would be postponed out of respect for the deceased person and the bereaved families. Families that had been bereaved in Mauritius remarked that such community solidarity was absent in Mauritius, where the bereaved family alone bore the responsibility and cost of organising the wake, funeral, and prayer sessions. Several complained that their Mauritian neighbours had continued to socialise normally and cause disturbances during the mourning period.

Narratives depicting such stark contrasts between Chagos and Mauritius were fully developed by time of my fieldwork, and few Chagos islanders sought to express alternative views. Isolated voices within the Chagossian community, however, have been critical of the blanket romanticisation of their homeland. A Chagossian man in his fifties, whose more public utterances were consistent with the standardised idealisation of Chagos, told me privately that while most Chagos islanders say that Chagos was harmonious, in fact:

> Chagossians conceal information … there are Chagossians who say Chagos is paradise, but that's not true … for a true history you have to tell the bad as well as the good: we were dominated by the colonial power; when you cut coconuts you have to be careful; we didn't have the right to do lots of things, and if you didn't work, you didn't eat … There was a lot of voodoo, which is a serious matter and is kept secret, and there were struggles for leadership amongst islanders, in which those who were weak had to stay quiet because they had no power, whereas those who were dominant could take the others' women.

His references to harsh working conditions, internal power struggles and secret rituals deployed against one another, and infidelity and the sexual oppression of women immediately recall the recurrent themes of the lyrics of songs composed in Chagos.

Depicting the displacement

Although locally produced *seggae* (and ragga and rap) were more popular among younger Afro-Creoles in Mauritius, Ton Vié's lyrics enabled his *seggae* music to cross the generational divide. His songs appealed equally to older generations of Chagos islanders because of their depictions of life in Chagos and the Chagossian community's experiences of displacement, loss, and suffering in exile. Ton Vié's song *Peros vert*, which describes the displacement of the Chagos islanders from the Chagos Archipelago, was especially popular amongst Chagossians. Since its release in 2002, *Peros vert* has been played (usually several times) at every Chagossian party I have attended, invariably filling the dance floor with people singing along and swaying to the music. In *Peros vert*, Ton Vié describes the displacement as follows:

Green Peros, its people are black,	*Peros vert, so pep nwar,*
We black people, we were uprooted.	*Nu pep nwar, nu'nn derasine.*
Birds cried, dogs barked,	*Zwazo kriye, lisyen zape,*
I've lost my island.	*Mo'nn perdi mo zil.*
Goodbye green Peros,	*Goodbye Peros vert,*
Goodbye Salomon,	*Goodbye Salomon,*
Goodbye Diego.	*Goodbye Diego.*
I'll never see you again, my island.	*Ki zame mo pu truv zot, mo lil.*
The sun, the land where my umbilical	*Soley, later mo lombri,*
cord is buried, my island.	*mo lil.*

Ton Vié's evocation of dogs barking is a reference to when the then BIOT Commissioner Bruce Greatbatch ordered that the islanders' dogs be killed prior to the final deportations from Diego Garcia in 1971: the dogs were eventually rounded up and gassed in the building used for drying copra (see Chapter 1). This event also featured in many oral narratives of the displacement, serving to illustrate that islanders were concerned for their own safety and thus intimidated into obeying the orders to leave.

Another aspect of the final deportation that has become a common feature in songs and oral narratives about the displacement are references to the *Nordvær*, the ship that made most of the voyages between the Chagos islands and Seychelles and Mauritius from 1968 onwards, including the final deportations from Diego Garcia in 1971, Salomon in 1972 and Peros Banhos in 1973. In 2004, the professional Chagossian *segatye* Claude Lafoudre, who was born on Peros Banhos in 1959 and left Chagos aged six in 1965, released an album called *Dieu ti kré l'homme* [God created man]. His song *Bourik mo tonton* [My uncle's donkey] appeals to popular memory of the displacement by describing the deportation as follows:

My uncle tells the story of his uprooted life:	*Mo tonton rakonte so lavi derasine:*
He never thought that one day he would leave his natal land.	*Li pa ti espere si en zur li pu kit so later natal.*
The *Nordvær* ship came to take them away.	*Bato* Nordvær *ti vini pu vinn prend zot pu ale.*
The day they embarked on the ship,	*Sa zur ki embarke lor bato,*
They had sadness in their hearts and tears in their eyes.	*Regre dan leker, larm kule.*

Standardised descriptions of the gassing of the dogs and conditions on the *Nordvær* also feature in oral narratives of the displacement not only by those who experienced the displacement themselves, but also by some islanders who left Chagos prior to the final deportations, and, moreover, in the collective historical imagination of descendants born in exile. This was dramatically illustrated to me by the inclusion of both events in a series of sketches about the displacement prepared and performed by young Mauritius-born descendants of Chagossian parentage or grand-parentage at a Chagossian Youth Group [*Grup Zanfan Zilwa*] workshop in 2003. The collective historical imagination developed through such devices as song lyrics and oral narratives thus focuses on a few key themes that evoke shared experiences and promote particular representations of the displacement.

Suffering in exile and the right to return

Chagossian songs composed in exile also describe the sense of loss caused by the displacement. In *Bato ale laba* [The ship goes over there], Jessy Marcelin sings:

Don't cry, don't be sad,	*Pa plore pa sagrin,*
Console yourself, we're leaving.	*Konsole nu pe ale.*
We have sadness in our hearts,	*Regre nu ena dan nu leker,*
For what we've left in the earth.	*Seki nu'nn kit enba later.*
The ship goes over there,	*Bato ale laba,*

It's lost on the horizon.	*Li perdi dan lorison.*
It's lost on the horizon,	*Li perdi dan lorison,*
We've lost our riches.	*Nu fi'nn perdi nu la rises.*

She told me that 'what we've left in the earth' referred both to the bodies of deceased ancestors and to the umbilical cords and placentas buried on Chagos, reflecting connections to the land stretching over several generations and life cycles.

Jessy Marcelin's reference to riches in the last line refers both to cultural loss and to the loss of property. Similarly, in *Peros vert*, Ton Vié sings 'Sitting, we remember where we left our riches, on our little islands in the ocean' [*Assize, nu mazine kot nu bann rises nu'nn fini kite, dan nu ti zil, dan losean*), and the lyrics of *Zilois* evoke the loss both of culture and of property:

Sitting, we remember,	*Assize nu mazine,*
Our cheeks in our hands,	*Nu lame lor nu lazu,*
Tears flowing from our eyes.	*Nu larm lizye kule,*
When we remember our islands,	*Letan nu mazinn nu zil,*
Over there where we lived,	*Laba kot nu ti ete,*
We feel sorrow.	*Nu santi nu dan la tristess.*
We islanders had our houses,	*Zilwa en zilwa, zilwa ti ena so lakaz,*
We islanders had our hearths …	*Zilwa en zilwa, zilwa ti ena nu fwaye …*
Our culture is suffering, islanders,	*Sufer nu kiltir, zilwa,*
We have been waiting a long time,	*Depi longtan nu pe attan,*
When can we return to our islands?	*Kan nu pu returne, laba dan nu ti zil?*
Up to now we can't return.	*Ziska zordi, nu pa pu returne.*

He thus concludes his description of sorrow at the physical and cultural losses by conveying a shared and ongoing desire to return to the Chagos Archipelago.

Several other Chagossian singer-activists have likewise used their song lyrics to appeal for Chagossian unity and collective mobilisation in the Chagossian struggles. In *Dan Diego*, Léonide Jaffar sings:

We can't return,	*Turne pa kapav turne,*
The military base prevents us.	*Baz militer pe bann nu.*
Mothers and fathers,	*Bann mama bann papa,*
Let's put our heads together	*Nu met latet ensam*
for our return to Diego.	*pu nu returne dan Diego.*

Similarly, in *Payanke dan lizur*, Jessy Marcelin sings:

Raise your hands, friends,	*Donn nu lamen kamarad,*
We'll send our message	*Nu envoy nu messaz*
round the world:	*dan lemond:*
There's a naval base in our ocean,	*Baz naval dan nu losean,*
The people of Diego are living	*Pep Diego pe pass*
in poverty.	*mizer.*
Gather together, friends,	*Koste zepol kamarad,*
We'll seek our compensation	*Nu al rod nu rekompens*
for Diego.	*lil Diego.*

As we shall see, these standardised portrayals of the Chagossian experience have helped and hindered different aspects of the Chagossian struggle in exile.

Mobilising the community and galvanising support

Romanticised portrayals of life on the Chagos Archipelago have been used effectively to elicit political, legal, financial, institutional, and moral support from diverse outsiders such as journalists, politicians, non-governmental activists, and lawyers. During my fieldwork, I observed the filming of several documentaries and noticed that journalists sought very particular representations of life on Chagos and in Mauritius. These representations coincided with those in recent Chagossian cultural innovations in oral narratives and song lyrics.

A team from the US television network CBS filmed a documentary with Chagossians in Mauritius for a *60 Minutes* programme entitled 'Diego Garcia: Exiles Still Barred' (Tkach 2003). During an interview with the CRG leader Olivier Bancoult, the CNN reporter Christiane Amanpour asked him what life was like on the islands, whether 'it was a fairly simple, but good life'. This prompted Bancoult to concur that 'it was a simple but good life on the islands'. In 'Winning Back Paradise', a documentary produced by Dateline Australia, the voiceover remarks that the copra companies on the islands provided basic foodstuffs, education, and medicines, so 'life was sweet'. Concurring with this view, a Chagossian interviewee recalls that their 'life was like a fish in water' (Lazaredes 2002), which is reminiscent of the natural metaphors in some of the song lyrics quoted above. Recent documentaries have explicitly characterised the Chagos Archipelago as 'paradise' and routinely juxtapose scenes evoking the 'idyllic' and 'simple' life on Chagos with scenes conveying the Chagossians' suffering and 'abject poverty' in Mauritius (Lazaredes 2002; Lenette-Kisnorbo 2003; Pilger 2004; Tkach 2003). Crucially, these documentaries have included recordings of Chagossian songs composed in exile by Ton Vié (Lenette-Kisnorbo 2003), Charlesia Alexis (Pilger 2004) and Serge Elysée (Lazaredes 2002; Pilger 2004). Songs composed on Chagos before the displacement did not tend to be used.

In November 2003 I attended a ceremony facilitated by the Mauritian Ministry of Arts and Culture for the 'Unveiling of a Commemorative Stele to mark the Arrival of Chagossians in Mauritius following their Inhuman Uprooting from the Chagos Archipelago Islands'. This event further illustrates the kinds of representations deployed by the CRG to mobilise the Chagossian community and galvanise support from outsiders. Over one thousand people, Chagos islanders and their descendants alike, attended the ceremony. Guests of honour included such high-profile Mauritian dignitaries as church leaders, the former President Cassam Uteem, the then Prime Minister Paul Bérenger, and several members of his cabinet.

The event was dominated by speeches by Mauritian politicians interspersed with contributions from prominent Chagos islanders, starting with the CRG leader Olivier Bancoult, who thanked individual Mauritian politicians for their support and reiterated the CRG's requests for additional support from the Mauritian Government. Later in the ceremony, Ton Vié introduced his song *Peros vert* as an expression of 'all our suffering, all our culture', and gave a live performance to an audience of Chagossians almost all standing, singing, and swaying, with many in tears. A senior member of the CRG, Rosemond Saminaden, who was born on Salomon in 1936, gave an extremely moving account of his experience of his uprooting from Peros Banhos on the *Nordvær*'s penultimate voyage in 1973 and the difficulties his young family faced on arrival in Mauritius:

> When we left Chagos we were told that we would get everything we needed in Mauritius, so we came because there was no food left there. When we arrived in Mauritius we didn't have houses, animals, or money ... We suffered. We had a difficult time in Mauritius. Neither the Government nor the Catholic Church helped us. We didn't need money but we needed people's support because we were affected morally and physically.

Such powerful and public performances depict the Chagossians as a community with shared experiences of displacement, dislocation from native land, and suffering and loss of cultural heritage in exile. These elements contribute to attempts by the CRG leadership to inspire collective identification and political mobilisation among Chagossians. From the perspective of the networking CRG leadership, moreover, such cultural occasions allow Chagossians to demonstrate through songs and oral narrative the ongoing vitality of Chagossian culture in an evocative manner, which, they hope, encourages outsiders to lend their support to the Chagossian struggles for compensation and the right to return.

How Chagos was remembered and represented by public representatives such as lyricists and community leaders was politically important for the Chagossian struggle in exile. Critical engagement with the problems of the colonial Chagos Archipelago, which used to find an outlet through a vibrant tradition of lyrical expression, was no longer appropriate because of the detrimental effects such negative portrayals of Chagos could have on the Chagossian struggle for the right to return and on Chagossian unity, optimism, and activism. Emergent Chagossian songs and oral narratives in the public sphere blend two key elements: first, romanticised visions of the homeland, which explain and give impetus to the campaign for the right to return; and second, evocations of shared experiences of displacement, loss and suffering in exile, which justify the campaign for compensation. Such representations form part of attempts by the Chagossian leadership both to inspire collective identification and mobilisation among Chagossians and to elicit external support for these struggles (see Jeffery 2007).

Collective narratives in court

Whilst standardised collective historical narratives have successfully provided a focus for community identification and elicited support for the Chagossian cause, however, they have also come to pose major problems for the Chagossians' legal struggle for compensation and the right to return because of the more positivistic understanding of history imposed by formal concepts of legal evidence.

In 2002, as described in Chapter 2, the CRG formed a coalition with the DGIC and the Chagossian committee in Seychelles. The Chagossian coalition launched a preliminary hearing against the UK Government to determine whether any Chagossians might be eligible for further compensation from the UK Government. The Chagossian coalition and its legal team collected written witness statements from all of the claimants, and selected witnesses to give oral evidence in the High Court in London. All of the fourteen witnesses selected were Chagossian community leaders and active members of the CRG, the DGIC, or the Seychelles committee.

Over the course of the organised Chagossian struggle in Mauritius, several such Chagossian activists have become public representatives of the community and have become accustomed to recounting the community's collective experiences at meetings with the press and with government officials. Several do not exclusively describe their own individual experiences. Rather, in describing life in the Chagos Archipelago, the displacement, or the Chagossian struggle in exile, they recount a generalised description of how 'we' lived in Chagos, what happened to 'us', and how 'we' have suffered and struggled in exile. This conveys a shared Chagossian experience of displacement and suffering in exile. There was a high degree of concurrence that the crucial facts of the Chagossian story are the shared experience of displacement and the stark contrast between life in the Chagos Archipelago and life in Mauritius. Moreover, descriptions have become standardised to the extent that Chagossian community representatives have reproduced the same historical narratives almost verbatim in interviews with journalists and academics and in written witness statements and oral testimony produced for the court.

In his 2003 judgment, Mr Justice Ouseley ruled against the Chagossians, and in 2004 three Appeal Court judges concurred with his decision. Mr Justice Ouseley ruled against each of the Chagossian coalition's causes of action but was particularly critical of the witness evidence given by Chagossian witnesses, noting that 'evidence was ... given, as if at first hand, about events which the witness could not have seen or heard'.[4] He dismissed several Chagossian witnesses as unreliable and inconsistent because they initially presented as first hand eyewitness evidence stories that later appeared to have been based not on individual experience but rather on 'collective memory'.[5]

One example taken from the written statements is the surprisingly large number who claimed to have been on the final voyage from Diego Garcia to Seychelles on the *Nordvær* in 1971. In September 1971, the then BIOT Commissioner, Bruce Greatbatch, requested that the five horses on Diego Garcia be rounded up and accommodated in horseboxes on the *Nordvær* for the journey to Mahé in Seychelles.[6] Passenger lists indicated that there had been only thirty Chagos islanders (plus many more Seychellois workers) on this particular voyage.[7] Whilst collecting evidence for the court case, members of the Chagossian coalition's own legal team were surprised by the much higher number of Chagossian claimants who told the legal team that they had left Diego Garcia with the horses on the *Nordvær* in 1971, when according to their own chronology and the passenger lists they could not have done so. Mr Justice Ouseley, too, noted inconsistencies in the various statements made by claimants regarding when and on which ship they left from which Chagos island.[8] In relation to Lisette Talate, for instance, he noted that: 'In her witness statement, she referred to there being horses on the voyage she was on, but in her oral evidence she denied that there had been horses on it'.[9] In her oral evidence she recounted that she left Diego Garcia in 1971 not for Mauritius but for Peros Banhos, from where she was finally evicted in 1973.

Another example comes from inconsistencies noted by Mr Justice Ouseley between witnesses' written statements and subsequent oral evidence. In particular, some witnesses' written statements recounted aspects of the displacement in the first person as if the individual had been an eyewitness, but their subsequent oral evidence revealed that their accounts were based on hearsay.[10] For instance, Mr Justice Ouseley noted that Lisette Talate's written statement narrated two events that, as she later admitted in oral evidence, she did not witness personally but had heard about from others. The first concerns her description of a woman who was so shocked at the news that she would have to leave Chagos that she had a heart attack and died immediately.[11] The second concerns her account of the suicide of a man who had jumped overboard *en route* to Mauritius.[12] Like the *Nordvær* voyage with the horses, these two traumatic deaths had evidently been incorporated into her recollections of the displacement, but it emerged under questioning that she had not actually witnessed either death at first hand.

As a Chagossian activist, however, Lisette Talate has often been interviewed by journalists, lawyers, and other researchers, and has long been used to being expected to recount a generalised picture of life on Chagos, experiences of the displacement, and life in exile. Rather than talking in the singular and referring uniquely to her own individual experience, she has routinely used the collective voice to convey a shared Chagossian experience of forced displacement, suffering in exile, and solidarity in the Chagossian struggles for compensation and the right to return. In court, unfortunately, this collective narrative style resulted in a clash between the legal team's production of the Chagossian accounts and the judge's strict interpretation of the laws of evidence. The wholesale transposition of standardised accounts of the Chagossian experience into the court as witness evidence had a demonstrably detrimental effect on their case because this collective historical narrative style was at odds with the more formal individual eyewitness accounts expected and sought by the judge (see Jeffery 2006c).

Representing Chagos and the displacement

Popular music can be a means of making history both by retrospectively redefining history and by acting as a form of social action directed towards realising a particular future (Waterman 1990: 369). Recent Chagossian songs and oral narratives illustrate both of these features. Firstly, they retrospectively redefine the colonial Chagos Archipelago as an idyllic island paradise rather than as a complex plantation economy with both positive and negative attributes. Secondly, they seek to inspire collective identification amongst Chagossians and to mobilise Chagossians and others to support Chagossian campaigns for compensation and the right to return to Chagos. Chagossian narrators have successfully deployed eloquent recitation of romanticised representations of the homeland and of standardised accounts of displacement, dislocation, and suffering in exile to mobilise Chagossians and to elicit support for the Chagossian cause from diverse sources.

On the other hand, however, there have been some counter-productive aspects of the collective historical imagination of which these songs form a part. When transposed directly into the High Court as witness evidence in a compensation case launched against the UK Government, for instance, such collective narratives did not withstand the judge's scrutiny, and they have thus posed problems for the Chagossians' legal campaigns for compensation. Strategic cultural essentialism in the form of romanticised and standardised representations of the past has clearly brought significant benefits to displaced peoples and other groups seeking redress for mistreatment. In a world in which claims to rights are increasingly made in the 'evidence'-based domain of law courts, however, this case study demonstrates that such essentialism can, in certain legal contexts, be a hindrance rather than a help. The challenge, then, is to seek ways of harnessing the potential benefits of such powerful collective representations without becoming vulnerable to any potentially counter-productive side-effects.

Notes

1 See www.masa.mu.
2 My transcriptions should not be assumed to be reproductions of songs as they were actually sung on Chagos since there are no previous transcriptions of these songs, which will have evolved and changed in the decades since their composition. In any case they were usually sung to me by a descendant of the songwriter rather than the songwriter herself. Indeed, even their complicated polyphonic character itself may have evolved over time. *Sega* is improvisational, so lyrics may vary between performances, and are only standardised for copyright purposes. The Chagos Tambour Group's eponymous album (2004) contains many of the *sega* songs referred to in this chapter, but my transcriptions are based on independent recordings, so the lyrics are not necessarily identical. All translations of song lyrics are my own.
3 At the time of my fieldwork, Jessy Marcelin lived in Seychelles and was not a member of the Mauritius-based Chagos Tambour Group, although she was active in the CRG's partner organisation in Seychelles. The Chagossian activist Charlesia Alexis sang very similar lyrics in John Pilger's documentary, and I have not been able reliably to ascertain the song's provenance.
4 *Chagos Islanders v Attorney General and HM BIOT Commissioner* [2003] EWHC QB 2222: paragraph 161.
5 *Ibid.*
6 *Ibid.*: paragraph 332.
7 *Ibid.*: paragraphs 37–38.
8 *Ibid.*: appendix paragraphs 397–405.
9 *Ibid.*: appendix paragraphs 400.
10 *Ibid.*: appendix paragraphs 332–405.
11 *Ibid.*: appendix paragraph 355.
12 *Ibid.*: appendix paragraph 399.

4

The politics of culture in exile

This chapter explores the politics of cultural expression among the Chagossian community in exile. Culture [*kiltir*] has been an issue for displaced Chagos islanders in Mauritius for two reasons connected to the Chagossian struggle. First, in order to make a case for special treatment – compensation, the right of return, UK citizenship – they must show cultural uniqueness and demonstrate their distinctiveness from other Mauritian citizens and lack of integration into Mauritian society. Second, in order to be recognised as victims – and therefore deserving of recompense of various kinds – they must demonstrate suffering and loss as a result of the displacement. These two requirements imply contrasting (but not necessarily contradictory) notions of the characteristics of culture. On the one hand, emphasising distinctiveness implies certain static, authentic, or essential characteristics of 'Chagossian culture' distinguishing it from correspondingly authentic 'Mauritian culture'. On the other hand, emphasising loss indicates that Chagossian culture underwent transformations as a result of the displacement, which requires recognition that culture is not static but changeable. This chapter investigates how Chagossian socio-political and socio-cultural groups have responded to the dual challenge of needing to represent both cultural continuity and cultural change. It starts by outlining the main issues in the anthropology of the politics of culture. It then explores how Chagos islanders came to identify collectively as Chagossians. Next, it illuminates processes of Chagossian cultural revival and gendered transmission in exile. Finally, it shows how Chagossians have simultaneously associated with and dissociated from other Indian Ocean island Creole cultures.

The politics of culture

Since the mid-twentieth century, anthropologists have criticised the assumptions, attributed to functionalism and to interpretive cultural anthropology, that 'a culture' has authentic, traditional, essential, and static characteristics and that individuals have a bounded and fixed cultural identity (Barth 1969; Baumann 1996: 9–36; Handler & Linnekin 1984; Leach 2000 [1977]; Turner 1993: 411–412). Social scientists increasingly see cultural identification as a process of doing and becoming rather than cultural identity as a state of having and being (Baumann 1996: 9–14; Brubaker & Cooper 2000: 14–15; Hall 1993: 392–394). Analysis of 'culture' and 'tradition' is not, however, restricted to academics. It also engages social actors, who have their own ideas about cultural authenticity, ethnic boundaries, and the transmission of tradition. Partly as a result, social scientists are increasingly wary of the potential social and political implications of how they represent and theorise cultural practices, including claims to tradition, authenticity, and boundedness.

Handler and Linnekin, for instance, are clear that 'tradition cannot be defined in terms of boundedness, givenness, or essence. Rather, tradition refers to an interpretive process that embodies both continuity and discontinuity' (Handler & Linnekin 1984: 273). Analysing national and ethnic identification in Quebec and Hawaii, however, they show how ethnographically inspired theories about cultural traits and ethnic boundaries have provided apparently scientific academic justification for nationalist movements built on seemingly natural and objective categories such as a culture, ethnic group, or nation (Handler & Linnekin 1984). Thus conceptualisations of culture and identity may have real-life social and political implications for individuals and socio-political groups, which may incorporate favourable theories of boundedness and may participate actively in debates about the characteristics of culture.

Extending Handler and Linnekin's concerns about essentialism in nationalist movements, Adam Kuper has argued that indigenous land claims 'rely on obsolete anthropological notions and on a romantic and false ethnographic vision' (Kuper 2003: 395). Others, however, have criticised Kuper's own homogenising representation of 'the indigenous rights movement' (for example, see Kenrick & Lewis 2004: 8–9; Robins 2003). His critics point out that Kuper's argument was based on portrayals of indigenous peoples in particular political and legal contexts in which the indigenous claimants were required to represent themselves in specific and essentialised ways.

Contrasting academic definitions of culture have been transposed into legal debates in court cases, which can have detrimental implications for marginalised claimants. On the one hand, land claims tribunals in the Americas and Australasia have required indigenous peoples to demonstrate continuous cultural practices and ongoing connections to territory. Change and movement were assumed to be evidence either that indigenous groups had successfully assimilated into local settler communities or that the rupture in question happened too long ago to have ongoing significance for descendants or to be reversible via land allocation (Clifford 1988; Culhane 1998; Sutton 2003; Weiner 1999). A famous example is a land rights case in Cape Cod in which the Mashpee Wampanoag Tribal Council were required to demonstrate unbroken residence and cultural continuity with the past, a blinkered approach which neglected the 'complex historical processes of appropriation, compromise, subversion, masking, invention, and revival' (Clifford 1988: 337–339). In sharp contrast, the Nuclear Claims Tribunal in the Marshall Islands required that the former inhabitants of Rongelap, evacuated as a result of US nuclear tests there, demonstrated that their experience had been one of loss and complete rupture with the past (Kirsch 2001: 171). A search for cultural loss challenges more recent anthropological conceptions of culture as 'a process that continually undergoes change rather than something which can be damaged or lost' (Kirsch 2001: 168). Kirsch set the challenge that anthropological models of culture 'must be able to account for the contradictory demands that the courts placed on the Mashpee and the people of Rongelap: to recognize change while simultaneously acknowledging loss' (Kirsch 2001: 177).

One way to respond to this challenge is to ask how indigenous peoples conceptualise 'culture' outside the narrow confines of law courts (Kenrick & Lewis 2004: 9; Omura 2003: 396). For instance, Jean Jackson noted that members of the Tukanoan indigenous rights movement in Colombia had to strike a series of delicate balances: to respect the past without appearing reactionary, to promote development without threatening cultural uniqueness, and to advocate group-based rights without endorsing separatism (Jackson 1995: 12). Through the indigenous rights movement, Tukanoans and their supporters embraced a complex notion of culture that incorporated aspects of authenticity and preservation on the one hand and of change and development on the other. Jackson concluded that:

> Culture is not a primordial legacy from the past; cultures are not static, homogeneous systems on which change is imposed. Rather, cultures are systems whose very foundations are characterized by dynamism, negotiation, and contestation. (Jackson 1995: 20)

Viewing cultural activity as a (political) process, therefore, enables recognition that there can be elements of both continuity and change: some practices may continue apparently unchanged while others are lost or forgotten, and yet others are transformed or created anew. Even among groups that have experienced collective trauma such as dislocation, loss may not be total. Practices of cultural revival and transformation complicate any picture of cultural change, although highlighting cultural innovation may unfairly be interpreted as denying cultural authenticity (Jackson 1989: 127). Furthermore, as anthropologists in the Americas and Australasia have realised, acknowledging cultural change has provided a legal get-out clause for governments attempting for political reasons to demonstrate that indigenous connections to land are no more essential, timeless, or real than those of settler communities (Harrison 1999a; Kirsch 2001; Sutton 2003; Weiner 1999). In this context, academics need to be keenly aware of the possible implications of particular ways of theorising culture (Handler 1985; Jackson 1989; Spencer 1990).

In this chapter I explore Chagossian understandings of culture, illustrating how, among Chagossians, the concept of *kiltir* has diverse – but not mutually exclusive – characteristics. These characteristics range from authenticity, uniqueness, and continuity to loss, revival, and transformation. My Chagossian friends and acquaintances sometimes viewed culture in terms of tangible and unchanging trappings. They also recognised that their own culture had been prone to loss (as a result of displacement and dispossession) and change (as a result of changing circumstances in exile) without necessarily becoming inauthentic. Crucially, they felt that loss and change did not remove key distinctions between Chagossians and non-Chagossian others. Thus I respond to Kirsch's challenge by showing how Chagossian notions of culture can be used to reconcile recent anthropological theories about processes of cultural identification with real-life experiences of loss. Chagossians engage with diverse contemporary conceptualisations of culture much as others do. Their nuanced understandings of culture validate their simultaneous claims of cultural loss and ongoing cultural distinctiveness in exile.

Identification as Chagossians

My lineage is of black skin,	*Mo desandan lapo nwar,*
I was born on Peros Banhos.	*Mo'nn ne mo nesans lor Peros Banhos.*
My elders brought me to Mauritius,	*Mo gran fami ti amen mwa Moris,*
To this day I'm still here.	*Ziska ler mo ankor la mem.*
I was born on Peros,	*Mo'nn ne Peros,*
I've never seen it, what it's like.	*Zame mo'nn truv li, kuma li ete.*
I was born on Peros Banhos,	*Mo'nn ne mo nesans lor Peros Banhos,*
They called me 'that islander there'.	*Ti apel mwa 'sa zilwa-la'.*
Oh, it's the truth:	*Ay-o la verite,*
I was born on the islands.	*Mo'nn ne dan zil.*
I'm a little islander,	*Mwa mo en ti-ilwa,*
I was born on Peros.	*Mo'nn ne Peros.*
What am I, in this land?	*Ki mo ete, lor sa later la?*
Those born on Rodrigues,	*Seki'nn ne Rodrige,*
You call Rodriguan.	*To dir Rodrige.*
Those born in Seychelles,	*Seki'nn ne Seysel,*
You call Seychellois.	*To dir Seyselwa.*
Those born on Réunion,	*Seki'nn ne la Reynon,*
You call Réunionais.	*To dir Reynone.*
Those born in Mauritius,	*Seki'nn ne Moris,*
You call Mauritian.	*To dir Morisyen.*
Diego, there was Salomon,	*Diego, ti ena Salomon,*
there was Peros.	*ti ena Peros.*
Oh, I was born on Peros.	*Ay-o mon ne Peros.*
What am I, on this land?	*Ki mo ete, lor sa later la?*

(Claude Lafoudre, *Divas Sega* [*Sega* Divas], 2003)

Changes in the collective names used by others to describe the Chagos islanders and used by Chagos islanders to describe themselves reveal important changes in self-perception and reflect the mobilisation of the displaced community. During the nineteenth century, slave owners classified enslaved labourers throughout the Indian Ocean according to place of birth, which was sometimes mistakenly conflated with port of embarkation in Africa (Scott 1961: 2). Enslaved labourers brought to Mauritius and its dependencies from East Africa or Madagascar were registered as *Mozambique* (from the Mozambique coast) or *Malgasche* (from

Madagascar) as appropriate. Those born on Mauritius or one of its dependencies were registered as *Créole de Maurice* [Creole of Mauritius], *Créole de Diego Garcia*, *Créole de Peros Banhos*, *Créole de Salomon*, and so forth.

Following the abolition of slavery, colonial visitors to the Chagos Archipelago continued to distinguish between those workers who had been born on Chagos islands and those who had been born in Mauritius. After a Catholic mission in 1933–34, the Roman Catholic priest Roger Dussercle referred to those born on the Chagos islands as *enfants des îles* [children of the islands] and *Ilois* [islanders] (Dussercle 1934: 9–10). The report of the visit in 1969 of the then BIOT administrator John Todd implies that at that time, *Créoles des Iles* [Creoles of the islands] and *Ilois* [islanders] were the terms most often used to refer to those born on the Chagos Archipelago rather than in Mauritius and Seychelles (Todd 1969: 19). By the 1980s, Chagos islanders in Mauritius seem to have referred to themselves and to have been known by others as *Ilois* rather than as *Créoles des Iles* (Botte 1980; Walker 1986). By the time of my fieldwork in Mauritius in 2002–4, Chagos islanders only very rarely mentioned the term *Créoles des Iles*, and they described themselves as *Chagossien* far more often than as *Ilois*. Here I outline first the islanders' dissociation from the appellation *Ilois* and second their identification with the appellation Chagossian.

On the Chagos Archipelago, the appellations *Créoles des Iles* and *Ilois* distinguished between islanders who were born on Chagos (i.e. insiders) and migrant workers from elsewhere (i.e. outsiders), and the terms apparently had no pejorative connotations. On arrival in Mauritius, however, the distinction became one between the local Mauritians (i.e. insiders) and *Ilois* from elsewhere (i.e. outsiders). Chagossians frequently asserted to me that Mauritians had judged Chagos islanders to be inferior and had attached negative connotations to the term *Ilois* (see also Anyangwe 2001: 17). Older Chagos islanders told me that some Mauritians had used the word *Ilois* as a general insult meaning a fool or an uneducated or ignorant person, and would comment 'look at that *Ilois* over there' [*get sa zilwa la*] whenever they saw people (not necessarily Chagos islanders) behaving foolishly. Many Chagossians claimed that once they had been labelled as *Ilois*, Mauritians would mock them and attempt to deceive them. As Josephine, a retired Chagossian woman, put it,

> They say: 'you're savage', 'the *Ilois* don't know how to read', 'they've come from the islands to fill our places' … We changed the name *Ilois* because people abused us with that name, they treated us as if we were ignorant.

Thus islanders from Chagos became increasingly unwilling to identify themselves as *Ilois* due to the pejorative connotations attributed to the category and the experience of actual discrimination as a result of categorisation as *Ilois*.

The name *Ilois* also became problematic because it meant islander in general, was not specific to the Chagos islanders, and could be applied to islanders from any of the 'lesser dependencies' or 'smaller island dependencies' (Houbert 1992: 471). For many in Mauritius, *Ilois* refers to islanders of the smaller Indian Ocean islands in general rather than from the Chagos Archipelago in particular. In articles about the Mauritius outer island Agalega, for instance, Mauritian journalists have referred to Agalegans as *Ilois* (see, for example, Quirin & Achille 2003). Some Chagossians told me that *Ilois* referred to the inhabitants of all the Indian Ocean islands regardless of ethnic or religious background. Others disagreed with the inclusion of non-Creoles in the category *Ilois*, specifying instead that *Ilois* referred to slaves and their descendants. A Mauritius Broadcasting Corporation (MBC) programme about the 2003 Creole Festival in Rodrigues, for instance, used the terms *esklav* [slaves] and *Ilois* [islander] almost interchangeably in its overview of the history of Rodrigues. Whether interpreted as islander or as islander with slave ancestry, the appellation *Ilois* was unproblematic when on Chagos. In Mauritius, however, it could not adequately identify them as a distinct category of displaced islanders originating specifically from the Chagos Archipelago. Whereas those identified as Mauritian or Seychellois are directly associated with the territories of Mauritius and Seychelles respectively, the word *Ilois* indicates no connection to any particular territory.

In the mid- to late 1990s, as outlined in Chapter 2, the CSC was the dominant Chagossian organisation. Believing that a people's collective name should reflect their connection to a specific territory, the CSC's Mauritian barrister, Hervé Lassemillante, coined the collective name Chagossian (spelt *Chagossien* in French) to make explicit the link between the Chagos islanders and the Chagos Archipelago. There was no precolonial population on the Chagos Archipelago, and the name Chagos (evidently the only name the Archipelago has ever had) dates from the Portuguese discovery of the islands in the first half of the sixteenth century. Its meaning is obscure; the Mauritian historian Alain Toussaint suggested that Chagos might be a derivation of the Portuguese word *chagas* (Toussaint 1966: 110), meaning wound or disease.[1]

At CSC meetings I attended, the CSC leader Fernand Mandarin reasserted several times that, unlike the appellation *Ilois*, the collective name Chagossian reflects the particular history of the Chagos islanders in terms of their connection to the Chagos Archipelago and their displacement from their homeland. It was well known that the word Chagossian was devised by Lassemillante and was therefore associated with the CSC in particular. Nevertheless, the vast majority of Chagossians I knew, regardless of socio-political affiliation, accepted his logic and have gradually replaced self-identification as *Ilois* with self-identification as Chagossian. Thus, the original collective name for islanders born on the Chagos Archipelago, *Ilois* [islander], was indexical and adequate on Chagos, but it became derogatory and imprecise in Mauritius, where it has been replaced by the collective name Chagossian, which implies a precise and direct connection to the Chagos Archipelago.

Gendered cultural responsibility

In addition to emphasising their link to the Chagos Archipelago, Chagossian socio-cultural groups in exile have also sought to elaborate the content of Chagossian culture. During my fieldwork in Mauritius in 2002–4, the CRG was engaged in an attempt to preserve Chagossian culture, promote Chagossian collective identity, and transmit Chagossian traditions to the younger generations in exile. These goals were approached through the formalisation of residual Chagossian cultural practices and the establishment and entrenchment of new markers. These activities centred on *sega* music (which was a mixed-sex activity in relation to composition, singing and dancing) and cuisine (which was generally seen as the preserve of women).

In numerous ethnographic contexts, women are seen as markers and repositories of an 'authentic' cultural identity. Among diasporic communities women are often assigned the role of 'cultural carriers' who are responsible for the retention and transmission of cultural knowledge to future generations (Anthias & Yuval-Davis 1992; Yuval-Davis 1997). Chagossian cultural practices suggest that Chagossian women in Mauritius were seen as sites of authentic cultural knowledge about life in the Chagos Archipelago. Women were assumed to have the primary responsibility for the revival of cultural practices and transmission of the connection to the land and knowledge of traditions to their descendants born in exile.

Under colonial rule, Creoles in Seychelles and Creoles at the bottom of the socio-economic stratum in Mauritius developed a working-class matrifocal family structure akin to that of former colonial plantation societies in the Caribbean (Benedict 1965: 29; Benedict & Benedict 1982: 104; cf. Smith 1996). A matrifocal household consists of a woman and her children plus, in some cases, a peripheral male partner and father figure. He might give some of his wages to the female head of household, who controls the purchase of subsistence items (Benedict & Benedict 1982: 215–216). In Seychelles, the rate of marriage halved and the percentage of children born outwith marriage doubled between 1891 and 1971 (Benedict & Benedict 1982: 221–225). An increasing proportion of couples turned to living *en ménage* (cohabiting without marrying), which was evidently less durable than marriage, so a woman might have children by several different men over the course of her reproductive years (Benedict & Benedict 1982: 137, 223). A mother would build up obligations so that her children would support her as she and they grew older. She would be likely to encourage her own daughters to marry in order to gain another source of income, but discourage her sons from marrying in order to keep them as wage earners in the matrifocal household (Benedict & Benedict 1982: 210, 260).

In common with other matrifocal post-slavery societies in the Indian Ocean and the Caribbean, the colonial Chagos Archipelago was characterised by women-headed households, a relative instability of sexual relationships, and a low incidence of marriage (Botte 1980: 22–23; Brooks 1875: 37; Walker 1986: 15–18). Chagos islanders told me that they did not necessarily get married to their partners, both because they were not encouraged to do so and because it was not expected that the union would be for life. I was told several times that the home was based around the mother and her children, and that many men did not want to take responsibility for fatherhood, and so they did not settle in one household with one woman. Some men moved between houses and fathered children with several different women in quick succession. Women were also able to instigate separations. For example, a fisherman posted temporarily to distant small islands might find on his return that his female partner had replaced him with another live-in male partner (see also Botte 1980: 2).

Due to recruitment patterns, men outnumbered women throughout the colonial settlement of the Chagos Archipelago. As described in Chapter 1, the copra companies employed men and women to do different work. All workers received the same rations but different work received different pay. Overall, women's work was paid less than men's work, and women generally worked shorter hours in employment so that they could also do housework and provide childcare, although male and female workers alike also had the opportunity to do overtime, which was relatively better paid. Prior to the depopulation of the islands, then, most women on Chagos were in formal employment and had both economic and domestic roles.

This changed after the displacement. Many Chagossian women who used to be employed on Chagos became housewives in Mauritius, where employment was not guaranteed as it had been in Chagos. Thus their former economic roles declined while their social and domestic roles (with primary responsibility for cooking, cleaning, shopping, and childcare) took precedence. These changes were accompanied by suggestions that women had greater responsibility than men for the preservation of culture and its transmission to future generations. Certainly, among Chagossians in general there was a sense that women ought to uphold Chagossian culture by cooking distinctively Chagossian coconut-based dishes [*seraz*] for their families. When I asked Josephine, a retired Chagossian woman, whether she thought that her children could imagine life on Chagos, she replied:

> They know our culture, they know a bit, because sometimes my own children say to me 'why don't you cook your island food, why don't you cook Chagossian food?' My son says 'Ma, cook *seraz*, we'll eat it'.

In 2003, the Ilois Support Trust (IST) organised a young leaders' workshop for the CRG's youth group, the *Grup Zanfan Zilwa*. A session about the difference between male and female responsibilities revealed some ideas among Chagos islanders and their descendants about the gendered nature of responsibility to culture in exile. The young women in one group suggested that men should become more active in the Chagossian struggle. Meanwhile, the young men in another group declared that (Chagossian) women do not do enough to preserve their culture since, for example, many do not know how to cook *seraz*. The IST's Mauritian facilitator, Paula Lew Fai, who ran the session, remarked that the young women talked of seeking 'equality' with men while the young men talked of the need for women to preserve and transmit 'tradition'. She queried the assumption that Chagossian men have no culture to pass on to their descendants. An adult male participant responded that, 'it's the women who are in the house, spending time on culture and cuisine while the men are at work'. Lew Fai commented that culture was not cuisine alone, but there was no further discussion of what else culture might be, what culture men knew and could teach, or how responsibility for the preservation and transmission of culture was distributed. No mention was made, for instance, of Chagossian men's traditional skills such as fishing or working with coconuts.

The Chagossian Women's Group

The IST project with the CRG included the establishment in 2002 of a socio-cultural group for women, the Chagossian Women's Group [*Grup Fam Chagossienne*].[2] At the group's strategic planning session, Paula Lew Fai asked the Chagossian women present to list their aims for the group. With her encouragement and input, the group eventually produced a mission statement with the following aims:

1. To foster knowledge, skills, know-how and well-being
2. To protect and promote our traditional cultural identity
3. To share traditional ways of life between Chagossians and non-Chagossians

Throughout my fieldwork in Mauritius, the Chagossian Women's Group focused on two main aspects of Chagossian culture (*sega* music and cuisine) and on two main activities (revival and transmission). First, the group convened with the intention of remembering, standardising, rehearsing, and performing Chagossian *sega*. Second, members shared recipes for Chagossian cuisine, which they prepared and served to Chagossians and outsiders at special events. These sets of activities entailed debates about cultural authenticity and the emergence of new cultural practices.

The first elements of the cultural revival were attempts by Chagossian Women's Group members to remember and rehearse Chagossian *sega*. The group leader, Mimose Furcy (the elder sister of the CRG leader Olivier Bancoult), asked members to try to remember songs from Chagos. She said that even younger Chagos islanders such as herself – she was born in 1955 and was a teenage girl when her family left Peros Banhos in 1968 – should try to remember songs their elders sang. Mimose sang as much as she could remember of a song composed by her grandmother, Alexandrine Petrisseur, whereupon the CRG deputy leader Lisette Talate, who was born in 1941 and was in her early thirties when she was removed from Chagos, said she recognised the song and recalled the circumstances in which it had been composed.

Over the next few months, Chagossian Women's Group members attempted to remember songs from Chagos and worked together on different recollections of the lyrics to devise an agreed version, after which a rough recording was made so that lyrics could be transcribed and distributed for memorisation by members. This process resulted in some notable conflicts, such as when two senior Chagossian women disputed the sex of the principal voice in one song, each insisting that she was correct since the story relied on the narrator being male or female respectively. On another occasion one woman complained that the singer had sung a song's verses in the wrong order, and remarked that this should have been evident from the chronology of the story. Realising that the process of establishing a single authorised version was problematic, one singer reiterated that if she sometimes got the lyrics 'wrong', it was not because she was 'lying' but because she could not remember all of the words.

Once the women had remembered, memorised, and rehearsed several of their own and their elders' songs from Chagos, they formed the musical ensemble Chagos Tambour Group, in which women sang, women and men danced together, and men played the goatskin drum [*ravanne*].[3] One performance was attended by a French documentary filmmaker, Michel Daëron, who suggested that the Chagos Tambour Group should have a costume. This idea was somewhat controversial among older Chagossian women, however, because, as Lisette Talate put it,

> Journalists don't know about *sega*. Our culture on the islands was that at dances everyone could wear whatever they had and it did not have to be the same, everyone just knew to wear a white petticoat and a coloured skirt.

Thus she expected that women would wear the same kinds of clothes (that is, a white petticoat under a coloured skirt), but she saw as inauthentic the idea that the colour and style should be prescribed and matching.

Nevertheless, most Chagos Tambour Group members agreed that as a performing *sega* ensemble, they ought to perform in a specifically Chagossian costume. For inspiration they turned to a Chagossian banner designed in 1999 by Nicole Bésage, a Chagossian woman living in Switzerland, which was already the basis for the CRG's colour code. The banner consists of three horizontal stripes: orange at the top (representing the bright sun at dawn and dusk), black in the middle (representing the islands), and blue at the bottom (representing the sea and lagoons of the archipelago).[4] In 2002, the CRG painted this banner above the entrance to their office in Mauritius, and committee members call it the *pavyon Chagossien* [Chagossian flag], although it was recognisable only to active members of the CRG. The Chagos Tambour Group based their costume on these colours. Women wore orange or blue headscarves and plain black tops with orange, black and blue striped skirts over white petticoats. Men wore black trousers with orange and blue panelled shirts without collars. The establishment of a colour-coded flag and costume indicates that the CRG had started to collect symbols that immediately signified a uniquely Chagossian collective identity.

The second aspect of the Chagossian cultural revival was the representation of this unique culture to outsiders through public demonstrations of various aspects of culture, such as cuisine. On a daily basis, Chagossians' diets were indistinguishable from the diets of other urban working-class people in Mauritius. For breakfast, most people ate baguettes or crusty white bread rolls with butter, cheese, or jam. Lunches and dinners were usually rice (or crusty white bread) accompanied with a curried meat or vegetable sauce. Likewise, on Catholic festivals such as Easter, weddings, baptisms and first communions, and on other special occasions such as birthday parties, Chagossians and Mauritian Creoles served the same range of party finger food, such as fried meat snacks, sandwiches, and cakes.

Chagossian cuisine was served only on specifically Chagossian special occasions such as the fundraising Chagossian Day [*Journée Chagossienne*], the Creole Day [*Journée Créole*] in Port Louis and the Creole Festival [*Festival Kréol*] in Rodrigues (where Chagossian groups participated expressly as Chagossians), or when VIPs or potential supporters had been invited to dine at the CRG office.[5] On these occasions, all connected to patronage, political campaigning and representing the group to outsiders, members of the Chagossian Women's Group were called upon to serve Chagossian feasts. Such feasts were intended to show that they had their own culture: as Olivier Bancoult put it, 'they took us from the islands, but we have kept our culture'.

The Chagossian cuisine offered at these events was a standardised set menu of popular dishes.[6] The main course invariably consisted of rice and flatbread [*roti*] accompanied with coconut-based *seraz* dishes of chicken, fish, or octopus (depending on availability and finances), lentils in coconut milk [*seraz lentil*], coconut chutney [*satini koko*], fried green leaves [*tufe bred*] and chillies. On occasions when dessert was offered, it was rice flour and coconut milk dumplings [*muf*] and wheat flour and coconut milk dumplings [*matuftwa*], sugared coconut [*gato koko*] and peanut crunch [*nuga pistas*] or sweet potato in coconut milk [*seraz patat*]. I was told that they could not make dishes based on wildfowl and certain fish and seafood since these were not available in Mauritius. Chagos islanders also mentioned *seraz* dishes made with banana, breadfruit and pumpkin that I never saw made, not necessarily due to the scarcity or expense of crucial ingredients since all three were abundant and cheap in Mauritius: perhaps these variants were just less popular. Certainly there was very little debate among Chagossians about the authenticity of the Chagossian cuisine offered in Mauritius. They reiterated that people might legitimately cook differently. As one member of the Chagossian Women's Group put it, 'everyone has their own method of preparation'. They agreed, however, that a key characteristic of Chagossian cooking was that it was naturally flavoursome and did not require the herbs and spices popular in Indo-, Sino- and Franco-Mauritian dishes. Cuisine was an important but less controversial repository of Chagossian culture than was *sega*, as we shall see below.

Sega music, Creole cuisines, and Kreol languages

In addition to elaborating the content of Chagossian culture, Chagossian sociocultural groups in exile have also sought to define Chagossian collective identity in relation to other Creole cultures of the Indian Ocean. Chagossians frequently reflected both on the overlaps between their culture and other Creole cultures and on the differences between Chagossian culture and other cultures, emphasising what it means to be specifically Chagossian.

As outlined in Chapter 1, many of the islands of the Indian Ocean share similar colonial histories. Early French colonialists started to populate the islands with slaves from East Africa and Madagascar. Later, British colonialists brought indentured labourers from India and China. During the French and the early British colonial periods, the term 'Creole' referred to those born in the colonies, but gradually it became an ethnic designation for Mauritians of primarily African or mixed ancestry (see Vaughan 2005: 2–3, 272). In this, the trajectory of the concept of 'Creole' in the Indian Ocean differs somewhat from its trajectory in the Caribbean. In the Caribbean, 'Creole' likewise originally meant those born locally, but there the concept of creolisation developed principally in reference to new, hybrid cultural forms that emerged locally through colonial plantation encounters between indigenous peoples, colonists, and enslaved and indentured labourers (Palmié 2006). By contrast, in postcolonial Mauritius and elsewhere in the Indian Ocean, the term 'Creole' instead increasingly referred to those of primarily African descent, or at least those whose mixed ethnic backgrounds included African ancestry (Boswell 2006: 42–76; Eisenlohr 2006: 22–65; Eriksen 1998: 15, 50–52; Teelock 1999: 3–4).

Chagossians and other Creoles I met in Mauritius, Rodrigues, and Seychelles frequently compared and contrasted Creole cultures of the smaller Indian Ocean islands. On the one hand they emphasised the similarities amongst Creole cultures in contradistinction with other local cultures originating in Euro-American or Asian traditions. On the other hand they pointed out the differences between the Creole cultures of different islands, with each asserting the uniqueness of their particular island culture. Thus they marked both a shared Indian Ocean Creole identity and the uniqueness of each island's Creole identity. As we shall see, Creole culture was principally conceived as *sega* music, Creole cuisine, and Kreol languages.

Every October, a week-long popular Creole Festival is celebrated in Mauritius, Seychelles, and Réunion. In the Republic of Mauritius, the Creole Festival is supported by the Nelson Mandela Centre for African Culture, which operates under the aegis of the Ministry of Education, Culture and Human Resources.[7] Particularly on the island of Rodrigues, which has a proportionately much higher Afro-Creole population than mainland Mauritius, the Creole Festival has been a forum for the emergence of collective identification amongst Creoles from various Indian Ocean islands on the basis of African ancestry, a shared history of slavery, and Afro-Creole cultural practices. Festival organisers routinely promoted their desire for more widespread recognition of the 'value' of Afro-Creole cultures, which Creole activists throughout the Indian Ocean widely perceived to be threatened by dominant Euro-American and Asian cultures.

One of the main cultural practices promoted at the Creole Festivals is Indian Ocean *sega* music. *Sega* is performed throughout the Indian Ocean islands at events ranging from small-scale private celebrations (for example, parties and weddings) and professional performances (such as cultural shows in hotels), to national events (such as Independence Day celebrations) and inter-state cultural shows (including the Creole Festival). The press supports the Creole Festivals as an important demonstration of African heritage, and audience attendance at public performances is high.

In October 2003, the Rodrigues Regional Assembly (RRA) invited the CRG's *sega* ensemble, the Chagos Tambour Group [*Grup Tambour Chagos*] to perform at the Creole Festival in Rodrigues, and the group invited me to accompany them.

The day after the Chagos Tambour Group's performance, one of the Rodriguan festival organisers, Michel Menn, announced:

> We must not let our culture fall; we must give it its value. Yesterday I heard the Chagossian group singing. They sing the same *sega* as we do, and I realised that we are an important people of the Indian Ocean with the same mentality. We need to open our eyes to our culture.

At the same time, however, festival organisers and performers alike frequently emphasised not only the commonalities but also the differences between the *sega* music from the islands of Mauritius, Rodrigues, Chagos, Réunion, and Seychelles. In particular, they noted differences in instrumentation, tempo, dance style, and costume (see Lee 1990: 28–29; Nelson Mandela Centre for African Culture 2003), but did not comment on lyrical or thematic content. While welcoming the Chagos Tambour Group to Rodrigues, for instance, the then Chief Commissioner of Rodrigues, Serge Clair, imitated the different *sega* dance styles of various Indian Ocean islands. He conveyed a tempo continuum from the languorous Seychellois *sega* at one extreme, via the slightly faster Chagossian *sega*, and then the more energetic Rodriguan *sega*, to the frenetic Mauritian *sega* at the other extreme. Mauritian *sega* dancing is considered to be most flamboyant and sexually provocative, whereas in Rodriguan *sega*, male and female dancers maintain a greater distance from each other. Mauritian and Rodriguan *sega* dancing is based on an elliptical hip movement aided by quick footwork, whereas in Chagossian *sega*, dancers twirl one way and then the other and shuffle their feet on the ground, which I was told was because they were used to dancing on sand.

The outfits worn by the *sega* dancers also have characteristics specific to each island. At cultural events I attended, there was little variation among male dancers, who wore a plain or patterned shirt, plain dark trousers and an optional straw hat (see Lee 1990: 32). There was, however, considerable variation in the attire worn by female dancers from different islands. Female Mauritian and Seychellois dancers wore a long, full, brightly patterned skirt with a matching cropped blouse, whereas female Rodriguan dancers wore plainer skirts and waist-length blouses. Female Chagos Tambour Group dancers, by contrast, covered their midriffs and wore full knee- or calf-length skirts that could be left open up the front to reveal white underskirts when twirling. Jean-Marie Richard, a Mauritian cultural events organiser, told me these differences relate to the fact that the Rodriguan *sega* was more 'traditional' than the 'westernised' Mauritian *sega*. He concluded that only Chagossians had kept the truly 'authentic' white underskirts and practice of twirling back and forth.

Classifications of these aspects of *sega* by Indian Ocean island state, however, were controversial, resulting in debates about cultural authenticity and borrowing. After the Chagos Tambour Group's performance at the Creole Festival opening ceremony, the CRG leader Olivier Bancoult complained:

> The way they beat the *ravannes* [drums] was the same as how Mauritians play. If there hadn't been dancing, people would have thought we were Mauritian, but the dancing is different.

This can partly be explained by the fact that the dancers were primarily middle-aged Chagossian women whereas the *ravanne* players were young Mauritius-born men of Chagossian parentage. Bancoult's explanation was that the (Mauritian-born) *ravanne*-playing musicians had been too influenced by Mauritian *sega*, suggesting that Chagossian cultural purity was becoming impure on contact with Mauritian *sega* (cf. Baily & Collyer 2006: 174; Harrison 1999b: 10). On return to Mauritius, Bancoult received further complaints from Chagossians in Mauritius (who had seen the performance on television) that the Chagos Tambour Group had not performed authentically Chagossian *sega*. The CRG deputy leader, Lisette Talate, concurred with Bancoult's assessment: 'those who don't know anything about it say it was good, but those who know Chagossian *sega* know that it was not good'.

Indian Ocean *sega* music is regulated by the beating of a *ravanne*, a goatskin tambour drum, accompanied by various optional extra instruments that vary according to island. In a commemorative exhibition opened on 1 February 2004, the anniversary of the abolition of slavery, the Mauritian musician Marclaine Antoine exhibited musical instruments separated into the categories Mauritius, Rodrigues, Chagos, Africa, and Madagascar (see also Ballgobin & Antoine 2003). The Mauritius, Rodrigues, and Chagos sections all included *ravannes*. In addition the Mauritius section contained a wooden one-stringed *makalopo* and several *maravanne* [rain-makers] and shakers. The Rodrigues section contained an accordion and stringed instruments such as violin, lute, and guitar. The Chagos section contained another *makalopo*, wooden and metal beaters, metal triangles, glass bottles, and cutlery. Whenever he heard the Mauritian *sega* singer Sandra Mayotte's song *Makalopo*, Olivier Bancoult complained that the *makalopo* was a traditional Chagossian instrument that had been appropriated by Mauritian musicians (cf. Ballgobin & Antoine 2003: 71, who do not mention its origins; see also Lassemillante 2001b). Thus the CRG leadership stressed the importance of dance, costume, and instrumentation in maintaining a specifically Chagossian *sega* distinct from the *sega* of other islands in general and from Mauritian *sega* in particular.

Throughout the Indian Ocean, cuisine is also widely considered to be a cultural mode. Creole cuisine has some features that are seen to distinguish it from other local cuisines, but there are also some key differences between the Creole cuisines of the different Indian Ocean islands. The Chagos Archipelago, the Mauritian outer island Agalega, and the Seychelles islands are abundant in coconut palms and have a coconut-based cuisine. Chagos islanders often remarked that this distinguishes Chagossian cuisine from Creole cuisine in Mauritius and Rodrigues, since the latter never had a coconut industry and did not develop a tradition of cooking with coconut. In Chagossian and Agalegan cuisine, creamy dishes based on coconut milk are called *seraz* (see Le Chartier 1991: 124, who does not mention the origins of the word). In Seychelles, dishes based on coconut milk are called *ladob* (from the French *la daube* [stew]). Savoury *seraz* is fowl (chicken or wildfowl), fish, octopus, or lentils stewed in coconut milk and salt, with the optional addition of ingredients such as ginger, garlic, chillies, turmeric and cinnamon (see Le Chartier 1991: 80–81, 105–106). Sweet *seraz* is fruit (e.g. banana or breadfruit) or vegetable (e.g. pumpkin or sweet potato) cooked in coconut milk with sugar (see Le Chartier 1991: 85). When the MBC food programme *Ki Ti Kwi* [What's Cooking?] showed a woman in Agalega making *seraz pule* [coconut and chicken], Chagossian friends told me her recipe was very similar to the Chagossian dish with the same name. Several Chagossians, however, contrasted their own rich *seraz* with the Seychellois *ladob*, which they said contains a lower ratio of coconut milk to meat and a higher volume of water.

On the Chagos Archipelago, islanders brewed *kalu* (fermented coconut palm sap) and *baka* (made by fermenting crushed maize flour, the juice of soaked lentils, pineapple skin and unrefined sugar). Chagos islanders explained that they could not make *kalu* in Mauritius because of the lack of coconut palms (and the consequently high cost of purchasing coconuts), but nor did I come across *kalu* during my trip to Seychelles, where I was told it was made only for special occasions.[8] In Mauritius, several Chagossian women prepared *baka* months in advance of Catholic festivals and other celebrations such as New Year, and commented that the long fermentation process distinguishes Chagossian *baka* from that made on Rodrigues. Thus they commented on the similarities among and differences between Creole cuisine of various Indian Ocean islands, and compared and contrasted techniques selectively: firstly to emphasise the similarities between Creole cuisine from the different islands (especially in comparison to that in Mauritius), and secondly to assert the uniqueness of each island.

As with *sega* and Creole cuisine, so in matters of language Chagossians compared and contrasted Kreol accents in order to emphasise differences with Mauritius on the one hand and similarity with Rodrigues on the other. Chagossians and Mauritians frequently told me that the Chagossian accent differs from the Mauritian accent, and older Chagos islanders told me that when they arrived in Mauritius, these differences posed two main problems for them in their relations with Mauritians. Firstly, Chagos islanders could not always understand what was being said to them, which enabled Mauritians to manipulate them. Secondly, they could be easily identified as Chagos islanders, which attracted discrimination. Several Chagos islanders asserted that the Chagossian accent was very similar to the Rodrigues accent and that they had been mistaken for Rodriguans. They therefore speculated that recent Rodriguan migrants to Mauritius face problems today that were similar to those faced by newly arrived Chagos islanders over thirty years ago. When I accompanied the CRG on a cultural exchange trip to Rodrigues, a Rodriguan trade unionist who had been listening to the Chagossians speaking told us that there was 'no difference between Rodriguans and Chagossians: we speak the same'.

Sega and Creole cuisine were routinely described as if they were standardised across the whole island of Mauritius and so there would be an identifiable Mauritian version of each. By contrast, internal differences within Mauritius were identified in relation to the Kreol language in the form of regional accents. *Ledikasyon Pu Travayer* [Education for Workers] provides adult literacy classes in Mauritian Kreol. Alain Ah-Vee, a former LPT employee, told me that linguistic differences within Mauritius were particularly noticeable in comparisons between the old and the young, and between urban and rural (see also Eriksen 1998: 76). A Mauritian Creole friend added an ethnic dimension by telling me that people in the Indo-Mauritian-dominated coastal countryside spoke what she called *Bhojpuri-Kreol* (Kreol influenced by the north Indian language Bhojpuri), those in the Franco-Mauritian-dominated suburban highlands spoke *Français-Kreol* (closer to French), and those in Afro-Creole dominated urban areas such as Port Louis spoke *Creole-Kreol* (see also Eisenlohr 2006: 113). Thus Mauritians identified different regional accents within the island of Mauritius. Islanders from other islands in the Republic of Mauritius – Rodrigues, Agalega, and the Chagos Archipelago – could be expected also to have accents that were somewhat different again. Moreover Chagossians sometimes commented that people from different Chagos islands had different accents. Differences in Kreol vocabulary and accent, then, were principally accounted for by regional variation.

Thus in a context in which music, cuisine, and language were considered to be key markers of cultural identity and cultural difference, Chagossians pointed to the specific characteristics of their *sega* music, dance and costume, their coconut-based cuisine, and their vocabulary and accents. This emphasis had three effects. First, it associated Chagossians with other Indian Ocean island Creole cultures (while allowing for differences among different Creole cultures). Second, it distinguished Chagossians from other Mauritians (including Mauritian Creoles). Third, it allowed them to assert their own cultural uniqueness.

Cultural loss, continuity, and change

I have used a range of Chagossian cultural processes to illustrate how Chagossians engage a range of conceptualisations of culture. Their keenness to emphasise and maintain the distinctions between Chagossian culture and other Creole cultures in Mauritius and the Indian Ocean suggests that some Chagossians sought to protect what they saw as authentic Chagossian culture against dominant cultural influences with which they were confronted daily. Since changing environmental, residential, and financial circumstances have resulted in cultural transformations, though, Chagossian culture was not necessarily assumed to be unchangeable. Chagossian cultural expressions reveal senses both of cultural loss and of cultural revival in exile, which were framed negatively and positively respectively. On the one hand, traditional Chagossian cultural practices – such as weekly *sega* parties and a cuisine dominated by coconuts and fresh fish and seafood – were difficult to sustain in Mauritius, where the population was impoverished and geographically dispersed, and where coconuts are rare and fresh fish and seafood are prohibitively expensive. On the other hand, emerging Chagossian socio-political and socio-cultural movements demonstrated a desire to remember, preserve, rehearse, demonstrate, and transmit Chagossian culture – in the form of Chagossian *sega*, collective historical narratives, and Chagossian cuisine – to outsiders and the younger generations. This cultural revival was surrounded by debates about authenticity and transformation. Chagossian culture in Mauritius is being rebuilt around expressions associated with exile – shared memories of Chagos, collective narratives of the displacement, and evocations of suffering in exile – which political activists hoped would bind Chagossians together through shared experiences.

Notes

1 The Portuguese named (but did not settle) many islands in the region during this period: in Chagos, Diego Garcia and Peros Banhos were named after Portuguese explorers (Toussaint 1966:110). The names of most of the smaller islands and place names in Chagos date from the later period of French settlement, although the British later translated many of these names into English. Chagossians referred to these smaller islands by their French or Kreol names.
2 There was no suggestion (in the IST proposal or subsequently) to establish a men's group or a mixed group, although the mixed-sex Chagos Tambour Group operates through the Chagossian Women's Group.
3 A couple of songs were composed and performed by men, and on occasion a man or woman would play percussion (such as using metal to tap glass bottles), but women in this ensemble did not play *ravanne*.
4 See www.chagos.org/home.htm.
5 The one exception to this generalisation is the alcoholic drink *baka*, which Chagossian women also made in preparation for special occasions.
6 Note the mixed provenance and etymology of these dishes, which blend recipes and names from India, East Africa, and France. Thus, for instance, *satini koko* combines the Indian word chutney with the European root for coconut, while *muf* and *matuftwa* are reminiscent of East African dumplings.
7 See www.gov.mu/portal/sites/ncb/mac/mnacc/index.htm.
8 For a description of the production and regulation of *kalu*, *baka*, and fermented fruit or vegetable purée in Seychelles, see Benedict & Benedict 1982: 191–192.

III

Onward migration

5

Echoes of marginalisation in Crawley

I hope it will be better for me there [in the UK]. Life here [in Mauritius] is hard. Here [in Mauritius] we work a lot for a little money, whereas there [in the UK] we will work a little for enough money. I hope to save a bit, to build my children's future, to make a stable life. I'm sacrificing myself for my family. (Claude, a father in his forties born in Mauritius to a Chagossian mother)

Displaced Chagos islanders' experiences of marginalisation and mobilisation in Mauritius were examined in Part I. This chapter revisits the themes explored there by examining the experiences of those Chagossians who have migrated to the UK since 2002, when Chagos islanders and their second-generation descendants were awarded UK citizenship under the British Overseas Territories Act. Chagossians have faced considerable hardships in exile, and most feel at best ambivalent towards their host states Mauritius and Seychelles, where they feel marginalised and excluded from full national membership and participation. In any case, many other Mauritians and Seychellois would likewise jump at an opportunity to migrate to Europe. In this context, it is not surprising that hundreds of Chagos islanders and their descendants applied for UK passports and sought to migrate to the UK.

During my fieldwork in Mauritius in 2002–4, the reasons Chagossian prospective emigrants gave for wanting to emigrate from Mauritius fell into three main categories: firstly, what they viewed as a low-quality and inequitable education system; secondly, high unemployment and unattractive employment opportunities, especially for those who felt structurally disadvantaged as a result of poor education and ethnic discrimination; and thirdly, the perceived chasm between low wages and high living costs. They imagined *la vie en rose* in the UK, anticipating that their families would benefit from a higher-quality and more equitable education system, the availability and accessibility of more jobs, and a presumed lower disparity between wages and the cost of living. Thus they sought to escape long-term marginalisation and disadvantage in Mauritius and hoped to build a more productive and comfortable future for their families in the UK.

Has life in the UK lived up to prospective migrants' high expectations? How do migrant Chagossians compare and contrast their recent experiences in the UK since 2002 with the experiences of displaced Chagos islanders on arrival in

Mauritius and Seychelles in the late 1960s and early 1970s? And in what ways do their experiences of family separation, ethnic discrimination, bureaucratic hurdles, education, employment and healthcare problems, and other challenges to a sense of belonging in the UK echo their earlier recollections of impoverishment and marginalisation in Mauritius? This chapter outlines some of the barriers to eligibility for UK citizenship, details Chagossian chain migration to Crawley in West Sussex, and analyses Chagossian experiences of employment and education in Crawley. It then offers ethnographic accounts of marginalisation and belonging to illustrate how Chagossians conceptualised their recent experiences in Crawley rather differently from how they conceptualised their experiences on arrival in Mauritius in the 1960s and 1970s.

Uneven eligibility for UK citizenship

Chagos islanders in Mauritius were granted Mauritian citizenship under the constitution when Mauritius became independent in 1968.[1] Exiled Chagos islanders also became eligible for British Dependent Territory (BDT) citizenship under the British Nationality Act 1981. In theory, BDT citizenship entitled them to visit but not to settle in the UK, but in practice most Chagos islanders did not apply for BDT passports because of costs and a lack of knowledge about their citizenship rights. In 2002, however, the citizenship status of Chagossians changed dramatically with the British Overseas Territories Act.[2] This Act reclassified the fourteen former BDTs as BOTs and replaced BDT citizenship with full UK citizenship. Islanders born on Chagos, who had been eligible for BDT citizenship under the British Nationality Act 1981, thus became eligible for full UK citizenship through their birth on British territory.

According to the British Overseas Territories Act, citizens of the BOTs can transmit the entitlement to UK citizenship to their children who were also born in a BOT. The initial proposals did not apply this provision to the children born to Chagos islanders in exile, since they were born not in a BOT but in the independent republics of Mauritius and Seychelles. In response to this situation, the CRG staged a sleep-in protest outside the British High Commission in the Mauritian capital Port Louis. Their campaign was supported in the UK by the Labour MPs Tam Dalyell (who was then Father of the House) and Jeremy Corbyn, who repeatedly put the Chagossian case on the parliamentary agenda. They emphasised that the Chagos islanders' residence outwith the Chagos Archipelago was a result of their forcible displacement from that territory rather than choice. Accepting this logic, the UK Government introduced a supplementary clause to provide for the transmission of UK citizenship to Chagos islanders' children born in exile after 26 April 1969. There remain, however, three key problems in the clause that make for uneven eligibility.

Firstly, the legislation provides for Chagos-born islanders and their children born in exile, but not for their grandchildren or subsequent generations of descendants born in exile. The UK Government's rationale was that extending eligibility to subsequent generations would privilege Chagos islanders vis-à-vis other BOT citizens by descent, who could not pass their citizenship to future generations born outwith a BOT.[3] The House of Commons Foreign Affairs Committee (FAC) took evidence from the leaders of three Chagossian organisations in 2008. The FAC agreed that the fact that the islanders were no longer living in a BOT was 'a consequence of exile rather than their own choice'. It recommended that citizenship 'should be extended to third generation descendants of exiled Chagossians'.[4] Similarly, in its briefing for a House of Lords Committee debate on the Borders, Citizenship and Immigration Bill in 2009, the Immigration Law Practitioners' Association noted that the fact that 'the children of Chagossians are born outside the UK or a qualifying territory is no fault of their own but the result of their enforced exile'. The briefing concluded: 'few can have as compelling a claim to British citizenship as those children'.[5] Despite these high-level recommendations, however, the restriction has remained in place.

Secondly, the British Overseas Territories Act 2002 covers Chagos islanders' second-generation descendants only if they were born in exile after 26 April 1969, which the UK Government selected as the start date of the 'policy of exclusion' from the Chagos Archipelago.[6] Writing this start date into the BOT legislation was a way to avoid awarding UK citizenship to the children of those islanders deemed by British officials to have left Chagos 'voluntarily' prior to the forced depopulation of the territory. This start date has been highly contested: regardless of when the forced deportations actually began, the BIOT was established in 1965, and islanders visiting Mauritius or Seychelles were prevented from returning to Chagos from the mid-1960s onwards. An obvious example is the Bancoult family, which travelled to Mauritius in 1968 to seek medical attention for a daughter injured in an accident with a donkey cart, and was prevented from returning to Chagos after her death. As a result of the anomalous 1969 cut-off date, numerous Chagossian families comprise siblings born in exile prior to 1969 who are ineligible for UK citizenship plus siblings born in exile after 1969 who are eligible for UK citizenship. The Immigration Law Practitioners' Association recommended removing this cut-off date to 'ensure that Chagos Islanders ... born in exile before 26 April 1969 are British Citizens'[7], but again, the restriction has remained in place.

Thirdly, according to the British Nationality Act 1981, whereas an unmarried British woman can pass her citizenship to her children, an unmarried British man cannot pass his citizenship to his children born outwith marriage (unless the parents subsequently marry). The problem for the Chagossian community, as described in Chapter 4, is that the matrifocal Chagos Archipelago was characterised by a low incidence of marriage (Botte 1980: 22–23; Brooks 1875: 37; Walker 1986: 15–18). Although most of its inhabitants were nominally Roman Catholic, the Chagos Archipelago did not have a resident priest. An itinerant priest travelled around the Mauritius outer islands to perform important ceremonies such as baptisms, christenings, and weddings. In between these visits, administrators apparently conducted weekly services, but not other ceremonies (Descroizilles & Mülnier 1999: 26; Dussercle 1934: 10). Chagos islanders did not necessarily get married to their partners, both because they were not encouraged to do so, and because it was not expected that the union would be for life. Thus many Chagossians feel that the privileging of 'legitimate' children in UK citizenship legislation discriminates against those for whom marriage was not promoted by the British authorities. In particular, this rule affects the children born in exile to an unmarried Chagossian man and a non-Chagossian woman, who comprise a relatively common category as a result of the flows of people amongst all of the dependencies of colonial Mauritius.

Strategies for onward migration to the UK

Ongoing campaigns for amendments to the British Overseas Territories Act aside, at present the effect of these features – the ineligibility of grandchildren and subsequent generations, the 1969 cut-off date, and the privileging of marriage – is that all extended Chagossian families thus comprise some individuals eligible for UK citizenship and others ineligible for UK citizenship. Eligibility for UK citizenship – rather than, say, English-language skills or employability – was the key criterion used to determine who in a family would migrate first. Chagos islanders and their second-generation descendants have therefore tended to migrate ahead of their Mauritian or Seychellois spouses and third and subsequent generations of descendants. In a significant number of cases, this has meant that Chagossian women who were full-time mothers and housewives in Mauritius or Seychelles might be the first in their families to emigrate, temporarily leaving the rest of the family behind. Generally, the family would mobilise extended family networks to raise the funds to purchase a UK passport and an aeroplane ticket for the initial migrant.

Over one hundred initial migrants migrated as part of a series of groups organised from Mauritius. The DGIC organised three groups, totalling 85 people, between 2002 and 2004. For its part, the CRG organised two groups, totalling 30 people, in 2002 and 2003. On arrival at Gatwick Airport in September 2002, the first DGIC group staged a spontaneous sit-in at the airport, which concluded only when the local West Sussex County Council (WSCC) social services awarded the group bed and breakfast accommodation in the nearby town of Crawley, plus £30 per week for living expenses for a period of up to six months. During this time the migrants were expected to undertake English courses or other training if necessary in order to improve employability. The subsequent DGIC groups, as well as the CRG's second group, similarly remained in the arrival lounge at Gatwick Airport for periods of between two days and a fortnight until they received the same support.

Most Chagossian migrants, however, have not migrated as part of an organised group. Rather, as individuals, they mobilised their own networks of extended family and friends in order to migrate alone, and did not take up the offer of social services support. Instead, most initially shared rooms (or even beds in shifts) in houses rented by earlier migrants from Mauritius. They supported themselves financially with money brought from Mauritius or by relying on the hospitality of their hosts, and concentrated on establishing themselves in the UK.

The first step is to obtain a National Insurance (NI) number, which is required by all UK residents (citizens and non-citizens alike) to work legally in the UK. It is also the system by which UK governments manage taxes, National Insurance pension contributions, and some state social security benefits.[8] Other important tasks include setting up a bank account, finding a job, and establishing adequate accommodation. All of these can be long-drawn-out processes, especially when, in order to provide the proof of address required for a bank account, applicants need to be long enough established at an address to hold accounts and pay bills in their own names. Additionally, some applicants evidently received contradictory advice. For example, some were told by employers that they needed an NI number in order to apply for jobs. They were then told by staff at the Jobcentre Plus, which deals with applications for NI numbers, that they should have a job lined up in order to qualify for an NI number. Not surprisingly, recent migrants often complained about these complex and contradictory bureaucratic processes. Many also resented their powerlessness and reliance on others during this period, and were in turn resented by their hosts or sponsors when they were felt to have outstayed their welcome, failed adequately to contribute to the household, or refused later to repay these debts.

At the same time, many initial onward migrants also struggled with being separated from the families they left behind. Family separations are central to the entire history of the Chagossian community. Firstly, Chagos was populated via slavery, which routinely broke up family units by sending members to different territories. Secondly, during the settled colonial period, Chagossian fishermen could be posted to distant Chagos outer islands for up to several months at a time, and were separated from their families for the duration. Thirdly, the forced displacement from Chagos resulted in the separation of many extended families and social networks split between Mauritius and Seychelles or geographically dispersed within these countries. Now, as a result of uneven citizenship eligibility, Chagossians migrate to the UK individually in the first instance, leaving behind family members that in some cases include a spouse and young children. Spousal separation has resulted in several cases of marital breakdown. According to a social worker I spoke to in Crawley, several very young children initially left behind in Mauritius by their parents have displayed truncated progression through key developmental stages such as toilet training and speech acquisition.

After six months in the UK, those who have the right to reside in the UK satisfy the Habitual Residence Test. This entitles them to a range of benefits including Income Support, income-based Jobseeker's Allowance, Housing Benefit and Council Tax Benefit, Child Benefit, and Pension Credits.[9] Within a year or two, most initial migrants find accommodation and jobs. Many are also able to send adequate remittances back to Mauritius and Seychelles to repay their debts. Savings are often put towards aeroplane tickets and UK passports or short-term Settlement Visas (for those not entitled to UK passports) for close family members to migrate to the UK. The family could then move out of shared accommodation into a family house, where they might take in newly arrived friends or relatives for a time as the chain migration continues. In many respects these patterns resemble Chagossian experiences on arrival in Mauritius and Seychelles in the late 1960s and early 1970s, when recent arrivals from Chagos had to rely upon the hospitality of extended family and friends around Port Louis (cf. Chapter 1). The key differences are that these onward migrants have chosen to emigrate, have benefited considerably from the UK welfare state's provision of housing and income, and have the option of returning one day to Mauritius or Seychelles.

Socio-economic and ethnic diversity in Crawley

Chagossian organisations now based in the UK estimate that over one thousand people from the extended Chagossian community – displaced islanders and their spouses plus children and grandchildren born in exile – migrated from Mauritius and Seychelles to the UK in the first five years following the British Overseas Territories Act 2002. Chagossian migration from Mauritius to the UK has taken the form of a steady chain migration to Crawley in West Sussex. The vast majority of Chagossians from Mauritius still lived in Crawley at the time of my fieldwork there in 2006–7, while smaller numbers lived nearby in West Sussex (particularly Haywards Heath), Surrey (particularly Horley), and Greater London (particularly East Croydon and Purley) (see Map 6). Others lived further afield, predominantly in Manchester.[10] What then were the characteristics of Crawley as a site of in-migration?

Crawley was developed as one of the New Towns designed after the Second World War to disperse people and jobs from London (Cole 2004: 94; Gwynne 1990: 155). Located fifty kilometres south of London, *en route* to Brighton in East Sussex, the West Sussex settlements of Crawley, Ifield, and Three Bridges were considered to be a good site for a New Town (see Map 6). The area already had good road and rail links and was near the aerodrome that was to become Gatwick Airport. Additionally, the land was agriculturally poor, and water provision and sewage disposal opportunities were good (Gwynne 1990: 155). The plans were met with considerable resistance – both from locals who feared the loss of the area's village atmosphere and from Londoners who said they would prefer to move to a more rural location – but nonetheless Crawley was designated a New Town in 1947 (see Gwynne 1990: 155). Commentators have reported tensions between 'Old Crawley' and the 'New Towners', noting that central and local government employment, management, shop staff, and the voluntary sector have been dominated by those whose families moved to Crawley since the New Town's development rather than those whose families had a prior connection to the area (Gwynne 1990: 161–162). Original plans were for a New Town numbering between 20,000 and 40,000 people (Gwynne 1990: 155, 161–171), but Crawley's population has grown steadily from 10,000 in 1951 to almost 100,000 in the 2001 census. At the time of my fieldwork, the extended Chagossian community in Crawley probably comprised around one thousand people – that is, 1 per cent of the town's population.

Crawley's thirteen residential neighbourhoods – Bewbush, Broadfield, Furnace Green, Ifield, Gossops Green, Langley Green, Maidenbower, Northgate,

Pound Hill, Southgate, Three Bridges, Tilgate, and West Green – were built up gradually in a radial pattern around the town centre (see Map 7). From the start there was an explicit policy to promote socio-economic diversity across the city through the provision of mixed housing stock in all areas. Each neighbour-hood was to comprise 80 per cent three-bedroom 'manual standard' houses, 15 per cent four-bedroom 'intermediate' houses, and 5 per cent five-bedroom 'detached' houses (Cole 2004: 95; Gwynne 1990: 157). Much of Crawley's housing was originally owned by the Council, but since 1980 most has been purchased by residents under the Right to Buy scheme.[11] By the 2001 census, 69 per cent of the population lived in owner-occupied properties, 23 per cent in Council housing, 3 per cent in housing associations, 3 per cent in privately rented houses, and the remainder with friends or relatives or in property tied to employment (Crawley Together 2001: chapter 5).

The Manor Royal industrial estate was opened near Gatwick Airport in 1950. In 1952 the UK Government decided that Gatwick would be developed as London's second airport after Heathrow (Gwynne 1990: 160). When it re-opened after expansion in 1958, Gatwick Airport employed 1,200 people; by 1967 it employed 5,200, and by 2004 the number had reached 25,000 (Cole 2004: 98, 111). Local jobs in the airport, the industrial estate, and the town itself are predominantly low-skilled and low-waged. However, unemployment rates in Crawley are consistently very low compared to national averages, sometimes representing the lowest unemployment levels in the UK (Gwynne 1990: 167, 171).

UK Government surveys in 1998, 2000, and 2004 suggest that deprivation in West Sussex is concentrated on the coast and in western Crawley, and that there is wide disparity between neighbourhoods in Crawley. The most deprived areas in Crawley are Broadfield, Bewbush, and Langley Green, although the 2000 survey also reports significant levels of deprivation in Southgate, Furnace Green, and Ifield. Furthermore, the 2004 survey concluded that some areas in Bewbush, Broadfield, and Southgate are in the lowest decile in West Sussex (Crawley Together 2001: chapter 4; Office of the Deputy Prime Minister 2004).[12] The cor-relation between deprivation and poor health is confirmed by evidence that the lowest life expectancy and highest mortality rates are in Bewbush, Broadfield, Ifield, and Southgate, along with West Green (Connellan 2007; Crawley Together 2001: chapter 7). Disadvantaged areas typically have higher levels of crime than other areas. Broadfield Parade shopping arcade has a particularly bad reputation locally for drug abuse and associated crime.

According to the 2001 census, Crawley's 'ethnic minority' population (i.e. all groups other than 'white', 'white other', and 'white Irish') was 10.3 per cent. This is the highest in West Sussex, where the county average is 2.9 per cent, compared to a South East England average of 4.4 per cent, and an England average of 7.9 per cent (Crawley Together 2001: chapter 2; Southdown Housing Association 2006: 9–10). The vast majority of Crawley's so-called 'Black and Minority Ethnic' residents are of South Asian origin, with those of Indian origin comprising 4.4 per cent and those of Pakistani origin comprising 3 per cent of the town's total population respectively (Southdown Housing Association 2006: 9). Crawley has a long history of in-migration from South Asia, China, Uganda, West Africa, and the Caribbean. More recently, there has been in-migration from Afghanistan since the war in 2001, from Mauritius and Seychelles since the awarding of UK citizenship to Chagossians in 2002, and from Eastern Europe since the expansion of the European Union in 2004 and 2007.

Crawley parliamentary constituency was created in 1983. It was held by the Conservatives until 1997, and then by Labour until 2010, when it returned to the Conservatives.[13] There has been very limited and ineffectual activity by the extreme right-wing British National Front, and the town has generally escaped the occasionally explosive ethnic tensions that have sporadically plagued other ethnically diverse towns and cities in England. By design each neighbourhood has an Anglican church, and most neighbourhoods also have another church or two representing numerous Christian denominations, while there are Sunni mosques in Langley Green and Broadfield, Hindu temples in Langley Green and West Green, and a Sikh gurdwara in West Green. Crawley hit the national news headlines in 2004 when three young men who had attended local schools and the Langley Green mosque were among a group of eight UK-born men of Pakistani descent arrested, accused, and eventually convicted of planning terrorist activities. This sparked a debate in the local press about the level of interaction between people of different ethnic and religious backgrounds in the multicultural town.

Southdown Housing Association is a not-for-profit organisation which provides advice and housing assistance for around one thousand vulnerable people across Sussex. According to the association's annual report for 2006, there has been a strong tendency for new arrivals in Crawley, particularly those from ethnic minorities, to settle in the deprived (and cheaper) neighbourhoods described above (Southdown Housing Association 2006: 13). According to the 2001 census, ethnic minority populations were most concentrated in Langley Green, Bewbush, and Broadfield, where they comprised approximately 27.9 per cent, 17.3 per cent, and 15 per cent of the neighbourhood population respectively.[14] Migrants from Mauritius have followed this general trend. Whilst Chagossians had scattered throughout Crawley, they were particularly concentrated in Bewbush, Broadfield, and Langley Green. Significant but smaller numbers lived in Northgate, Southgate, Ifield, Tilgate, and Furnace Green.

Education and employment in Crawley

Educational attainment levels of Crawley residents have been lower than the county averages (Crawley Together 2001: chapter 9), but there is considerable diversity within the town. While Maidenbower and Pound Hill scored slightly above national averages, the lack of qualifications was reportedly most acute in Bewbush, Tilgate, and Broadfield.[15] The two non-denominational secondary schools in Three Bridges and Maidenbower, the Church of England secondary school in Gossops Green, and the Catholic school in Southgate (all of which sometimes score above the national average) have consistently outperformed the two community colleges in Ifield and Tilgate. These latter schools tend to score considerably below the national average and have more challenging pupil profiles, including significant numbers for whom English is not their first language.

Most in Mauritius expected education in the UK to be superior to that in Mauritius, thus delivering better prospects for employment and higher earnings in the future. On arrival in Crawley, pupils from Mauritius had to adapt to new disciplinary regimes and styles of learning. However, English as an Additional Language teachers in Crawley schools told me that many of their pupils from Mauritius settled in quite quickly compared to other pupils from other countries, and were expected to perform adequately in exams. One reason for this may be that the Mauritian education system was based on the English system, and Mauritian schools – in theory at least – function in the English language. This is likely to give pupils from Mauritius a relative advantage over pupils from countries with completely different education systems and more limited exposure to the English language. A handful of children from relatively well-educated Chagossian families adapted extremely well to secondary schools in the UK and planned further education at college or university.

Several migrants told me, however, that education in the UK did not meet their expectations of higher standards. Many felt that the greater degree of autonomy for pupils in the UK made outcomes more unpredictable than in Mauritius. Local primary school teachers told me that interactive teaching methods tended either to open up Mauritian children's imaginations or to prompt them to challenge authority and reject learning. A similar problem arises in relation to secondary education. Thomas, a teenage boy born in Mauritius to a Chagossian father, told me that 'the level here is lower because there's too much freedom, there's no discipline'.

Lydia, born in Mauritius, became eligible for a UK passport through her Chagossian parents. She migrated to Crawley in 2003, followed by her non-Chagossian husband Luke and then their two teenage children Robert and Sara in 2004. When I asked the family about their impressions of the British education system, they complained about the lower emphasis on discipline in their Crawley secondary school than in their Mauritian school:

> LUKE: The education system here is worse than in Mauritius.

> SARA: Over there, people learn more.

> ROBERT: That's because there you're forced to learn, whereas here the students talk back to the teachers.

> LUKE: We are worried that the children aren't learning anything here, because in Mauritius they had lots of homework, but here they just play on the computer. In Mauritius a child's room might be full of books because of the quantity that you have to buy.

Several other parents from Mauritius similarly complained about their children's lack of educational materials and their apparently limited homework. In Mauritius, they told me, schoolchildren would have to come home from school and spend hours on their homework so as not to get into trouble at school the follow-ing day. Schoolchildren in Crawley, by contrast, either had far less homework or else could get away with not doing their homework. Consequently, they had far more leisure time, which parents feared was not necessarily well-spent, especially if the parents were at work until later in the evening and could not monitor their children's after-school activities.

For their part, teachers at local schools in Crawley told me that they were worried that the parents of many of their pupils from Mauritius were unable to provide much academic support. They reported that most Chagossian parents had limited English, limited literacy, a general lack of books and other educa-tional materials in the home, and a lack of knowledge about local educational services such as free library membership. Evidently one major problem has been high truancy rates, which were compounded by lack of communication between parents and the school. Teachers at several local schools told me that the parents of pupils from Mauritius overwhelmingly did not attend parents' evenings, which they suggested may be a result of a combination of the parents' unsocial working hours, their lack of spoken English (which inhibited communication), and their relative lack of formal education (which fostered a sense of being unable to assist one's children's education).

Thomas Bennett Community College is a secondary school in Tilgate attended by 23 pupils from Mauritius in the academic year 2006–7. An English as an Addi-tional Language teacher at the school told me that pupils from Mauritius, whose own English-language skills may be better than their parents' English-language skills, occasionally accompanied their parents to appointments with doctors and careers advisors in order to translate for them. However, some pupils had started to play the system by using their parents' communication problems as an excuse for all of their (increasingly frequent) absences. Many Chagossian adults, whose own educational trajectories in Chagos or Mauritius had been truncated or limited, felt unable actively to support their children's learning, but wanted their children to do well at school. Parents often told me they were disappointed by their children's lack of commitment to studying, especially considering the sacrifices that had been made to bring them to the UK.

Many Chagossian adults from Mauritius complained that their own lack of English, poor reading and writing skills, and low education in general put them at a relative disadvantage in their job searches. At the same time, however, many were impressed with what they felt was a lack of ethnic discrimination in the UK in comparison to their experiences of seeking work in Mauritius. As Serge, a Chagossian man in his fifties, put it, 'there is a system of meritocracy in education and work here. Nobody looks at your face before giving you work: if you deserve it, you get it'.

On the other hand, most of their employment opportunities have been in comparatively undesirable jobs dominated by recent immigrants. Over half of working Chagossians in Crawley found jobs at Gatwick Airport, where the vast majority work for airport and aircraft cleaning companies, for aeroplane food production companies, or for fast-food and other commercial outlets in the terminal buildings. Most other working Chagossians were based in and around Crawley town, where they worked as cashiers or shelf stackers in supermarkets or department stores, warehouse assistants in the nearby Manor Royal industrial estate, cleaners or carers in care homes, cleaners or childminders in private homes, hairdressers in local Afro hair salons, security guards, freelance dressmakers, or painter-decorators.

In 2006–7, unskilled commercial cleaning and industrial labouring jobs paid around or just above the national minimum wage, at £5.35–£7.07 per hour. This resulted in a pre-tax weekly income of around £214–£282.80, around half of median national earnings (£447 per week in 2006, or £470 in the South East). This puts them in the lowest 10 per cent of earners nationally, on a par with sales occupations, the lowest-paid full-time employment.[16] Most Chagossians were cleaners, fishermen, dock labourers or factory helpers in Mauritius, and tend to consider their new unskilled manual jobs to be equivalent to the manual labouring jobs they held in Mauritius.[17] On the whole, their general assessment was that they worked harder but were paid better than in Mauritius, and this enabled them to achieve a higher standard of living.[18] This contrasts with their general preconceptions before migrating, as described in this chapter's opening quote, that relatively higher wages would enable them to work less hard whilst achieving a better standard of living than in Mauritius.

Echoes of marginalisation in Crawley

In contrast to their almost uniformly negative reports of their reception by Mauritians on arrival in Mauritius, Chagossians report a wide range of experiences in relation to their reception in Crawley, ranging from discrimination to neighbourliness. Serge, a Chagos islander in his fifties, worked in the Port Louis docks before bringing his family to Crawley and working as a cleaner at Gatwick Airport. Having been friends for five years and having discussed contentious issues on numerous occasions, one day I decided to pose Serge some direct questions. As this excerpt shows, he inverted my questions in order to foreground his own agenda: highlighting the comparison he saw between his mistreatment in Mauritius and his positive experiences in the UK.

LJ: Have you encountered racism here?

SERGE: Since I've come here I haven't observed any racist situation. Everyone has welcomed me. On the contrary, it's here that we learned to respect people. For example, when I'm waiting for the bus, if there's someone behind me, then that person will let me get on the bus before they do. This is a civilised way of doing things. We weren't treated like that in Mauritius because of our black skin.

LJ: Are people badly behaved here?

SERGE: Badly behaved? You get that everywhere, particularly rude young people. I don't worry about that. I haven't had any problems with people at all yet. In Mauritius we were mistreated: people said we were islanders [*Ilois*] who didn't even know how to wear shoes. By contrast, we don't get that here.

LJ: Have British people helped you?

SERGE: My neighbours … are very kind, they helped us get schools, helped us run errands that we had to do. They are still helping us, for example when we need a lift somewhere they never refuse us.

Thus he dismissed youthful anti-social behaviour as a universal problem and focused instead on the contrast between the racial discrimination he had suffered in Mauritius and the respectful and friendly welcome he felt he received in Crawley in general and in his neighbourhood in particular.

Others report being held at arm's length by locals uninterested in foreign newcomers. Irene, a Chagossian woman in her fifties, told me: 'Most British people are not interested in speaking to us, they aren't interested in learning about where we're from'. Her daughter Yvette, who works in a local supermarket, agreed: 'In Mauritius we knew our neighbours, but here we don't know them. Nobody has the time to talk, they're not even interested, and they're racist'. Madeleine, a Chagossian woman in her forties, told me she had had some unpleasant encounters at work at Gatwick Airport:

The British are racist. For example at work we don't have the right to say anything. We have to listen to what they say. British people always protect other British people, even if a boy says we're dirty because he doesn't like black people.

In several situations, though, various local authorities have intervened. Two of my interviewees told me that their children had been bullied and called 'negro' or 'black' by other children at their local primary school. One told me that her daughter had cried when she was told by a fellow pupil that she had no right to be there, which prompted her teacher to chastise the offending pupil. Conversely, several Chagossians who worked at Gatwick Airport told me that they have been cautioned at work for breaking guidelines by calling other black colleagues 'negro' or 'nigger' in jest.

This raises the question of relations between Chagossians and other ethnic minority communities in Crawley. Renée, a woman in her forties born in Mauritius to Chagossian parents, told me two stories illustrating how she had experienced both a harsh rejection and a warm welcome in her adult education classes at Central Sussex College, where she studied English for Speakers of Other Languages. On the one hand, the Muslim women students in her class had declared that they did not want to share the class with non-Muslim students. In response the teacher (a Hindu woman of South Asian origin) had separated the students, seating the Muslim and the Mauritian students at opposite sides of the classroom. On the other hand, when Renée broke down during a private tutorial with this teacher and revealed that she didn't have any money to buy food for her family, her teacher later presented her with a gift of three bags of foodstuffs. In a similar vein, a Pakistani shopkeeper who owned a shop on Broadfield Parade – he claimed already to speak seven languages – was renowned amongst Chagossians for making an effort to learn French and Kreol so that he could communicate with his new customers.

In accommodation, Chagossians reported a wide range of experiences of renting, from claims of dishonest and profiteering landlords who were inattentive to necessary house improvements, to reports of mutually beneficial relationships with friendly landlords.[19] Many Chagossians found that a large proportion of their landlords, co-workers, managers, and employers in Crawley were of South Asian origin.[20] With this in mind Luke remarked:

> Chagossians want to leave Mauritius because Creoles are disadvantaged and discriminated against by Hindus and Muslims, but they come here and find that Hindus and Muslims are ahead here too because a long time ago they were the first to be given the chance to come here and work, and by their intelligence they've succeeded.

In a certain sense, he implies, history was repeating itself for Chagossians and their families. They had been given the opportunity of a fresh start in the UK, but still found themselves struggling to overcome the fact that educationally and professionally they were several steps behind South Asians and others who had been able to migrate to the UK before them.

For some, preconceptions of a wide gulf between life in Mauritius and life in the UK had to be rethought when high expectations of life in the UK were dashed by unexpected hardships. This was revealed particularly clearly in a discussion I had in a dingy shared house with two unemployed men of Chagossian parentage. Bruno, a man in his forties born in Mauritius to a Chagossian father, had left his wife and children behind in Mauritius when he came to the UK. His friend Nathaniel (who had also migrated from Mauritius) was a single man in his twenties. I asked them about the contrasts between their prior expectations and their actual experiences of life in the UK.

> LJ: When I gave English classes in Mauritius, people assumed *la vie en rose* in the UK, and didn't believe me when I said that there is racism and poverty in the UK.
>
> BRUNO: Do you know why people didn't want to believe you? Because people say that Mauritius is paradise but it's not, it's hell – racism, corruption, important people [*gran-dimunn*] remain important, insignificant people [*ti-dimunn*] remain insignificant – but they think it's not like that here [in the UK], that everyone's equal. They see big limousines in films and they hear that everyone in the UK has a house and a car, and they think our life is good, but even though I have a car, I find that life is difficult. I was never depressed until I came to the UK. It's not the weather that depresses me, it's because this is a terrible country, and now I think it would have been better to stay in Mauritius.
>
> NATHANIEL: I got depressed here too.
>
> BRUNO: The Chagossian community is a lost people [*enn lepep perdi*]. Poverty [*lamizer*] has made them come [to the UK]. I've seen lots of people who are living like animals [*bebet*] but they don't even know it. They say 'I have my house, my car, my life is OK', but they will be slaves for white people for their whole lives.
>
> NATHANIEL: There's lots of racism here, dogs get better treatment than Chagossians here because of our black skin. You'd have to say that we aren't living here, we're surviving [*nu pa pe viv isi, nu pe surviv*].

I was particularly struck by Bruno's evocation of the Chagossian community as 'a lost people' working like slaves, and by Nathaniel's assertion that dogs were treated better than Chagossians due to racism in the UK. Both phrases were exactly the same as phrases I had heard many times from Chagossians describing their problems in Mauritius (see Chapter 1). The key change was that the identity of the archetypal racist ethnic Other had been transferred from Indo-Mauritians in Mauritius to white Britons in the UK. My point is not to claim that they had decided that Mauritius was not as bad as they had previously thought. Rather it is to highlight their sense of disillusionment that the UK was not undeniably an improvement. Both men were immensely disappointed because they had emigrated from Mauritius to escape discrimination and hardship, and had anticipated that the UK would offer them an opportunity to improve their situations. Instead they found that they encountered similar problems in the UK.

Onward migration and echoes of marginalisation

This chapter has revealed that Chagossian migrants' descriptions of their experiences in the UK since 2002 often echo displaced Chagos islanders' recollections of their experiences upon arrival in Mauritius in the late 1960s and 1970s. In several instances the same tropes reappear in the new context. For instance, families were often separated between the UK and Mauritius or Seychelles as a result of uneven eligibility for UK citizenship and the relatively high cost of migration. This is reminiscent of the break-up of families who found themselves divided between Mauritius and Seychelles or dispersed within Mauritius and Seychelles after the displacement from Chagos. Likewise, as in Mauritius, Chagossians in Crawley have faced educational and socio-economic challenges connected to their chain migration to deprived neighbourhoods and their dispersal within Crawley. Finally, also as in Mauritius, Chagossians in Crawley reported experiences of ethnic discrimination. At the same time, however, Chagossian migrants' accounts of life in the UK were much more varied than their almost uniformly negative accounts (when in Mauritius) of life in Mauritius. Some recounted lower levels of ethnic discrimination, more positive employment experiences, and an ability to sustain a higher standard of living than in Mauritius.

On the one hand, the similarities I have outlined in this chapter illustrate that uprooting and relocation – whatever the characteristics of the 'home' and 'host' societies, and regardless of whether the movement is forced or voluntary – are routinely fraught with difficulties, including feelings of homesickness and concerns about social exclusion. On the other hand, the more varied accounts of onward migration to the UK highlight that there are key distinctions between the historical case of forced displacement from Chagos to Mauritius and Seychelles and the current option of onward migration to the UK. In the first case, Chagos islanders were forced from their homeland to turbulent late colonial Mauritius and Seychelles and had no option of returning to Chagos, whereas in the second case, members of the extended Chagossian community can choose whether or not to try their luck in the UK in the relatively stable early twenty-first century, and can later reverse this decision through return migration if desired. Chapter 6 investigates how the experiences that have challenged Chagossians' preconceptions about life in the UK have also led to reformulations of life in Mauritius, showing that such reformulations have implications for their changing visions of the future.

Notes

1 Chagossians in Seychelles, by contrast, were not automatically awarded Seychellois citizenship, and had to survive as non-citizens, or else pay for naturalisation.

2 UK National Archives website: www.opsi.gov.uk/Acts/acts2002/ukpga_20020008_en_1.

3 House of Commons Standing Committee D, 6 December 2001 (pt 1), online at: www.publications.parliament.uk/pa/cm200102/cmstand/d/st011206/am/11206s04.htm.

4 House of Commons FAC (2008) report on the Overseas Territories: paragraph 74. Online at: www.publications.parliament.uk/pa/cm200708/cmselect/cmfaff/147/147i.pdf.

5 Immigration Law Practitioners' Association briefings for the House of Lords Committee debate (2 March 2009) on the Borders Immigration and Citizenship Bill Part 2 (Citizenship): pages 1 & 8. Online at: www.ilpa.org.uk/briefings/BCI%20HL%20Comm/09.02.23%20ILPA%20HL%20Comm%20Chagos.pdf.

6 House of Commons Standing Committee D, 6 December 2001 (pt 1), online at: www.publications.parliament.uk/pa/cm200102/cmstand/d/st011206/am/11206s05.htm.

7 Immigration Law Practitioners' Association briefings for the House of Lords Committee debate (2 March 2009) on the Borders Immigration and Citizenship Bill Part 2 (Citizenship): page 1. www.ilpa.org.uk/briefings/BCI%20HL%20Comm/09.02.23%20ILPA%20HL%20Comm%20Chagos.pdf.

8 See Directgov (www.direct.gov.uk) or Department for Work and Pensions (www.dwp.gov.uk).

9 Eligibility for these particular benefits is reliant on habitual residency in the UK rather than on UK citizenship or on having made sufficient National Insurance contributions in the past. For information on the Habitual Residence Test, see the Department for Work and Pensions website: www.dwp.gov.uk.

10 An estimated sixty people from the extended Chagossian community in Mauritius lived in about thirteen households in Manchester at that time (although this number is also increasing). I have no reliable figures for the numbers who settled in London and elsewhere. Chagossians from Seychelles, who by and large have received more formal education and have had more experience with the English language than those from Mauritius, have tended to settle in London boroughs rather than in Crawley, and have generally managed to get better paid and more highly skilled jobs (although not necessarily jobs of the same or similar status to the careers they left behind in Seychelles).

11 For information on the scheme, see the Directgov website: www.direct.gov.uk.

12 Crawley deprivation statistics: www.crawley.gov.uk/stellent/groups/public/documents/report/int010685.pdf and www.westsussex.gov.uk/ccm/cms-service/stream/asset/?asset_id=2240589.

13 Crawley's Conservative MP Henry Smith (elected in 2010), used his maiden speech in the House of Commons to declare his support for the Chagossians' right of return to Chagos. Crawley's previous Labour MP Laura Moffat (1997–2010) had supported the Crawley-based DGS (led by Allen Vincatassin), facilitating a visit to the Chagos

Archipelago by six islanders in 2008. The other Crawley-based Chagossian organisation, the CICA (led by Hengride Permal), received considerable support from local branches of various trades unions and by the Workers Revolutionary Party. At the time of my fieldwork in 2006–7, the Mauritius-based CRG (led by Olivier Bancoult) had not yet established strong local connections in Crawley, but had much stronger links nationally with lawyers and politicians.

14 Crawley demographic statistics: www.crawley.gov.uk/stellent/groups/public/documents /report/int010668.pdf.

15 Crawley education statistics: www.crawley.gov.uk/stellent/groups/public/documents/ report/int010671.pdf.

16 UK Office for National Statistics online service: www.statistics.gov.uk.

17 For the small minority of Chagossians who have some qualifications, taking cleaning work in Gatwick has entailed a loss of status, at least in the first instance. A few young migrants experienced in IT, cabinet-making, nursery nursing, dressmaking or secretarial work, for instance, were compelled initially to work as cleaners, and a few trained police initially worked in the security industry. A few years later, having settled in and improved their English, they are better equipped to obtain work that is more commensurate with their previous training and experience.

18 For an exploration of Chagossians' distinctions between standard of life and quality of life, see Jeffery 2010.

19 Both extremes worryingly often seem to lack formalised Tenancy Agreements to protect tenants' rights.

20 This came about as a result of the numerical dominance in Crawley of immigrants from South Asia, their concentration in neighbourhoods dominated by ethnic minorities and recent immigrants, the Right to Buy council houses scheme, and the popularity of Buy to Let mortgage schemes.

6

Making home in exile

This concluding chapter continues Chapter 5's ethnographic focus on the Chagossian community in Crawley, while revisiting the themes of home and homeland explored in Part II. This chapter starts by revisiting debates amongst scholars of migration and displacement about the distinction between 'forced displacement' and 'voluntary migration'. It asks to what extent Chagossians contrast their forced displacement from Chagos to Mauritius with their onward migration from Mauritius to the UK. My data reveal that experiences of onward migration to the UK and settlement in Crawley have challenged Chagossians' preconceptions of Britons and of life in the UK and subtly altered their assessments of Mauritians and life in Mauritius. Next, this chapter examines the degree to which experiences of migration and settlement in the UK and changing visions of the future are delineated according to stage in the life course. It concludes that, despite very different experience of forced displacement and onward migration, claims of a desire to return to Mauritius take much the same form amongst migrant Chagossians in Crawley as claims of a desire to return to Chagos take amongst displaced Chagos islanders in Mauritius.

Forced displacement and onward migration

Scholars of migration and displacement have debated the value of attempts to distinguish types of human movement according to whether they are relatively 'voluntary', which tends to imply economic migration, or relatively 'forced', which tends to refer to political exodus (cf. Richmond 1994; Turton 2003; Van Hear 1998). Nick Van Hear suggests a distinction between the 'voluntary migration' of labour migrants, professional migrants, traders, tourists, and students, and the 'involuntary migration' of refugees, internal displacement, development-induced displacement, forcible relocation, and disaster displacement. He then notes that the distinctions are blurred since most migration involves a combination of compulsion and choice (Van Hear 1998: 42). A supposedly 'voluntary' choice made on economic grounds may be the only way of preventing death by starvation. Conversely, even when political upheaval creates a mass 'forced' exodus, there are some who choose to stay behind, and who may face violence as a result.

Deploying Anthony Richmond's (1994: 55–61) continuum from proactive migration (for example retirees and returnees) to reactive migration (for example, war victims and slaves), Van Hear proposes a continuum from 'more options' to 'few options' (Van Hear 1998: 42–45). He then distinguishes three categories. At the more proactive and voluntary extreme are tourists, visitors, students, professional transients, and business travellers. In the middle, implying a blend of choice and compulsion, are economic or labour migrants, rural-to-urban migrants, anticipatory refugees, and people induced to move. At the more reactive and forced extreme are refugees, expellees, internally displaced people, and those displaced by development projects or disasters.

For his part, David Turton has argued that 'forced' or 'compulsory' are linguistically more appropriate oppositions to 'voluntary' than is 'involuntary', which usually implies something unintentional or entirely lacking in volition, such as a physical twitch (Turton 2003: 8–9). Moreover, he has noted that 'forced migration' entails a logical contradiction in that 'migration' implies agency while 'force' denies agency. Since, as he puts it, 'people can be moved and displaced but not "migrated"', he suggests that 'involuntary migration' is more appropriately rendered 'compulsory' or 'forced' displacement (Turton 2003: 9). However, he also disputes the implication that those forcibly displaced have little or no agency, arguing that we should recognise them as 'purposive actors' and 'ordinary people' because, 'even in the most constrained of circumstances, human beings struggle to maintain some area of individual decision making' (Turton 2003: 8). His point applies well to refugees who make the decision that their lives, livelihoods, or lifestyles are so endangered that they must leave their homes. Cases of state-driven development- or military-induced displacement and relocation, though, often involve the forcible removal of already-marginalised sectors of the population, who have no future option to return (Turton 2003: 2–5). Whilst displaced persons are clearly 'purposive actors' in other aspects of their lives, it seems appropriate to describe their displacement as 'forced' or 'compulsory' (Turton 2003: 8–9).

This is certainly how all commentators view the forced displacement of the Chagos islanders, who clearly had no choice about being displaced and relocated. As detailed in Chapter 1, making distinctions between types of human movement – forced versus voluntary – has been of great significance to displaced Chagos islanders in Mauritius. Chagossians often sought to distinguish between the historical and piecemeal displacements entailed in populating Mauritius and the uprooting of the entire population of the Chagos Archipelago, which furthermore occurred within living memory. They also distinguished themselves from more recent migrants within the Republic of Mauritius, including islanders from the smaller Mauritian island of Rodrigues, who they typically characterised as 'voluntary' or 'economic' migrants seeking to escape unemployment, lack of opportunity, and poverty in Rodrigues.

Such distinctions between forced displacement and voluntary migration have remained central to discussions about onward migration to the UK. Chagossians have never seen the option of onward 'voluntary' or 'economic' migration to the UK in isolation from the community's earlier forced displacement. Rather, they have always seen onward migration as a potentially positive outcome of the community's previous negative experiences. Madeleine, a Chagossian single mother in her forties, migrated to the UK alone, leaving her dependent children with relatives in Mauritius until she got a job and could afford to bring them to Crawley seven months later. When I asked her why she had come to the UK, she replied:

> We got [UK] passports, and life in Mauritius was already difficult. Everything is expensive, you can't do what you want to do, like build the children's future, so I decided to come here.

Like many others, she saw emigration as a solution to problems such as the high cost of living and the lack of opportunities for young people in Mauritius. Having been awarded UK citizenship, the logical choice from her perspective was to migrate to the UK.

Bruno (whose father was a Chagos islander) was in his forties when he left his family in Mauritius and moved to the UK in 2005. Bruno critiqued the assumption of choice in my line of questioning and downplayed his own agency in the migration:

> LJ: Can you tell me how you decided to come to the UK?

> BRUNO: I didn't decide to come. I came by obligation. I'm a descendant of the Chagossian community, with a British passport, and life was difficult in my country [i.e. Mauritius]. As a British citizen, I thought I could change my life, improve my life. I saved money, sold things to buy the ticket. When I arrived here, as soon as I put my feet down on the ground, I already knew that it would not be easy for me to live in this country. I tried to integrate, I'm always trying to integrate, but I miss lots of things: firstly my family, secondly my work. I don't receive enough money to live and eat as well as send for my family, so my situation is difficult.

While seeing onward migration as an obligation rather than a choice, Bruno clearly felt (like Madeleine) that making use of their eligibility for UK citizenship was a logical solution to the problems they faced in Mauritius, where they or their parents had been forcibly relocated.

The suggestion that coming to the UK was a matter of 'obligation' rather than 'choice' was not uniformly accepted amongst migrants from Mauritius. Claude and Nina, a couple in their forties of mixed Chagossian and Mauritian parentage, came to the UK with their children in 2004. One day, Claude complained to assembled friends: 'I miss my island. Sometimes I remember Rose Hill and Beau Bassin, the same as the old people say they miss their islands'.[1] A mutual friend (also from Mauritius) shook his head, retorting: 'it was *your* choice to come, whereas *they* didn't have any choice: *they* were uprooted'. On a separate occasion, a native Chagos islander recounted at a DGS meeting how 'they took people from Diego and put them on Salomon and Peros, and then took people from Salomon and Peros and took them to Mauritius'. A younger woman (born in Mauritius to Chagossian parents) added: 'and then they took people from Mauritius and brought them here', but the assembled Chagos islanders present disagreed with her, saying, 'no, no, people must understand that coming to the UK is a personal decision, not forced'. Thus those forcibly displaced from Chagos took issue with an attempt by someone born in exile to conflate the community's initial experience of forced displacement from Chagos with subsequent individual experiences of onward migration to the UK.

From the perspective of the Chagossian struggle in Mauritius, the UK Government was wrong to depopulate the Chagos Archipelago at all. When I started speaking to Chagossians in Crawley, I noticed that their perspectives on the original policy of displacement and relocation had begun to change. Numerous people – including former Chagossian activists, Chagos islanders, and their descendants alike – now took for granted the decision to depopulate the islands to make way for the US military base on Diego Garcia. They suggested that the UK Government's mistake had been to send the Chagos islanders to Mauritius without making proper arrangements for them or putting enough pressure on the Mauritian Government for them to receive land, houses, and jobs equivalent to those they had left behind on Chagos. For its part, they said, the Mauritian Government's mistake had been not to welcome Chagos islanders in Mauritius by providing adequate accommodation and appropriate employment. From their perspective, this explained why Chagossians had reacted against their treatment in exile and why they were eager to emigrate from Mauritius once they were awarded UK citizenship. People now suggested that the original problem of the displacement would have been alleviated had the UK Government brought the Chagos islanders directly to the UK rather than sending them first to Mauritius or Seychelles.

Christophe and Lucette, a Chagossian couple who were in their twenties when they left Chagos in the 1960s, moved to Crawley in 2003 when they were in their sixties. Christophe had worked as a fisherman, but Lucette had not had paid employment in Mauritius, where she had been a housewife and looked after their six children. When I asked why they had come to the UK, Christophe responded: 'We had to re-uproot [re-derasine] ourselves. Why? Because we didn't receive a place [i.e. in Mauritius] for us to live the same as we lived there [i.e. in Chagos]'.

CHRISTOPHE: The UK Government gave lots of money to help the Chagossians but the Mauritian Government didn't do what it was supposed to with the Chagossians' money. The Mauritian Government is finding that people are leaving Mauritius and coming to the UK, but if when we had left Diego or Peros or Salomon we had got a house the same as we had on Diego or Peros or Salomon, those who were young could have worked, and there wouldn't have been this distress [bulverse]. People wouldn't have thought 'let's protest', 'let's go to England'. If someone is born here in England, you can't remove them and send them somewhere else. The mistake that the UK Government made when it did that was not to put pressure on the Mauritian Government ... Instead of blaming the UK Government, we should blame the Mauritian Government. If I had got a house in Mauritius I wouldn't have come here.[2] Why did I come here? Because of the difficulties in Mauritius. Otherwise no Chagossian would have had the idea of coming here. They would have come on holiday but wouldn't have stayed ... If you have money, it's better to stay in Mauritius, but when I retired in Mauritius, I still had children at school, and I found myself in difficulty. Sometimes I was unable to go fishing, and then the children didn't have transport money for school and had to stay at home. My pension ... wasn't enough, and Lucette never worked. Allen [Vincatassin from the DGIC] decided to come here, and when he returned to Mauritius he told us that life was easier than in Mauritius, and it's true. When we came here we had patience, we spent thirteen months in a hotel, but we succeeded in getting a pension, and our children got into a school. At the age I've reached, in Mauritius when there was nothing to do we would organise an outing and go to the sea, but here in England, we just stay at home because we've found it difficult to go out. The language question is a problem, and even though we've been here for four years, we haven't adapted to the winter.

LUCETTE: For old people like us, who had become accustomed [abitye] to the Mauritian weather, it's not possible to adapt here.

CHRISTOPHE: But for the young it's fine, if I was young it would have been fine.

LUCETTE: You could have worked and contributed. As it is we've become old without contributing, but for young people there are lots of opportunities, it would have been better to have removed us from the islands and brought us straight here.

Thus they painted a picture of missing out on opportunities as a result of the UK Government's decision to move the Chagossians to Mauritius and only later to offer them UK citizenship.

A similar impression emerged from an interview with Serge, whose family had left Chagos when he was a 10-year-old boy:

I'm sad that I've reached the age I am. I would have been happier if they had brought us straight here when I was ten years old, because I have a vision that I would have done something ... If I had come here aged ten I could have had my own house, a professional certificate, and good work, not as a cleaner. It would have enabled me to learn lots of things. I would have made lots of advances in my life.

Like Christophe and Lucette, Serge felt that it was harder for middle-aged or retired adults than for children and young adults to adapt to life in the UK. He frequently mentioned his own problems: the cold, the long shifts and heavy workload at Gatwick, the high cost of housing, and his trouble learning English. Also like the older couple, he saw coming to the UK as a way to provide better opportunities for the younger generations:

In Mauritian schools there's competition, and children have to have stress-ful private tuition, but when they finish school it's not easy to get into univer-sity there, and it's not easy to get a good job because of the system of sectarian [kominote] discrimination. That's why we wanted to leave and come to England. But I don't want to spend the rest of my life in England. Why not? Because I don't feel at home, I can't adapt, I miss my native country – not Mauritius, but my own country.

These Chagos islanders wished that – had the depopulation of Chagos been strictly necessary for security reasons – the Chagossian community should have been brought directly to the UK in the 1960s and early 1970s. They felt that this would have given them greater opportunities in life than did relocation to Mauritius. Their arguments illuminate how the decision they later took independently and voluntarily to migrate onwards from Mauritius to the UK was always seen through the lens of the original forcible displacement from the Chagos Archipelago.

Reassessing Mauritius and the UK

Comparing Chagossians' conceptualisations of forced displacement from Chagos to Mauritius and onward migration from the Indian Ocean to the UK brings me to consider how representations of Mauritius have been transformed through these experiences of onward migration. As demonstrated in Chapter 3, representations of the Chagos Archipelago have become increasingly standardised and romanticised in exile. Political, economic, sexual, and racial inequalities and conflict were routinely downplayed in public recollections of Chagos, and emerged only in private discussions with individuals. Older Chagos islanders who remembered life on Chagos uniformly characterised community life there as based on solidarity and sharing between families, in contrast to material hardship and social isolation in Mauritius.

This standardised account of solidarity in Chagos compared with isolation in Mauritius was echoed by the contrast drawn by older Chagos islanders between the traditional solidarity within the 'Chagossian community' and the individualism they attributed to their descendants. Older Chagos islanders frequently claimed that responsibility to the community had been replaced with individuals acting in the best interests of themselves and their own families. This could be seen in the attitudes of the younger generations – younger Chagos islanders born in the final few years prior to the depopulation of Chagos, plus the descendants of Chagos islanders – towards participation in the Chagossian struggle and the various potential types of recompense for the displacement. The main charges laid by senior Chagossian activists against their descendants were that the latter were not interested in their ancestral Chagossian history, culture, and traditions. Chagos islanders in Mauritius accused their juniors of being unwilling to participate in the struggle for the collective right to return to Chagos, or to contribute to projects that sought to benefit the most disadvantaged sectors of the Chagossian community. They reprimanded the younger generations for associating themselves with the Chagossian community only when it was in their own best interests. For example, they accused the younger generations of becoming more involved when they became eligible for UK citizenship and could use this right to emigrate with their own families, without due respect for the fact that these benefits came about as a result of the sustained campaigns led by their elders over several decades in exile.

How were Chagossian representations of life in Mauritius affected by their experiences of onward migration to the UK and of life in Crawley? First of all, several socio-political criticisms of Mauritius remained strong. As noted in Chapter 2, the majority of Chagossians (like the majority of other Afro-Creoles in Mauritius) historically aligned themselves with the anti-communalist MMM, rather than with the MLP, which has been more closely associated with Indo-Mauritian (and particularly Hindu) communities. Thus it is not surprising that they were highly critical of political changes in Mauritius when the MLP returned to power in 2005. In Crawley, newly arrived Chagossians and those returning from visits to Mauritius frequently recounted stories of rapid inflation, lack of jobs, low wages, and widespread drug abuse and violent crime back in Mauritius, which they blamed on Navin Ramgoolam's MLP Government. Lucette and Christophe put it as follows:

> LUCETTE: It was the Mauritian Government that made us poor, and it's getting even worse, children have no work, it's inflamed [*dan dife*].

> CHRISTOPHE: There's a political problem over there [i.e. in Mauritius]: black skin always comes last, we have no backing from the Government, there's terrible discrimination and dirty politics. Insignificant people [*ti-dimunn*] suffer because of this. I worked in Mauritius, you'd have to say I spent my whole life there, but when you see the work people are doing here, it's not the same.

> LUCETTE: Over there it's like slavery: you work day and night for very little cash. My sister is a widow who lives alone in her house. She receives a pension ... but after paying for her rent, gas, and water, her money runs out before the end of the month. There are lots of problems in Mauritius. Tourists live it up but those who actually live there have lots of problems. They never make a budget that helps the insignificant people. They should reduce what those at the top have and give it to those who are small. People tell us that all the children are turning to drugs. Why? There's no work, or if a mother works there's no-one to look after her children. If you work, you work a lot, but you don't get much pay.

> CHRISTOPHE: The problem is that there are too many ethnicities [*nasyon*].

> LUCETTE: There's no co-operation, so the Government does whatever it wants, it's domineering [*dominer*]. The people have no say.

Thus they recounted problems such as ongoing ethnic stratification and an economic system that benefits those at the top, particularly Indo-Mauritians, Franco-Mauritians, and Sino-Mauritians, and further disadvantages those at the bottom, especially Chagossians and other Afro-Creoles.

In other ways, however, experiences in Britain have transformed conceptualisations of life in Mauritius. Lydia, whose family was introduced in Chapter 5, was a dressmaker in her late thirties. She obtained UK citizenship through her Chagossian parents, and migrated to the UK in one of the first groups in 2003. Her non-Chagossian husband Luke joined her in early 2004, and their dependent teenage children, who had been left with Lydia's mother in Mauritius when Luke emigrated, joined them later that year.

> LUKE: We feel rich because we live in a rich country with a high standard of living, we have what we need, and we live much better than most people in the world.

> LYDIA: I now know that even Mauritius is better than most of the world.

They concluded that – in socio-economic terms – their life in the UK compared favourably with their life in Mauritius. At the same time, exposure to the British media and a growing awareness of poverty elsewhere in the world had made them rethink the degree of their economic hardship in Mauritius.

Interactions with British people and with other immigrants also transformed their attitudes towards Mauritian people. Over a series of discussions, Luke told me:

> I've learned a lot here. In Mauritius I thought that the Mauritian mentality [*mantalite Morisyen*] was bad, but now I know that people everywhere are bad ... British people don't know anything: the Government offers them lots but they don't benefit. I know that I don't want to stay here because of this mentality. Asians and Africans have a slave mentality and they know that they've got to save, but the British people don't benefit. It's obvious that British people are less intelligent than people from India and other countries ... The only reason the UK is strong is because the pound is strong, otherwise it would not have power over the rest of the world, and if Mauritians had the facilities that British people have, Mauritius would become much stronger than the UK.

His previous conception, that a weak 'mentality' was a uniquely Mauritian trait, was no longer plausible since he had now identified equivalent or greater deficiencies amongst many of the British people he had met since moving to the UK. Thus experiences in the UK have challenged migrants' often rose-tinted preconceptions about life in the UK. At the same time, they have precipitated a subtle rethinking of their previous negative conceptualisations of Mauritians and of life in Mauritius.

Reformulating the Chagossian community

Concepts of a stereotypically 'Mauritian' or 'Creole mentality' also played a significant role in internal Chagossian critiques of the 'Chagossian community' in Crawley. A group of Chagossian migrants organised and sold tickets for a Chagossian New Year's Eve party in the Langley Green community centre in 2006. Many Chagossians in Crawley complained that too many tickets had been sold considering the small size of the venue, and that they had not enjoyed the party because of the lack of space. Lydia, however, told me:

> I won't criticise it even if space was tight [*sere-sere*] because people here don't get the chance to see their friends because they're always working, so everyone wanted to come and celebrate the New Year together ... Lots of people have come here now. There are lots of people I didn't know in Mauritius but have met here, for example at work, and it's good that we're all crushed [*sere-sere*] in Crawley because then people sometimes get a chance to see their family.

Like Lydia, many other young migrants originally chose to settle in Crawley because they had family there. On arrival, they liked the fact that they already knew and could meet up with friends in the town and therefore did not feel isolated or lonely. Chain migration to Crawley, however, has given rise to a number of criticisms of the community from within.[3]

A common complaint among earlier migrants was that their newly arrived relatives – including children, parents, or siblings – abused their hospitality by staying with them too long, not contributing enough financially or in terms of household tasks, or conducting illicit relationships in their homes. To give an example, one young woman ended up being circulated around the various households of an extended Chagossian family. Her successive hosts became exasperated when she spent whole days at home watching television, refused to contribute to childcare, housework, or shopping, failed to apply for jobs, ran up large telephone bills calling her family in Mauritius, and started sneaking out at night to go on dates. Her first host in Crawley confided to me that she was unable to keep a close enough eye on the girl because of her long working hours, and she feared having to face the girl's mother (in Mauritius) if the girl fell pregnant. The girl was moved to a household inhabited by a more watchful stay-at-home mother, but eventually she was asked to leave this household too.

One outcome of the chain migration to Crawley was that there were 'too many Chagossian families in Crawley' [tro buku fami Chagossien dan Crawley] and consequently 'too much gossip' [tro buku palab]. A major concern for many migrants was that news about their social activities – such as drinking, nightclubbing, and dating – was likely to travel back to the Indian Ocean via the Chagossian grapevine to reach the ears of family members, and particularly their parents. They dreaded their relatives in Mauritius seeking to exert their influence over their religious, sexual, or financial behaviour. For example, they did not want to be reminded that they still had a partner and family back in Mauritius, or that they still owed money to extended family members who financed their passage to the UK. One story that had got back to Mauritius was that young women of Chagossian parentage had started wearing knee-high boots and working as barmaids in the UK. This was problematic for the reputations of the young women in question since both knee-high boots and bartending are considered symbols of prostitution in Mauritius. Other major topics of gossip included discussions of whose Mauritian family members had or had not managed to get Indefinite Leave to Remain in the UK, how best to access state benefits, and how much money other people were making. For instance, many observers attributed the fact that one particular family was able to buy a house in Crawley to their additional income acquired by renting out their house in Mauritius. This was both a source of envy and of criticism since many commentators felt that the family should have made their house freely available to poorer relatives in Mauritius.

The tendencies to keep an eye on one another's business [vey zafer dimunn] and to spread gossip about one another [koz palab], were generally considered to be part of a Mauritian Creole 'mentality' [mantalite] that had become worse [anpire] in England, the land of twitching lace curtains. Related to spying and gossip is jealousy [zaluzi] and the concept of gran nwar, which refers to people thinking too highly of themselves, getting ideas above their station, or becoming too big for their boots (see Ledikasyon Pu Travayer 1993: 91). People might be considered to be *gran nwar* if, as their purchasing power increases, they become conspicuous consumers of goods that would have been beyond their budget in Mauritius. For instance, many people remarked that whereas people in Mauritius would exchange second-hand children's clothes because new clothes were too expensive, in the UK they wouldn't take up offers of second-hand clothes because they preferred to show that they could now afford to buy new clothes for their children.

In the context of low levels of education and career development amongst the older generations, responses to the successes of the younger generations illumi-nate the complex internal relations within the extended community. Countless Chagossians told me that if a Chagossian worker obtained a good supervisory job, or a Chagossian pupil achieved good grades at school, other Chagossians would not be proud [*fyer*] of the achievements and improved fortunes of members of the community. Rather, they would be jealous [*zalu*] and accuse the worker or pupil of being *gran nwar*, with the effect of depressing ambition. As evidence, several people asserted that 'all Chagossians in Crawley are cleaners', whereas Indo-Mauritian migrants in London were stereotypically assumed to be students or nurses. Bruno (born in Mauritius to a Chagossian father) had left his family in Mauritius and was living in a shared house with others of Chagossian descent. He described the problem as follows:

> Mauritians spy on one another, they talk nonsense [*ninport*], and they're jealous. If I see that my brother over there is in difficulty I won't help him, and will gossip about him with other people, but if I see that he is doing well I will visit him. The problem is that Mauritians who come to Europe should change their way of life and live like Europeans.

As a result of a fear of spying, gossip, jealousy, and criticism, many migrants told me that they preferred not to socialise with others from Mauritius. Aline (whose mother was a Chagos islander), was in her late twenties and worked in a care home in Crawley. She put it as follows:

> The Mauritian mentality is in a bad state of affairs [*dan bez*]: jealousy, always spying on one another. They'll never be able to live like Europeans because of this troublesome mentality [*mantalite bez*]. That's why we prefer to associate with strangers than with family [*pli kontan frekante ek etranze ki fami*].

Such criticisms, however, were confronted by admonitions that 'other' Chagos-sians in Crawley were forgetting their Chagossian roots. Some said that people who had been friendly in Mauritius or Seychelles had broken all ties and even started ignoring one another in the street or on buses since moving to Crawley. On the other hand, however, for most Chagossians in the UK – even those who criticised 'the Chagossian community' for its alleged tendencies towards spying, gossip, and jealousy – most social interaction was with other Chagossian mi-grants, although opportunities for socialising were limited by long, irregular, or unsocial working hours.

Migration and the life course

From the perspective of many Chagossians, the various forms that recompense could take had differential values depending on one's stage in the life course. Most of the older Chagos islanders and all of the Chagossian socio-political community leaders consistently asserted their desire to return to resettle the Chagos Archipelago. They saw the right of return – plus the financial assistance to do so – as the most appropriate form of recompense for Chagos islanders who had experienced the displacement first-hand and who wished to return to their homeland. Financial compensation was seen as something that would benefit all members of the extended Chagossian community. The granting of UK citizenship, by contrast, was seen as a form of recompense directed primarily towards younger people: Chagos islanders who were born shortly prior to the depopulation of Chagos, and the descendants of Chagos islanders born in exile. This was because older people were considered less likely to uproot themselves from Mauritius and make a new start in the UK, where they would expect to have more trouble finding employment than would their younger and better educated descendants.

Janine, a Chagos islander in her fifties based in Mauritius who occasionally visited her children in Crawley, told me that she would not move to the UK herself because:

> I have my job in Mauritius. I can't leave it and come here … I wouldn't get a job here because I don't know English and I don't really know how to read and write. Wait until my Chagossian work is finished, then I'll see. But I'm not happy either here or there. If one day my islands are opened I'll go there, even if I'm old and can't walk I'll tell people to take me there.

Like many other older displaced islanders, she saw UK citizenship as something that would not necessarily benefit older displaced islanders, whose overarching aim was to return to resettle Chagos.

The majority of those who migrated from Mauritius and Seychelles to the UK were young adults and parents with dependent children. Many migrants in Crawley were concerned about the effect of their exodus on their Chagossian elders in Mauritius, but did not view the UK as an ideal place for elderly people. Lydia commented that many of the older Chagos islanders in Mauritius (including her own mother) complained that they had been abandoned and forgotten by their descendants in the UK. She sympathised with the sadness felt by older people when the younger generations moved to the UK:

> When I came here, my mother was strong, but during the past four years she's got thin with sadness. Why? She was happy to have brought up her children, but now they're all leaving her and coming to England.

According to Lydia, the older Chagos islanders thought that all of their problems (such as poverty and ill-health) were due to living in Mauritius, and imagined that moving to the UK would solve these problems. They were mistaken, she said. To start with, she argued, elderly people would find it impossible to adapt to the cold British weather and to having to climb the stairs in two-storey houses. Moreover, Chagos islanders in Mauritius often lived with relatives and were surrounded by neighbours who looked out for them. In Crawley, by contrast, the whole family would be out all day, and they could not rely on neighbours to take care of the elderly like they did in Mauritius. According to Lydia:

> People are more impoverished here than in Mauritius. Not in terms of food –
> they get plenty of food here – but in terms of interaction, communication, living
> together … People should find out about all these problems before they come,
> but the leaders made us believe that England is paradise.

While in Mauritius, life in Mauritius was represented as individualistic and lacking in solidarity in comparison to life on Chagos (see Chapter 3). But from the vantage point of Crawley, life in Mauritius appears positively neighbourly by comparison with life in the UK.

This raises the question of how older Chagossian migrants have actually experienced settling in the UK. Older Chagos islanders certainly agreed that there were fewer activities for older people in the UK, where people were confined to the indoors because of the colder weather, than in Mauritius, where much of social life takes place outdoors. Many older migrants, including Christophe and Lucette, therefore felt that they were more isolated in the UK than they were in Mauritius. Asked about their daily activities, they told me:

> CHRISTOPHE: When we sit at home all day watching television, sometimes it
> makes you want to leave, because in Mauritius we can go to the seaside, but here
> there's no beach. They should have put us somewhere where there was a beach
> because we're used to being by the sea.

> LUCETTE: It is frustrating to stay at home, but where could we have a party at
> the seaside here? Christophe's family is here [in Crawley], but my family is there
> [in Mauritius]. If they told me to come back I might go because then my whole
> family would be together. Here it's only when you go into town that you meet
> other Chagossians.

Thus their complaint about life in the UK was that there was a lack of activities for older people and a lack of opportunities to meet others. Because of the cold weather and the long distance from the seaside, they found that they spent their time indoors watching television.

Some older Chagossian migrants had a more positive experience of resettlement in the UK. Charlesia Alexis, a Chagossian woman in her seventies, migrated to the UK in 2004 with one of her teenage grandchildren. She received Pension Credits, Housing Benefit in the form of a sheltered flat paid for by the Council (apart from bills for water, electricity, and gas, which she paid herself), and Child Benefit on behalf of her grandchild. When I asked her what she thought of her life in the UK, she told me that:

> I like England, I'll stay here … I've seen how the Government helps old people
> and those with children, although those who don't speak English don't get work.
> In Mauritius, even if you work … it's not enough to save, whereas here people
> who work can save quickly.

Charlesia saved as much as possible from the benefits she received to send back to Mauritius to pay for the passage of other family members to the UK, where they eventually set up separate households. In Mauritius, Charlesia Alexis had long been active in the Chagossian struggle for the right to return (see Chapter 2). But when I asked her whether she was upset that she had not been able to join the boat trip to the Chagos Archipelago in 2006, she shrugged and replied that she was no longer concerned with the Chagossian struggle. As an elderly woman in poor physical health, she found that in the UK she received adequate benefits and regularly saw a GP for her chronic diabetes and resultant mobility problems, which eased the financial and healthcare problems she faced in Mauritius. From her perspective, living the rest of her life in the UK represented a realistic resettlement that overrode her prior commitment to the resettlement of the Chagos Archipelago. Thus her experience complicates the assumption of many of those in the Indian Ocean that migrating to the UK would automatically be of most interest to younger people.

Changing visions of the future

LJ: What about your children's futures?

CHRISTOPHE: The children will stay [in the UK].

LUCETTE: The children say they will work here for a long time and then return to Mauritius. There are people here whose lives weren't OK in Mauritius – sometimes they had no food, so they couldn't send their children to school, which is why lots of Chagossians don't have much education – but when they came here they didn't want to stay here.

By offering an example of onward migration and raising the issue of migration and stage in the life course, the Chagossian case study provides an intriguing opportunity to re-examine the 'myth of return' and visions of the future among displaced people and migrants. Among Chagos islanders and their descendants, experiences of forced displacement and onward migration have resulted in diverse visions of the future, based variably on return to Chagos, integration into Mauritius or Seychelles, or settlement in the UK. My research in Mauritius initially indicated that these visions were delineated primarily by age. Older displaced islanders consistently asserted their desire to return to and resettle the Chagos Archipelago, whilst the majority of their descendants – plus some younger Chagos islanders – dreamed of migrating to Europe, and a minority planned to remain in Mauritius. Having now worked with migrant Chagossians in the UK, I found that plans to retire to Mauritius were beginning to feature more prominently in more people's visions of the future.

Egon Kunz's concept of 'refugee vintages' distinguishes between 'majority-identified' refugees who identify ideologically with the nation they left behind (although not its current government), 'events-alienated' refugees who are ambivalent about their country and its people as a result of ethnic or religious discrimination and marginalisation, and 'self-alienated' refugees who have ideological reasons for not identifying with the nation (Kunz 1981: 42–43). Madawi Al-Rasheed has suggested that while majority-identified refugees are more likely to view their displacement as 'a temporary phase which will eventually lead to their return', events-alienated and self-alienated refugees are more likely to view migration as 'a permanent solution to their alienated existence' in their homeland (Al-Rasheed 1994: 209). While Kunz's typology applies most neatly to refugees who have fled their country for political reasons, it is clear that Chagossians are 'events-alienated' in the sense that they were embittered by their experiences of forced displacement, marginalisation, and ethnic discrimination, and they were ambivalent towards the Mauritian nation-state. The implication would be that Chagossian migrants in the UK would be unlikely to demonstrate a 'myth of return' to Mauritius. My fieldwork in Crawley revealed that this was not necessarily the case.

In a volume on migrants in the UK, James Watson noted that it may be difficult to 'distinguish between "settlers" who intend to remain permanently abroad and "sojourners" who plan to return to their home society … because they commonly share a "myth of return"' (Watson 1977: 5). Several ethnographers have shown that migrants may oscillate between seeing themselves as temporary 'sojourners' who plan one day to return to the 'homeland' and recognising that they no longer felt 'at home' in their 'homeland' and had become permanent 'settlers' abroad (see e.g. Chamberlain 1997: 70–90; Gardner 2002: 93; Olwig 1999: 73). For Madawi Al-Rasheed, the central issue 'is not whether refugees aspire to a "real" or "actual" return to their homeland but with their orientation and its social consequences' (Al-Rasheed 1994: 201). Likewise, Johnathan Bascom proposed that the 'myth of return' should be interpreted not as the intention to return but as a worldview that sustains refugees and their descendants through difficult or uncertain times in exile (Bascom 1998: 146–149). For Roger Zetter, the 'myth of return' may therefore be better conceptualised as a 'myth of home' which serves 'to reinforce political claims for repatriation and the restitution of property; to create symbolic security and permanency in conditions of uncertainty and disorder; to retain the bonds of family, household or kinship' (Zetter 1999: 6). Thus it can become central to a group's self-representation whether or not it implies actual intention to return (Jansen & Löfving 2009: 14), and can justify migrants' remittances to the home country, reflect their concerns about 'integration' and 'assimilation', and sustain collective identity in exile.

During my fieldwork in Mauritius, some prospective migrants had told me that they anticipated becoming permanent 'settlers' in the UK. Others anticipated that they would be temporary 'sojourners', seeing migration to the UK as a temporary measure to improve their children's education and employment opportunities and to enable them to save enough to retire comfortably to Mauritius. Now in Crawley, these same people often addressed the question of their plans for the future, so I explored with them whether and how their experiences in the UK had affected these future plans.

Madeleine was a cleaner in Mauritius before she migrated to Crawley and took work as a cleaner at Gatwick. She lived with her dependent descendants in

a house half paid for by the Council via Housing Benefit, and was unequivocal about her positive experience in the UK and her intention to remain in the UK for the foreseeable future:

> When I came I knew I wouldn't have a problem with staying here because I already had family here. Before I got work I felt discouraged, but as soon as I got a job I knew I would be able to stay and bring my children. I worked for seven months, and after seven months I was able to bring the children here. Fortunately I managed to do that. With my job in Mauritius I wasn't able to buy enough food, but here I can get everything I want that I couldn't get in Mauritius. Everything's possible here. My life in Mauritius was very, very hard. Here it's just houses that are expensive. If people say they can't stay here, that means they don't want to stay here. Here, if you work, you can eat and drink, you can get everything you need, and you can stay. In Mauritius, you have to wait a week before you can afford meat. Unfortunately there are people who have come here who don't want to work, they just want to hang out, and they forget their families, but they should build a future here. People must be able to bring their families here because the currency is worth more in Mauritius. If they don't do it, that means they don't want to do it. In Mauritius there are lots of drug addicts, crime, rape, and rising costs. Everything has become difficult in Mauritius, which encourages me to stay here. I'm not saying I'll never return to live in Mauritius because I don't know, but I'm not going for the moment, I'm doing well here.

On another occasion, when members of her extended family teased her for having put on weight since moving to the UK, she retorted that this was because in Mauritius she had been stressed by having to decide whether to pay bills or eat. In Crawley, she explained, she did not have to worry because she worked and knew she could pay for everything she needed.

A few Chagossian families managed to save adequate deposits and get mortgages to buy houses in Crawley, saying that this had helped them to 'settle' in the UK (although they did not necessarily plan to remain in Crawley in the long term). The majority of young adults, though, told me that they had come to the UK for the benefit of their children's education and employment prospects. They intended eventually to retire to and settle permanently in the Indian Ocean. Serge, who brought his family to the UK for the sake of his children's education, told me that he planned to return to the Indian Ocean when his youngest children have finished school and he has reached retirement age:

> LJ: What visions do you have for the future?
>
> SERGE: I don't want to die here. I want to die either in my country [i.e. Chagos] or in Mauritius. I have lots of ideas but I don't know if I'll succeed because of the age I've reached. My goal is to buy a house here, help my children, and get decent work, but I don't know if I'll manage it because of my age. I have no intention of spending the rest of my life as a cleaner in the airport.
>
> LJ: What about your children's futures?
>
> SERGE: None of them intends to return to Mauritius for the moment, and I think they're right because they're still young. They've only just come here for their education. They have their own visions.

Serge generally felt that he had settled well and had been welcomed by locals in Crawley. Nevertheless, he reiterated several times that he didn't want to spend the rest of his life as a cleaner at Gatwick, or to die in the UK, and instead wanted eventually to return, preferably to Chagos, or otherwise to Mauritius. Numerous other Chagossian migrants in Crawley likewise anticipated that they would eventually retire to Mauritius. They concluded that the UK offered better education and employment opportunities for younger people, but that Mauritius was preferable for an enjoyable retirement. These concerns reflect a tension (identified in Staeheli & Nagel 2006) between home as where one's parents belong(ed) and where one was raised (in the past), home as where one participates (in the present), and home as where one's children (will) belong (in the future).

The Chagossian case study is instructive because it provides an example of forced displacement followed by onward migration within the living memory of the Chagossian community. Onward migration offers an intriguing opportunity to re-examine ideas about home, return, and the future among displaced people and migrants. Analyses of the 'myth of return' (e.g. Al-Rasheed 1994: 217) rightly recognise that the presence or absence and strength or weakness of a desire to return 'home' varies according to refugees' or migrants' past and present political and socio-economic positioning in relation to their 'home' country and their 'host' country. This may not, however, tell the whole story. Onward migration was a very popular option for the extended Chagossian community. It will certainly have important consequences for the community, especially given the focus of the Chagossian struggles on the resettlement of the Chagos Archipelago. In Mauritius, the almost ubiquitous desire amongst older native Chagos islanders to return to Chagos can be explained in terms of their overwhelmingly negative experiences of forced displacement and relocation, and the comparison they drew between the 'good life' in Chagos and their poor circumstances in Mauritius. The troubles they experienced in Mauritius, plus their high expectations of life in the UK, were the reasons given for migrating from Mauritius to the UK. By and large, they continued to view Mauritius negatively, and they made much more varied (although generally less negative) assessments of life in the UK. It was therefore striking that so many nevertheless claimed that they wished one day to return to Mauritius. It is important to note, however, that with the passing years, even some of those Chagossians who said they wished to retire to Mauritius also recognised that returning was becoming increasingly unlikely as they and their families settled in the UK.

My conclusion is that the transformation in the imagined destination of return (from Chagos to Mauritius) can only be explained by understanding three elements explored in this chapter. First, experiences in the UK challenged migrants' preconceptions about the UK. Second, experiences in the UK brought about subtle reformulations of conceptions of Mauritius from 'host' to 'home'. Third, experiences in the UK have altered the focus of visions of the future. From the vantage point of Mauritius, life in Mauritius was depicted as uniformly inferior to life in Chagos. From the vantage point of Crawley, life in Mauritius was depicted as having certain benefits and drawbacks relative to life in the UK. In particular, the

UK was generally seen as preferable to Mauritius in terms of *standard* of life and employment opportunities for young people, while Mauritius was generally seen as preferable in terms of *quality* of life, particularly for retired people. Among the younger generations at least, this reassessment of Mauritius was accompanied by a concomitant reconfiguration of Chagos as ancestral homeland rather than viable future.

Onward migration versus return migration?

The ethnographic challenge that this book has sought to address is to understand how people experience, create, and sustain their links to specific territories through diverse processes and practices: from emphasising displacement, reformulating the homeland, and mobilising for return, to seeking to belong, strategising onward migration, and making home in exile. I have illustrated that attachment to territory is a contested process. As Jansen and Löfving succinctly put it, 'home is made and remade on an everyday basis through strategies of cultural continuity' (Jansen & Löfving 2009: 15). On the one hand, the similarities in experiences of forced displacement from the Chagos Archipelago to Mauritius and onward migration from Mauritius to the UK illustrate that uprooting and relocation – whatever the characteristics of the 'home' and 'host' societies, and regardless of whether the movement is forced or voluntary – are routinely fraught with difficulties, including feelings of homesickness and concerns about social exclusion. On the other hand, the more varied accounts of onward migration to the UK highlight that there are crucial distinctions between the historical case of forced displacement from Chagos to Mauritius and Seychelles and the contemporary option of onward migration to the UK. In the first case, Chagos islanders were forcibly removed from their homeland to turbulent late colonial and postcolonial Mauritius and Seychelles and had no option of returning to Chagos. In the second case, Chagossians can choose whether or not to try their luck in the prosperous UK, and can later reverse this decision through return migration if desired.

The big question that remains is whether the relocation of an increasing proportion of the Chagossian community from Mauritius and Seychelles to the UK necessarily has irrevocably negative implications for the Chagossian struggle based in Mauritius, which focuses on pursuing the right to return to the Chagos Archipelago. While I have shown that onward migration to the UK is highly significant for individual Chagossians and their families, I would conclude that it is not necessarily to the detriment of the Chagossian struggle. To start with, the onward migration has been dominated by the younger generations, who were already less involved in the Chagossian struggle than their Chagossian parents and grandparents. So far, most Chagos islanders have not chosen to emigrate from Mauritius. Many of those most active in the Chagossian struggle have remained in Mauritius, where they have continued to participate in Chagossian campaigns for compensation and the right to return to Chagos. Moreover, a recent feasibility study drawn up in conversation with Chagossians in Mauritius proposed a small initial construction of 150 houses, and concluded that the resettlement of Chagos could grow to a maximum of 400 families, since this delicate, remote and tiny archipelago could not accommodate the vast majority of those who say they wish to return (Howell 2008: 13). In the case of small-scale resettlement, then, the challenge will be how to continue to engage the small and increasingly geographically dispersed Chagossian community.

Notes

1 Interestingly, Claude referred not to the disadvantaged neighbourhoods on the out-skirts of Port Louis where he and his family had lived, but rather to the middle-class hill towns of Rose Hill and Beau Bassin, where he had spent very little time. This conforms to processes whereby migrants selectively recall and romanticise their homeland (see Chapter 3).
2 Christophe did own a house in Mauritius that he had received as part of the compen-sation package awarded in the mid-1980s (see also Chapter 1). His statement reflects collective opinion rather than his own decision-making process (see also Chapter 3).
3 Similarly, many of those Chagossians who decided to settle in Manchester instead of in Crawley explained this decision in terms of wanting to avoid the muddle or disarray [*pelmel*] of the Chagossian community in Crawley. Indeed, some of the earliest arrivals in Manchester complained that the growing community of Chagossians in Manchester was increasingly exhibiting the same unappealing tendencies towards spying, gossip, jealousy, and criticism as that in Crawley.

Postscript

Legal and environmental barriers to resettlement

Throughout their decades in exile, Chagossian groups have focused on their campaigns for compensation and the right to return to Chagos, while other interest groups have worked against the resettlement of the Chagos Archipelago. According to the terms of the 1966 Exchange of Notes, the UK Government made Diego Garcia available for US defence purposes for an initial period of fifty years, renewable for a further twenty years. Given the military significance of the US base on Diego Garcia, it seems likely that both governments will seek to renew the lease in 2016. Meanwhile, the UK Government has allocated considerable resources towards preventing Chagossians from returning to Chagos, directly through immigration legislation relating to the British Indian Ocean Territory (BIOT), and indirectly through the creation a Marine Protected Area (MPA) in Chagos.

BIOT immigration legislation and human rights

In 2000, when the Chagossians' legal team won their judicial review of the 1971 BIOT Immigration Ordinance, the then Foreign Secretary, Robin Cook, announced that the Government would not appeal the decision. The Government immediately introduced a new BIOT Immigration Ordinance that theoretically allowed Chagos islanders to return to the smaller outer islands (i.e. with the exception of Diego Garcia). In 2004, however, the UK Government used the Orders in Council – a royal prerogative that bypasses parliament – to enact a new BIOT Immigration Order preventing non-authorised persons (including Chagos islanders) from entering the entire territory. The Chagossians' legal team launched a judicial review against the FCO, successfully arguing its case both in the Divisional Court in 2006 and in the Court of Appeal in 2007. Judges in both courts accepted the argument made by the Chagos islanders' barrister, Sir Sydney Kentridge QC, that the BIOT Immigration Order 2004 was 'irrational' because it considered neither the Chagossians' best interests nor their 'legitimate expectation' of return following Robin Cook's statement in 2000. The FCO finally appealed to the House of Lords in 2008, where a majority verdict in the FCO's favour was agreed by Lord Hoffmann, Lord Rodger of Earlsferry, and

Lord Carswell, while dissenting minority opinions were handed down by Lord Bingham of Cornhill and Lord Mance.[1]

The majority opinion was that the UK Government was under no obligation to consider the islanders' interests to be paramount; on the contrary, it might have been deemed irrational *not* to consider the wider interests of the UK and its allies (paragraphs 53, 114, 132). First, Lord Hoffmann accepted the UK Government's argument that resettlement would be precarious and expensive, both environmentally and financially (paragraph 168). Second, he noted that the UK Government was entitled to take into consideration the US Government's opposition to resettlement on the grounds that resettlement would compromise the unique isolation and security of the US military base on Diego Garcia (paragraphs 26, 57). Third, Lords Hoffmann, Rodger and Carswell each denied that the statement made by Robin Cook after the first judicial review in 2000 amounted to a 'legitimate expectation' that resettlement would be permitted and facilitated (paragraphs 60–62, 115, 133–135). Lord Carswell claimed that 'the Government did not give the Chagossians a clear and unambiguous promise that they would be allowed to return and resettle permanently on the outer islands' (paragraph 143).

Each of these three conclusions was disputed in the two minority opinions. First, Lord Mance accepted Sir Sydney Kentridge's logic that a colony must consist first and foremost of its population, and exiling that population cannot be in the best interests of either the colony or its population (paragraph 157). Second, Lord Bingham criticised the 'highly imaginative letters written by American officials to strengthen the Secretary of State's hand in this litigation' (paragraph 72), and Lord Mance dismissed the claim that these letters offered clear evidence that the US considered resettlement to pose a major threat to the security of the military base (paragraphs 163–171).[2] Third, Lord Mance discussed at length the question of 'legitimate expectation' (paragraphs 173–186). He argued that the Chagossians interpreted Robin Cook's statement as a 'clear policy decision taken by the United Kingdom to recognise and give legal effect to a right to return' (paragraph 173; see also Lord Bingham's agreement in paragraph 73). The *Bancoult* cases in general and the 2008 House of Lords ruling in particular have wide political and legal ramifications, particularly in relation to the reliance on precedent in English law and to the application of indigenous rights frameworks and human rights legislation in the overseas territories.

Legal scholars and practitioners noted that the *Bancoult* cases had the potential to establish legal precedent regarding the reviewability (or otherwise) of the royal prerogative (see Elliott & Perreau-Saussine 2009). The opinions of the five Law Lords were unanimous on this issue: they rejected the extreme argument put forward by the Crown barrister, Jonathan Crow QC, that the royal prerogative is not subject to judicial review, and they agreed instead that the royal prerogative is indeed subject to judicial review (see paragraphs 33–40, 71, 105–106, 122, 141). Their disagreement lay in whether the Government was entitled to implement such a restrictive Immigration Order *in this case*, and therefore whether the lower courts were correct to use their powers to review this particular legislation. The two dissenting Law Lords took their critique of the royal prerogative further: in Lord Bingham's opinion, the royal prerogative itself is an 'anachronistic survival' that has rightly been eroded over the centuries (paragraph 69). Lords Bingham and Mance both questioned whether the royal prerogative could be used to exile an indigenous population from its homeland in a colonial territory, although they both concluded that such an outcome could be achieved legitimately through parliament (paragraph 70, 160–161). Thus even the two dissenting Law Lords did not focus their analysis on the exiling of an indigenous people from its homeland *per se*; rather, they denounced the undemocratic method deployed. The implications of this are not lost on the citizens of other British Overseas Territories concerned about their own residence rights.[3]

In their majority opinions, Lords Hoffmann and Carswell accepted the argument made on behalf of the FCO by Jonathan Crow QC that the Human Rights Act 1998 and the European Convention on Human Rights do not apply in the BIOT (paragraphs 64–65, 131). There is considerable concern within human rights organisations that this finding has worrying implications for the application of human rights in the overseas territories and the negligible international monitoring to which (overseas) military bases are subjected. In February 2008, the then foreign secretary David Miliband admitted that two US rendition flights carrying prisoners had transited via Diego Garcia.[4] The week after the judicial hearing in the House of Lords in July 2008, the House of Commons FAC published its report on the British Overseas Territories.[5] The FAC report cited evidence from the All-Party Parliamentary Group on Extraordinary Rendition and from the prisoners' human rights charity Reprieve that the US military had used Diego Garcia for extraordinary rendition flights and had held detainees on ships in Diego Garcia's territorial waters (paragraphs 52–60). The FAC report also criticised the US authorities for initially (and falsely) denying this charge (paragraph 69). Later the same month, an article in *Time* magazine cited an unidentified 'former senior American official' claiming that a CIA counter-terrorism official had twice admitted that the US had imprisoned and interrogated prisoners on Diego Garcia.[6] Thus mounting evidence supports widespread concerns that so-called 'terrorism suspects' (neither convicted nor even formally accused of any crime) have been sent from Diego Garcia to countries where they have been tortured, or have been tortured on Diego Garcia itself (or on ships in Diego Garcia's lagoon), where they are evidently denied recourse to the protection of international human rights legislation (Sand 2009: 115–116). The UK Government has further drawn a distinction between its territory and its territorial waters to deny that it has jurisdiction over US ships anchored off Diego Garcia, where landmines are stored (Sand 2010: 236–237). Moreover, in December 2010, a US Embassy cable released by the media organisation WikiLeaks revealed that the UK Government had devised a legal loophole to allow the US military to continue to store cluster bombs off Diego Garcia as 'temporary exceptions', contravening the international Convention on Cluster Munitions.[7]

While the judgment had potentially wide-ranging repercussions for legal precedent and human rights, it was also a terrible blow to the Chagossian struggle for the right to resettle the Chagos Archipelago. Faced with a challenge not to lose the momentum built up since their first victory in 2000, Chagossian leaders and their supporters pledged to continue their struggle for the right of return. Firstly, Olivier Bancoult urged British politicians to consult both the minority Law Lords' opinions and the FAC report, which concluded: 'there is a strong moral case for the UK permitting and supporting a return to the British Indian Ocean Territory for the Chagossians' (paragraph 69). Secondly, Chagossian leaders hoped that the changing political landscapes following general elections in the USA in 2008 and the UK in 2010 would offer opportunities for more constructive dialogues with the new governments than with their predecessors. Thirdly, Olivier Bancoult instructed his solicitor Richard Gifford to pursue a case in the ECHR, which they hoped would take a more progressive stance on the applicability of the European Convention on Human Rights in BIOT, the forcible uprooting of an indigenous people, and the subsequent prevention of their return.

The creation of a Marine Protected Area in Chagos

Meanwhile, however, another barrier to resettlement has emerged in the form of a powerful environmental lobby. In 2008, a group of nine conservation and environmental organisations formed the Chagos Environment Network (CEN).[8] In March 2009, at the Royal Society in London, the CEN launched its campaign recommending that the UK Government establish a Marine Protected Area (MPA) in the Chagos Archipelago.[9] This was followed up with a natural science workshop in August 2009 at the National Oceanography Centre in Southampton. The Southampton workshop report promoted an MPA on the basis of the scientific significance of Chagos: the Chagos Bank is the world's largest coral atoll, and is characterised by biodiversity and the comparatively high resilience of the Chagos coral reefs and fish stocks (attributed to the relatively low level of damaging human activities such as boat and diver damage, pollution and sedimentation, and overfishing).[10]

In response to the CEN's campaign, the FCO launched a consultation from November 2009 to March 2010 to gather views from stakeholders on whether to establish an MPA in the BIOT, and if so what form the MPA should take. The consultation document offered three options: a full no-take marine reserve for the whole of the territorial waters; a no-take marine reserve with exceptions for certain forms of fishing in certain zones at certain times of year; a no-take marine reserve for the vulnerable reef systems only.[11] Of these, the CEN favoured the first option,[12] and its call for people to respond to the FCO consultation in support of the first option was circulated to hundreds of thousands of people via online activist networks including Avaaz, Greenpeace, and Care2. The call made no mention of the Chagossians or their campaign for the right of return.

A workshop at Royal Holloway, University of London, in January 2010 considered the socio-economic implications of establishing an MPA in Chagos.[13] The workshop report criticised the exclusion of Chagossians from previous meetings (particularly the Southampton workshop), arguing that successful natural resource management relies on involvement of local communities even and especially at the planning stages. It suggested that the UK Government should consider how the management of the proposed MPA would be affected by the possibility of resettlement of Chagos (pending the ECHR decision), the renegotiation of the US military base on Diego Garcia (due in 2016), and the promised transfer of Chagos to Mauritian sovereignty (once the territory is no longer required for defence purposes). The Royal Holloway workshop report noted that the three no-take options proposed by the FCO would compromise resource use in the case of future resettlement. It suggested as an alternative a well-protected MPA that would enable resettled Chagossians to partake in subsistence and small-scale commercial fishing, agricultural production, and sustainable tourism, and to be involved in scientific research (including environmental monitoring) and fisheries protection.

The FCO made minimal effort to elicit Chagossian viewpoints during its consultation process despite the fact that elderly Chagos islanders in Mauritius and Seychelles in particular would be unlikely to be able to respond to the consultation online due to their lack of English, low levels of literacy, and limited access to computers and the internet. The elected representatives from the CRG gave their views via a video conference in Mauritius which was also attended by other Chagossians. A consultation meeting with the Chagossian association in Seychelles resulted in a written response to the FCO. In the UK, both the DGS and the CICA submitted written responses; the former's submission included views elicited during a consultative meeting and 250 questionnaires, while the latter's submission included a petition signed by 70 people. However, critics of the consultation process focused on the lack of consideration of Chagossian perspectives. Firstly, they argued that the FCO's original consultation document did not supply adequate information about potential Chagossian resettlement to enable other respondents – such as the hundreds of thousands of signatories of petitions circulated by Avaaz, Greenpeace, and Care2 – to make an informed contribution. Secondly, they suggested that Chagossians should have been involved at the design stage (in particular in drawing up the proposed options) rather than sought along with – and as if merely equal to – other kinds of stakeholders.

According to the FCO consultation report, over a quarter of a million people – a range of 'private individuals, academic and scientific institutions, environmental organisations and networks, fishing and yachting interests, members of the Chagossian community, British MPs and peers and representatives of other governments' – responded to the consultation.[14] Of respondents who supported one of the three options proposed by the FCO, the majority favoured a full no-take marine reserve on the basis of the projected conservation, climate change, and scientific benefits this would provide. Representatives of Indian Ocean tuna fishing companies, not surprisingly given their commercial interests, favoured the second and third options as the best way to protect the reefs while managing licensed fishing. By contrast, the majority of Chagossian respondents, plus 13 per cent of other respondents, did not support any of the three options, instead either rejecting the proposal entirely (in anticipation of the ECHR decision and fuller consultation with the Chagossian community) or proposing alternative solutions (such as establishing a no-take marine reserve with exceptions for resettled Chagossians). Another regional interest group not adequately represented in the consultation report is the Mauritian Government, which boycotted the consultation process in protest against the UK Government's failure first to discuss the proposal in bilateral talks concerning Mauritian sovereignty and regional fishing interests.[15]

In April 2010 – a month before general elections in both the UK and Mauritius, on a day when neither parliament was sitting – the UK Government announced that it would establish an MPA in the BIOT. This includes a 'no-take' marine reserve of 544,000 square kilometres with a ban on commercial fishing, constituting the world's largest site with this status, and doubling global coverage with full protection.[16] The then foreign secretary David Miliband claimed firstly that the creation of an MPA had no implications for the future ceding of Chagos to Mauritius and secondly that it was 'without prejudice' to the forthcoming ECHR proceedings. Critics have argued the opposite on both counts, suggesting instead that the Labour Government's emphasis on its environmental legacy was intended to conceal its ulterior motives: firstly to entrench British sovereignty in the guise of internationally recognised environmental stewardship; secondly to strengthen its assertion of the unfeasibility of Chagossian resettlement due to the alleged incompatibility between human resettlement and environmental conservation; and thirdly to protect the remote character of the US military base on Diego Garcia, which was specifically excluded from the MPA and is therefore not subject to the same stringent controls (Sand 2010: 232–233).

The intentions of the Labour Government were confirmed in a cable from the political counsellor Richard Mills at the US Embassy in London to the Secretary of State in Washington DC, published in December 2010 as part of the WikiLeaks mass release of confidential US government files.[17] During a meeting in May 2009, the BIOT Commissioner Colin Roberts asserted that designating the BIOT as a marine reserve would enhance the isolation of Diego Garcia by enabling the authorities to restrict all access except for scientific research (paragraph 9). The BIOT Administrator Joanne Yeadon indicated that the Chagossian campaign for the right of return to the outer islands would be further damaged if the US Government could be persuaded to reassert that the entire Chagos Archipelago (and not only Diego Garcia) was required to be unpopulated for defence purposes (paragraph 11). Commenting on the meeting, Mills noted: 'we are concerned that, long-term, both the British public and policy makers would come to see the existence of a marine reserve as inherently inconsistent with the military use of Diego Garcia' (paragraph 14). His conclusion, however, was that 'Establishing a marine reserve might, indeed, as the FCO's Roberts stated, be the most effective long-term way to prevent any of the Chagos Islands' former inhabitants or their descendants from resettling in the BIOT' (paragraph 15).

Plus ça change

Whilst in opposition, the Conservative MP William Hague and the Liberal Democrat leader Nick Clegg MP criticised the Labour Government's approach and voiced their support for a 'fair settlement' for the Chagossian community. When the coalition Conservative and Liberal Democrat Government was formed in May 2010, with Nick Clegg as Deputy Prime Minister and William Hague as Foreign Secretary, Chagossian leaders were therefore hopeful for a change in their fortunes. Since coming to power, however, the new Government has gradually revealed its intention 'not to change the fundamental policy on resettlement, compensation and on the Marine Protected Area'.[18] In relation to the MPA, the UK Government announced that it would retain the MPA, the last licences for fishing in BIOT expired at the end of October and the MPA came into effect at the beginning of November.[19] In relation to compensation, the Government declared that it concurred with Mr Justice Ouseley's ruling in 2004 that a 'full and final' settlement had already been reached and subsequent claims for further compensation were time-barred.[20] In relation to resettlement, the Government rejected the ECHR's suggestion that it offer a 'friendly solution' and announced instead that it would continue to contest the Chagossians' case in the ECHR because it had been convinced by the 'feasibility and defence security' arguments against resettlement.[21]

Chagossian leaders have been disappointed that the current Government intends to continue the approach of the previous Government. As I write, in December 2010, Chagossian leaders have expressed their outrage at the WikiLeaks revelations that the UK Government intended to use the MPA as a tool to prevent resettlement and that the US military has continued to use Diego Garcia for extraordinary renditions and munitions storage. Also in December 2010, the Mauritian Government launched a legal action under the compulsory dispute settlement provisions of the 1982 UN Convention on the Law of the Sea. The Mauritian Government argued firstly that the MPA is incompatible with the 1982 Convention, and secondly that the UK lacked the jurisdiction to create the MPA (since, it claimed, only the Republic Mauritius has the authority to declare an exclusive zone around Chagos). The Mauritian Government further noted its concern that the UK Government's main intention in creating an MPA appeared to be not environmental conservation but rather the prevention of resettlement by Chagossians. Chagossian groups in exile still await a response from the ECHR before proceeding with a judicial review of the MPA, although clearly a positive ruling on their right to return to Chagos will be confronted yet again by the determination of the UK and US Governments to prevent resettlement. Meanwhile, members of the extended Chagossian community – dispersed in Mauritius, Seychelles, the UK, and beyond – continue their struggles to make themselves at home in exile.

Notes

1 R (Bancoult) v Secretary of State for Foreign and Commonwealth Affairs [2008] UKHL 61.
2 Speculations in the US State Department letters – to the effect that resettlement of the outer islands would enable terrorists to operate in the territory – are described even in Lord Hoffmann's majority opinion as 'fanciful' (paragraph 57). Only Lord Mance's minority opinion, however, notes the unconventional admittance of these letters as evidence 'after the commencement of the proceedings in which they were produced' (paragraph 163).
3 For instance, see www.saint.fm/Independent/20081024.pdf.
4 www.publications.parliament.uk/pa/cm200708/cmhansrd/cm080221/debtext/80221-0008.htm.
5 www.publications.parliament.uk/pa/cm200708/cmselect/cmfaff/147/147i.pdf.
6 See www.time.com/time/world/article/0,8599,1828469,00.html.
7 See www.guardian.co.uk/world/us-embassy-cables-documents/208206.
8 See http://protectchagos.org.
9 See www.reefnewmedia.co.uk/cmt_chagos/uploads/PDF/Brochure/CCT_brochure-draft_lowres.pdf.
10 See http://protectchagos.org/wp-content/uploads/Southampton-BIOT-workshop-brochure-1.pdf.
11 See www.reefnewmedia.co.uk/cmt_chagos/uploads/PDF/Science/FCO%20consultation%20document.pdf.
12 http://protectchagos.org/wp-content/uploads/CEN_Submission-Final-FINAL.pdf.
13 See www.marineeducationtrust.org/chagos-campaign.
14 See www.fco.gov.uk/resources/en/pdf/3052790/2010/marine-life-apr-2010.
15 www.publications.parliament.uk/pa/cm200910/cmselect/cmfaff/memo/overseas/ucm42302.htm.
16 See www.fco.gov.uk/en/news/latest-news/?view=News&id=22014096.
17 www.guardian.co.uk/world/us-embassy-cables-documents/207149.
18 www.publications.parliament.uk/pa/cm201011/cmhansrd/cm101104/text/101104w0002.htm#10110460000022.
19 www.publications.parliament.uk/pa/cm201011/cmhansrd/cm101021/text/101021w0001.htm#10102149000029.
20 www.publications.parliament.uk/pa/cm201011/cmhansrd/cm101013/text/101013w0003.htm#10101334000006.
21 Ibid.

References

Ackroyd, J.H. 1878. *Report of the Acting Police and Stipendiary Magistrate of the Smaller Dependencies of Mauritius*. Colony of Mauritius report no. 7.

Al-Rasheed, M. 1994. 'The myth of return: Iraqi Arab and Assyrian Refugees in London'. *Journal of Refugee Studies* 7(2/3): 199–219.

Allen, R.B. 1999. *Slaves, Freedmen, and Indentured Laborers in Colonial Mauritius*. Cambridge: Cambridge University Press.

—. 2004. 'The Mascarene slave-trade and labour migration in the Indian Ocean during the eighteenth and nineteenth centuries'. In *The Structure of Slavery in Indian Ocean Africa and Asia* (ed.) G. Campbell. London: Frank Cass.

Anderson, B. 1998. 'Long-distance nationalism'. In *The Spectre of Comparisons: Nationalism, Southeast Asia and the World*. London: Verso.

Anderson, Charles. 1839. *Apprentices in the Islands Dependent on Mauritius*. Public Records Office Instructions to and Report of Mr. Special Justice Anderson for Sir William Nicolay despatch No. 105 of 23rd October 1838 CO 167/204.

Anderson, Clare. 2000. *Convicts in the Indian Ocean: Transportation from South Asia to Mauritius, 1815–53*. Basingstoke: MacMillan.

Anthias, F., & N. Yuval-Davis, in association with H. Cain. 1992. *Racialized Boundaries: Race, Nation, Gender, Colour and Class in the Anti-Racist Struggle*. London: Routledge.

Antoine, J.-C. 2003. 'Cassam Uteem, ex-président de la République: "En politique étrangère, Maurice est un paillasson des Américains"'. In *Week-end* (23 March), pp. 4–5. Port Louis, Mauritius.

Anwar, M. 1979. *The Myth of Return: Pakistanis in Britain*. London: Heineman.

Anyangwe, C. 2001. *Question of the Chagos Archipelago: Report on the fact-finding mission to Mauritius*. SAHRINGON.

Assone, S.R. 2003. 'Tendance musicale: Assistons-nous à une américanisation de notre folklore?' *Revi Kiltir Kreol* 3: 87–89.

Baily, J., & M. Collyer. 2006. 'Introduction: Music and migration'. *Journal of Ethnic and Migration Studies* 32(2): 167–182.

Baker, P. 1972. *Kreol. A Description of Mauritian Creole*. London: C. Hurst.

Ballgobin, D.V., & M. Antoine. 2003. 'Traditional musical instruments from oral tradition: Folk music in Mauritius'. *Revi Kiltir Kreol* 3: 69–82.

Ballinger, P. 2003. *History in Exile: Memory and Identity at the Borders of the Balkans*. Princeton: Princeton University Press.

Bandjunis, V.B. 2001. *Diego Garcia: Creation of the Indian Ocean Base*. San Jose, CA: Writer's Showcase.

Barnwell, P.J., & A. Toussaint. 1949. *A Short History of Mauritius*. London: Longmans, Green & Co.

Barth, F. 1969. Introduction. In *Ethnic Groups and Boundaries: The Social Organization of Culture Difference* (ed.) F. Barth. London: George Allen & Unwin.

Bascom, J. 1998. *Losing Place: Refugee Populations and Rural Transformations in East Africa*. Oxford: Berghahn.

Baumann, G. 1996. *Contesting Culture: Discourses of Identity in Multi-Ethnic London*. Cambridge: Cambridge University Press.

Benedict, B. 1961. *Indians in a Plural Society: A Report on Mauritius*. London: Her Majesty's Stationery Office.

—. 1965. *Mauritius: Problems of a Plural Society*. London: Pall Mall Press.

Benedict, M., & B. Benedict. 1982. *Men, Women and Money in the Seychelles*. Berkeley, CA: University of California Press.

Blunt, A., & R. Dowling. 2006. *Home*. Abingdon: Routledge.

Boolell, S. 2001. 'The fall out of the Bancoult case'. In *Le Mauricien* (27 February). Port Louis, Mauritius.

Boswell, R. 2002. 'Finding our roots – Transnationalism and political culture in Mauritius'. Paper presented to the EASA 7th Biennial Conference, Copenhagen, 2002.

—. 2006. *Le Malaise Créole: Ethnic Identity in Mauritius*. Oxford: Berghahn.

Botte, F. 1980. *The 'Ilois' Community and the 'Ilois' Women*. Unpublished report.

Bowman, L.W. 1991. *Mauritius: Democracy and Development in the Indian Ocean*. London: Dartmouth.

Bowman, L.W., & J.A. Lefebvre. 1985. 'The Indian Ocean: US military and strategic perspectives'. In *The Indian Ocean: Perspectives on a Strategic Approach* (eds) W.L. Dowdy & R.B. Trood. Durham: Duke University Press.

Brooks, E.P. 1875. *Report on the Lesser Dependencies of Mauritius*. Port Louis, Mauritius.

Brubaker, R., & F. Cooper. 2000. 'Beyond "identity"'. *Theory and Society* 29(1): 1–47.

Carroll, B.W., & T. Carroll. 2000. 'Accommodating ethnic diversity in a modernizing democratic state: Theory and practice in the case of Mauritius'. *Ethnic and Racial Studies* 23(1): 120–142.

Carroll, T. 1994. 'Owners, immigrants and ethnic conflict in Fiji and Mauritius'. *Ethnic and Racial Studies* 17(2): 301–324.

Carter, M. 1995. *Servants, Sirdars and Settlers: Indians in Mauritius, 1834–1874*. Delhi: Oxford University Press.

Central Statistics Office. 2000. *Mauritius in Figures 1999*. Government of Mauritius: Ministry of Economic Development, Financial Services & Corporate Affairs.

—. 2003a. *Annual Digest of Statistics 2002*. Government of Mauritius: Ministry of Economic Development, Financial Services & Corporate Affairs.

—. 2003b. *Mauritius in Figures 2002*. Government of Mauritius: Ministry of Economic Development, Financial Services & Corporate Affairs.

—. 2010. *Mauritius in Figures 2009*. Government of Mauritius: Ministry of Finance and Economic Development.

Cernea, M.M. 1997. 'The risks and reconstruction model for resettling displaced populations'. *World Development* 25(10): 1569–1587.

—. 2000. 'Risks, safeguards, and reconstruction: A model for population displacement and resettlement'. In *Risks and Reconstruction: Experiences of Resettlers and Refugees* (eds) M.M. Cernea & C. McDowell. Washington DC: The World Bank.

Chagossian Social Committee. 1997. *Un homme parmi les hommes*. Leaflet produced by Chagossian Social Committee and Indian Ocean Institute for Human Rights and

Democracy.

Chamberlain, M. 1997. *Narratives of Exile and Return*. London: Macmillan.

Chateau, T. 2000. *Février noir*. GRNW, Port Louis, Mauritius: Ledikasyon Pu Travayer.

—. 2002. 'Hervé Lassemillante parle de "piège anglais"'. In *Le Mauricien* (27 May), p. 3. Port Louis, Mauritius.

Chinniah, H., & V. Dhunputh. 2002. 'Interview: Me Siva Mardemootoo, Conseiller légal du *Grup Refuzié Chagos*'. In *University of Mauritius Law Society* newsletter (2002), pp. 84–85.

Clifford, J. 1988. 'Identity in Mashpee'. In *The Predicament of Culture: Twentieth-Century Ethnography, Literature, and Art*. Cambridge, MA: Harvard University Press.

Cole, B. 2004. *Crawley: A History and Celebration*. Salisbury, Wiltshire: Frith.

Collen, L., & R. Kistnasamy. 2002. 'Lalit dumunn ordiner kont baz US lor Chagos, pu reinifikasyon Repiblik Moris ek pu reparasyon'. In *Diego Garcia in Times of Globalization* (ed.) *Lalit*. GRNW, Port Louis, Mauritius: Ledikasyon Pu Travayer.

Colson, E. 1989. 'Overview'. *Annual Review of Anthropology* 18: 1–16.

—. 2003. 'Forced migration and the anthropological response'. *Journal of Refugee Studies* 16(1): 1–18.

Connellan, M. 2007. 'You could have a long life if you choose your neighbourhood well'. In *Crawley News* (11 April), p. 17.

Crawley Together. 2001. *Crawley: A Community Profile*. Report produced by Health and Social Policy Research Centre of Brighton University for Crawley Borough Council and West Sussex County Council.

Culhane, D. 1998. *The Pleasure of the Crown: Anthropology, Law and First Nations*. Burnaby, BC: Talon.

Daes, E.-I.A. 1996. *Standard-setting Activities: Evolution of Standards Concerning the Rights of Indigenous People: On the Concept of 'Indigenous Peoples'*. United Nations Sub-Commission on Prevention of Discrimination and Protection of Minorities. UN Doc. E/CN.4/Sub.2/AC.4/1996/2.

de l'Estrac, J.-C. 1983. *Report of the Select Committee on the Excision of the Chagos Archipelago*. Government of Mauritius report No. 2 of 1983.

Descroizilles, M., & A. Mülnier. 1999. *Bor'endan bor'déhor*. Stanley, Rose Hill, Mauritius: Editions de l'Océan Indien.

Diehl, K. 2002. *Echoes from Dharamsala: Music in the Life of a Tibetan Refugee Community*. Berkeley, CA: University of California Press.

Dinan, M. 2002. *Mauritius in the Making: Across the Censuses 1846–2000*. Port Louis, Mauritius: Nelson Mandela Centre for African Culture.

Dræbel, T. 1997. *Evaluation des besoins sociaux de la communauté déplacée de l'Archipel de Chagos, volet un: santé et éducation*. Unpublished report.

Dupont, I. 1884. *Report of the Magistrate for the Lesser Dependencies on his Visit to the Chagos Archipelago in December 1884*. Colony of Mauritius.

Dussercle, R.P.R. 1934. *Archipel de Chagos en mission 10 Novembre 1933 – 11 Janvier 1934*. Port Louis, Mauritius: The General Printing & Stationery Company Limited.

Edis, R. 2004 [1993]. *Peak of Limuria: The Story of Diego Garcia and the Chagos Archipelago*. London: Chagos Conservation Trust.

Eisenlohr, P. 2006. *Little India: Diaspora, Time, and Ethnolinguistic Belonging in Hindu Mauritius*. Berkeley, CA: University of California Press.

Elliott, M., & A. Perreau-Saussine. 2009. 'Pyrrhic public law: Bancoult and the sources, status and content of common law limitations on prerogative power'. *Public Law* 4: 697–722.

Eriksen, T.H. 1998. *Common Denominators: Ethnicity, Nation-Building and Compromise in Mauritius*. Oxford: Berg.

—. 2002. *Tu dimunn pu vin Kréol:* the Mauritian Creole and the concept of creolization. *Revi Kiltir Kreol* 1: 74–82.

Falzon, M.-A. 2009. 'Multi-sited ethnography: Theory, praxis and locality in contemporary research'. In *Multi-Sited Ethnography: Theory, Praxis and Locality in Contemporary Research* (ed.) M.-A. Falzon. Farnham: Ashgate.

Farquharson, C. 1864. *Report of Charles Farquharson, Esq., District and Stipendiary Magistrate, Seychelles, appointed Commissioner by His Excellency the Governor to visit the smaller Dependencies of Mauritius, and to enquire into the condition of the laborers employed therein*. Colony of Mauritius.

Foreign and Commonwealth Office. 1999. *Partnership for Progress and Prosperity: Britain and the Overseas Territories*. Foreign and Commonwealth Office. Cm 4264.

Fuglerud, Ø. 1999. *Life on the Outside: The Tamil Diaspora and Long-Distance Nationalism*. London: Pluto.

Gallo, E. 2009. 'In the right place at the right time? Reflections on multi-sited ethnography in the age of migration'. In *Multi-Sited Ethnography: Theory, Praxis and Locality in Contemporary Research* (ed.) M.-A. Falzon. Farnham: Ashgate.

Gardner, K. 2002. *Age, Narrative and Migration: The Life Course and Life Histories of Bengali Elders in London*. Oxford: Berg.

Gwynne, P. 1990. *A History of Crawley*. Chichester: Phillimore & Co. Ltd.

Hage, G. 2005. 'A not so multi-sited ethnography of a not so imagined community'. *Anthropological Theory* 5(4): 463–475.

Hall, S. 1993. 'Cultural identity and diaspora'. In *Colonial Discourse and Post-Colonial Theory: A Reader* (eds) P. Williams & L. Chrisman. Hemel Hempstead: Harvester Wheatsheaf.

Handler, R. 1985. 'On dialogue and destructive analysis: Problems in narrating nationalism and ethnicity'. *Journal of Anthropological Research* 41: 171–182.

Handler, R., & J. Linnekin. 1984. 'Tradition, genuine or spurious'. *Journal of American Folklore* 97(385): 273–290.

Harrison, S. 1999a. 'Identity as a scarce resource'. *Social Anthropology* 7(3): 239–251.

—. 1999b. Cultural boundaries. *Anthropology Today* 15(5): 10–13.

Higman, B.W. 1984. *Slave Populations of the British Caribbean*. Baltimore, MD: Johns Hopkins University Press.

Hills, M. 2002. 'The formal and informal management of diversity in the Republic of Mauritius'. *Social Identities* 8(2): 287–300.

Hirschon, R. 1998. *Heirs of the Greek Catastrophe: The Social Life of Asia Minor Refugees in Piraeus*. Oxford: Berghahn.

Houbert, J. 1992. 'The Indian Ocean Creole islands: Geo-politics and decolonisation'. *The Journal of Modern African Studies* 30(3): 465–484.

Howell, J. 2008. *Returning home: A proposal for the resettlement of the Chagos Islands*. Report produced for the Chagos Refugees Group and the UK Chagos Support Association.

Jackson, J. 1989. 'Is there a way to talk about making culture without making enemies?' *Dialectical Anthropology* 14: 127–143.

—. 1995. 'Culture, genuine and spurious: The politics of Indianness in the Vaupes, Colombia'. *American Ethnologist* 22(1): 3–27.

Jackson, M. 2000. *At Home in the World*. Durham: Duke University Press.

Jansen, S., & S. Löfving. 2009. 'Introduction: Towards an anthropology of violence, hope and the movement of people'. In *Struggles for Home: Violence, Hope and the Movement of People* (eds) S. Jansen & S. Löfving. Oxford: Berghahn.

Jawatkar, K.S. 1983. *Diego Garcia in International Diplomacy*. London: Sangam.

Jeffery, L. 2006a. 'The politics of victimhood among displaced Chagossians in Mauritius'. Unpublished PhD thesis: University of Cambridge.

—. 2006b. 'Victims and patrons: Strategic alliances and the anti-politics of victimhood among displaced Chagossians and their supporters'. *History and Anthropology* 17(4): 297–312.

—. 2006c. 'Historical narrative and legal evidence: Judging Chagossians' High Court testimonies'. *Political and Legal Anthropology Review* 29(2): 228–253.

—. 2007. 'How a plantation became paradise: Changing representations of the homeland among displaced Chagos islanders'. *Journal of the Royal Anthropological Institute* 13(4): 951–968.

—. 2009. 'Chagossians refused right to return home'. *Anthropology Today* 25(1): 24–26.

—. 2010. 'Forced displacement, onward migration, and reformulations of "home" by Chagossians in Crawley, West Sussex'. *Journal of Ethnic and Migration Studies* 36(7): 1099–1117.

Jeffery, L., & D. Vine. 2011. 'Sorrow, sadness, and impoverishment: the lives of Chagossians in Mauritius'. In *Eviction from the Chagos Islands: Displacement and Struggle for Identity Against Two World Powers* (ed.) S.J.T.M. Evers & M. Kooy. Leiden: Brill.

Jing, J. 1996. *The Temple of Memories: History, Power, and Morality in a Chinese Village*. Stanford, CA: Stanford University Press.

Kaiser, T. 2006. 'Songs, discos and dancing in Kiryandongo, Uganda'. *Journal of Ethnic and Migration Studies* 32(2): 183–202.

Kenrick, J., & J. Lewis. 2004. 'Indigenous peoples' rights and the politics of the term "indigenous"'. *Anthropology Today* 20(2): 4–9.

Kibreab, G. 1999. 'Revisiting the debate on people, place, identity and displacement'. *Journal of Refugee Studies* 12(4): 385–410.

Kirsch, S. 2001. 'Environmental disaster, "culture loss," and the law'. *Current Anthropology* 42(2): 167–198.

Kistnasamy, R., & L. Collen. 2002. 'Sityasyon Chagosyen zordi'. In *Diego Garcia in Times of Globalization* (ed.) Lalit. GRNW, Port Louis, Mauritius: Ledikasyon Pu Travayer.

Kunz, E. 1981. 'Exile and resettlement: Refugee theory'. *International Migration Review* 1(15): 42–51.

Kuper, A. 2003. 'The return of the native'. *Current Anthropology* 44(3): 389–402.

L'express. 1973. 'L'acceuil aux îlois: Le Premier Ministre donne des précisions'. In *L'express* (10 May), p. 1.

—. 1982. 'Purryag exprime l'espoir d'un règlement du problème des Ilois'. In *L'express* (23 March), p. 6. Port Louis, Mauritius.

—. 2001. '"Ilois Welfare Fund": Olivier Bancoult écrase Fernand Mandarin'. In *L'express* (19 March), p. 7. Riche Terre, Baie du Tombeau, Mauritius.

Lalit. 1986. *Program LALIT lor Repiblik*. GRNW, Port Louis, Mauritius: Ledikasyon Pu Travayer.

—. 1987. *Program LALIT lor internasyonalism ek lalit anti-imperyalis*. GRNW, Port Louis, Mauritius: Ledikasyon Pu Travayer.

— (ed.) 2002. *Diego Garcia in Times of Globalization*. GRNW, Port Louis, Mauritius: Ledikasyon Pu Travayer.

Lallah, R. 2002. 'AGOA – an instrument of the US ruling class'. In *Diego Garcia in Times of Globalization* (ed.) Lalit. GRNW, Port Louis, Mauritius: Ledikasyon Pu Travayer.

Lamusse, R. 2001. 'Macroeconomic policy and performance'. In *The Mauritian Economy: A Reader* (eds) R. Dabee & D. Greenaway. Houndsmill: Palgrave.

Lassemillante, H. 2000. 'Devinette Chagossienne: Cherchez l'homme'. In *Le Mauricien* (5 August). Port Louis, Mauritius.

—. 2001a. 'Chagos: "les intérêts mauriciens sont menacés"'. In *Le Mauricien* (1 March), p. 7. Port Louis, Mauritius.

—. 2001b. 'L'imaginaire Chagossien'. In *Le Mauricien* (9 November), p. 8. Port Louis, Mauritius.

—. 2002. 'R. v. Secretary of State Ex parte Bancoult'. In *University of Mauritius Law Society* newsletter (2002), pp. 86–90.

Lazaredes, N. 2002. 'Chagos Archipelago: Winning back paradise'. Documentary film directed by N. Lazaredes and produced by Journeyman Pictures for Dateline Australia.

Le Chartier, C. 1991. *Table et traditions créoles: Ile Maurice, Ile Rodrigues, Agaléga, Chagos*. Bell Village, Pailles, Mauritius: Centre Culturel Africain & Les Editions de l'Océan Indien.

Le Mauricien. 1973. 150 '"Ilois" explusés refusent de débarquer à Port-Louis'. In *Le Mauricien* (4 May), p. 4. Port Louis, Mauritius.

—. 1978. 'Trois des sept grévistes de la faim admiser à l'hôpital civil'. In *Le Mauricien* (21 September). Port Louis, Mauritius.

—. 1982a. 'L'affaire Iloise réglée'. In *Le Mauricien* (29 March), p. 1 & p. 5. Port Louis, Mauritius.

—. 1982b. 'Nouvelle proposition britannique hier aux négociations anglo-mauriciennes'. In *Le Mauricien* (23 March), p. 1 & p. 4. Port Louis, Mauritius.

—. 1982c. 'Les représentants du "Foreign Office" et les avocats du comité Ilois – O.F. arrivent demain'. In *Le Mauricien* (20 March 1982), p. 1 & p. 4. Port Louis, Mauritius.

—. 2002. 'SAHRINGON réclame la fermeture de la base de Diego Garcia'. In *Le Mauricien* (20 November), p. 7. Port Louis, Mauritius.

—. 2004. 'Au Social Forum, Mumbai, le GRC et Lalit chercheront un bateau pour aller à Diego'. In *Le Mauricien* (9 January), p. 1 & p. 5. Port Louis, Mauritius.

Leach, E. 2000 [1977]. 'Anthropos'. In *The Essential Edmund Leach volume 2: Culture and Human Nature* (eds) S. Hugh-Jones & J. Laidlaw. New Haven, CT: Yale University Press.

Ledikasyon Pu Travayer. 1993. *Diksyoner Kreol Angle*. GRNW, Port Louis, Mauritius: Ledikasyon Pu Travayer.

Lee, J.K. 1990. *Sega: The Mauritian Folk Dance*. London: Nautilus.

Lenette-Kisnorbo, M. 2003. 'A la recherche du paradis perdu'. Documentary film directed by M. Lenette-Kisnorbo.

Leonard, K.I. 2009. 'Changing places: The advantages of multi-sited ethnography'. In *Multi-Sited Ethnography: Theory, Praxis and Locality in Contemporary Research* (ed.) M.-A. Falzon. Farnham: Ashgate.

Ly-Tio-Fane, H., & S. Rajabalee. 1986. 'An account of Diego Garcia and its people'. *Journal of Mauritian Studies* 1(2): 90–107.

Ly-Tio-Fane Pineo, H. 1985. *Chinese Diaspora in Western Indian Ocean*. Port Louis, Mauritius: Editions de l'Océan Indien / Chinese Catholic Mission.

Madeley, J. 1985. *Diego Garcia: A Contrast to the Falklands*. Minority Rights Group report No. 54.

Malkki, L.H. 1995. *Purity and Exile: Violence, Memory and National Cosmology among Hutu Refugees in Tanzania*. Chicago, IL: University of Chicago Press.

Mallett, S. 2004. 'Understanding home: A critical review of the literature'. *The Sociological Review* 54(1): 62–89.

Marcus, G.E. 1995. 'Ethnography in/of the world system: The emergence of multi-sited ethnography'. *Annual Review of Anthropology* 24: 95–117.

Marimootoo, H. 1997. 'Diego Files'. In *Week-end* (weekly, 25 May 1997 – 10 August 1997). Port Louis, Mauritius.

—. 2000. 'M. Olivier Bancoult lance, à nouveau, un appel à l'unité des Chagossiens'. In *Week-end* (6 August), p. 11. Port Louis, Mauritius.

—. 2002. 'L'intérêt commun de la compensation rapproche les Chagossiens'. In *Week-end* (22 December), p. 69. Port Louis, Mauritius.

—. 2003. 'Les "coustics" honteux de la diplomatie mauricienne'. In *Week-end* (6 April), pp. 30–31. Port Louis, Mauritius.

Martinez Cobo, J. 1986. *Study on the Problem of Discrimination Against Indigenous Populations*. United Nations UN Sub-Commission on Prevention of Discrimination & Protection of Minorities. UN Doc. E/CN.4/Sub.2/1986/Add.4.

Mauritius Research Council. 1999. *Social fabric study phase II*. Mauritius Research Council.

Miles, W.F.S. 1999. 'The Creole malaise in Mauritius'. *African Affairs* 98(391): 211–228.

Minerve, J. 2000. 'L'archipel des Chagos: affirmons concrètement notre souveraineté!' In *Le Mauricien* (15 November): p. 7. Port Louis, Mauritius.

Nave, A. 2000. 'Marriage and the maintenance of ethnic group boundaries: the case of Mauritius'. *Ethnic and Racial Studies* 23(2): 329–352.

Nelson Mandela Centre for African Culture. 2003. *Festival Kréol 2003: Kréolité, découverte ek développement*. Rodnet Programme.

Office of the Deputy Prime Minister. 2004. 'Briefing – 2004 indices of multiple deprivation'. London: Office of the Deputy Prime Minister.

Olwig, K.F. 1999. 'Travelling makes a home: Mobility and identity among West Indians'. In *Ideal homes? Social Change and Domestic Life* (eds) T. Chapman & J. Hockey. London: Routledge.

—. 2007. *Caribbean Journeys: An Ethnography of Migration and Home in Three Family Networks*. Durham: Duke University Press.

Omura, K. 2003. 'Comment on Adam Kuper's "The return of the native"'. *Current Anthropology* 44(3): 395–396.

Palmié, S. 2006. 'Creolization and its discontents'. *Annual Review of Anthropology* 35, 433–456.

Pilger, J. 2004. 'Stealing a nation: A special report by John Pilger'. Documentary film directed by J. Pilger and produced by C. Martin for Granada Television.

Poché, J.-M. 2000. 'Maurice réclame l'ouverture immédiate des négociations sur sa souveraineté'. In *Le Mauricien* (7 November), p. 4. Port Louis, Mauritius.

Prosper, L. 2000. 'Anil Gayan, Ministre des Affaires étrangères: "La souveraineté sur les Chagos n'est pas négociable"'. In *Le Mauricien* (12 November), p. 11. Port Louis, Mauritius.

Prosser, A.R.G. 1976. *Visit to Mauritius from 24 January to 2 February: Mauritius – Resettlement of Persons Transferred from Chagos Archipelago*. Government of Mauritius.

Quirin, S., & J. Achille. 2003. 'Agaléens vivant à Maurice: *Exilés* en terre d'espoir'. In *Week-end* (16 November), pp. 25–26. Port Louis, Mauritius.

Rabinowitz, D. 1994. 'The common memory of loss: Political mobilization among Palestinian citizens in Israel'. *Journal of Anthropological Research* 50: 27–44.

Ramdas, J.-P.M. 2003. *Chagossian Desire for a Restoration and Resettlement Plan for Chagossian*. Report produced for Diego Garcia Island Council.

Richmond, A. 1994. *Global Apartheid: Refugees, Racism, and the New World Order*. Oxford: Oxford University Press.

Robins, S. 2003. 'Comment on Adam Kuper's "The return of the native"'. *Current Anthropology* 44(3): 398–399.

Salverda, T. 2004. 'Changing definitions of ethnic boundaries on Mauritius'. *International Institute of Asian Studies Newsletter* 33: 20.

Sand, P. 2009. 'Diego Garcia: British–American legal black hole in the Indian Ocean?' *Journal of Environmental Law* 21(1): 113–137.

—. 2010. 'The Chagos Archipelago: Footprint of empire, or world heritage?' *Environmental Policy and Law* 40(5): 232–242.

Sayigh, R. 1979. *Palestinians: From Peasants to Revolutionaries*. London: Zed.

Scott, R. 1961. *Limuria: The Lesser Dependencies of Mauritius*. London: Oxford University Press.

Selvon, S. 2001. *A Comprehensive History of Mauritius*. Mauritius: M.D.S.

Simmons, A.S. 1982. *Modern Mauritius: The Politics of Decolonization*. Bloomington, IN: Indiana University Press.

Smith, R.T. 1996. *The Matrifocal Family: Power, Pluralism, and Politics*. London: Routledge.

Southdown Housing Association. 2006. *Black and Minority Ethnic Project Report 2006*. Southdown Housing Association.

Spencer, J. 1990. 'Writing within: Anthropology, nationalism, and culture in Sri Lanka'. *Current Anthropology* 31(3): 283–300.

Srebrnik, H. 2002. '"Full of sound and fury": Three decades of parliamentary politics in Mauritius'. *Journal of Southern African Studies* 28(2): 277–289.

Staeheli, L.A., & C.R. Nagel. 2006. 'Topographies of home and citizenship: Arab-American activists in the United States'. *Environment and Planning A* 38(9): 1599–1614.

Subron, A. 2002. 'Losean Indyin zonn de pe ubyin zonn de ger?' In *Diego Garcia in Times of Globalization* (ed.) *Lalit*. GRNW, Port Louis, Mauritius: Ledikasyon Pu Travayer.

Sutton, P. 2003. *Native Title in Australia: An Ethnographic Perspective*. Cambridge: Cambridge University Press.

Sylva, H. 1981. *Report on the Survey on the Conditions of Living of the Ilois Community Displaced from the Chagos Archipelago*. Government of Mauritius.

Tally, A. 2003. 'Anil Gayan, ministre des Affaires étrangères: "L'Irak a besoin d'un gouvernement provisoire composé uniquement d'Irakiens"'. In *Week-end* (23 March), p. 12. Port Louis, Mauritius.

Teelock, V. 1999. 'The influence of slavery in the formation of Creole identity'. *Comparative Studies of South Asia, Africa and the Middle East* 19(2): 3–8.

—. 2001. *Mauritian History: From its Beginnings to Modern Times*. Moka: Mahatma Gandhi Institute.

Tinker, H. 1974. *A New System of Slavery: The Export of Indian Labour Overseas, 1830–1920*. London: Oxford University Press for the Institute of Race Relations.

Tkach, A. 2003. 'Diego Garcia: Exiles still barred'. Documentary film directed by A. Tkach for CBS *60 Minutes*.

Todd, J.R. 1969. *Notes on the islands of the British Indian Ocean Territory*. British Indian Ocean Territory Report of BIOT Administrator. SA.F2.507.

Toussaint, A. 1966. *History of the Indian Ocean* (trans.) J. Guicharnaud. London: Routledge & K. Paul.

—. 1977. *History of Mauritius*. London: Macmillan.

Turner, S. 2008. 'The waxing and waning of the political field in Burundi and its diaspora'. *Ethnic and Racial Studies* 31(4): 742–765.

Turner, T. 1993. 'Anthropology and multiculturalism: What is anthropology that multi-culturalists should be mindful of it?' *Cultural Anthropology* 8(4): 411–429.

Turton, D. 2003. *Refugees, forced resettlers and 'other forced migrants': Towards a unitary study of forced migration*. UNHCR Working Paper No. 94.

—. 2005. 'The meaning of place in a world of movement: Lessons from long-term field research in Southern Ethiopia'. *Journal of Refugee Studies* 18(3): 258–280.

Van Hear, N. 1998. *New Diasporas: The Mass Exodus, Dispersal and Regrouping of Migrant Communities*. London: UCL Press.

Vaughan, M. 2001. 'Slavery and colonial identity in eighteenth century Mauritius'. In *History, Memory and Identity* (eds) V. Teelock & E.A. Alpers. Port Louis, Mauritius: Nelson Mandela Centre for African Culture and the University of Mauritius.

—. 2005. *Creating the Creole Island: Slavery in Eighteenth Century Mauritius*. Durham: Duke University Press.

Vincatassin, S. 2001. *Bulletin du mercredi 22 août 2001*. Association Internationale pour le Développement Economique et Social de l'Archipel de Chagos.

Vine, D. 2006. 'The impoverishment of displacement: Models for documenting human rights abuses and the people of Diego Garcia'. *Human Rights Brief* 13(2): 21–24.

—. 2009. *Island of Shame: The Secret History of the U.S. Military Base on Diego Garcia*. Princeton, NJ: Princeton University Press.

Vine, D., & L. Jeffery. 2009. 'Give us back Diego Garcia: Unity and division among activists in the Indian Ocean'. In *The Bases of Empire: The Global Struggle against U.S. Military Posts* (ed.) C. Lutz. London: Pluto.

Vine, D., S.W. Sokolowski & P. Harvey. 2005. 'Dérasiné: The expulsion and impoverishment of the Chagossian people'. Unpublished report.

Walker, I. 1986. *Zaffer pe sanze: Ethnic Identity and Social Change among the Ilois in Mauritius*. Report produced for Mauritius Indian Ocean Committee.

Waterman, C.A. 1990. '"Our tradition is a very modern tradition": Popular music and the construction of Pan-Yoruba identity'. *Ethnomusicology* 34(3): 367–379.

Watson, J.L. 1977. 'Introduction: Immigration, ethnicity, and class in Britain'. In *Between Two Cultures: Migrants and Minorities in Britain* (ed.) J.L. Watson. Oxford: Basil Blackwell.

Week-end. 1997a. 'Lalit réclame l'inclusion des Chagos dans la zone africaine dénucléarisée'. In *Week-end* (9 February), p. 15. Port Louis, Mauritius.

—. 1997b. 'Le véritable combat (pacifique) pour les Chagos libres, a-t-il, enfin, commencé?' In *Week-end* (26 January), p. 15. Port Louis, Mauritius.

—. 1998. 'Le Komité Ran Nou Diego refléchit sur la décolonisation et la démilitarisation'. In *Week-end* (8 November), p. 6. Port Louis, Mauritius.

—. 2003a. '"Elle était évitable" déclare Paul Bérenger'. In *Week-end* (30 March), p. 18. Port Louis, Mauritius.

—. 2003b. 'Ramgoolam annonce l'organisation d'une marche de solidarité'. In *Week-end* (30 March), p. 8. Port Louis, Mauritius.

Weiner, J.F. 1999. 'Culture in a sealed envelope: The concealment of Australian Aboriginal heritage and tradition in the Hindmarsh island bridge affair'. *Journal of the Royal Anthropological Institute* 5(2): 193–210.

Yuval-Davis, N. 1997. *Gender and Nation*. London: SAGE.

Zetter, R. 1999. 'Reconceptualizing the myth of return: Continuity and transition amongst the Greek-Cypriot refugees of 1974'. *Journal of Refugee Studies* 12(1): 1–22.

Index